RESEARCH COMPLIANCE PROFESSIONAL'S HANDBOOK

3rd Edition

The Practical Guide to Building and Maintaining a Clinical Research Compliance & Ethics Program

HCCA™

Research Compliance Professional's Handbook, Third Edition is published and updated by the Health Care Compliance Association, Minneapolis, MN.

Copyright © 2019 by the Health Care Compliance Association.

Printed in the United States of America. All rights reserved.

This book or parts thereof may not be reproduced in any form without express written permission of the publisher.

ISBN: 978-1-7335986-1-3

This publication is designed to provide accurate, comprehensive and authoritative information in regard to the subject matter covered. However, the publisher does not warrant that information contained herein is complete or accurate. It is published with the understanding that the publisher is not engaged in rendering legal, accounting, or other professional service and that the authors are not offering such advice in this publication. If legal advice or other expert assistance is required, the services of a competent professional should be sought.

To order copies of this publication contact:

Health Care Compliance Association
6500 Barrie Road, Suite 250
Minneapolis, MN 55435

888-580-8373 or 952-988-0141 (phone); 952-988-0146 (fax);

www.hcca-info.org | helpteam@hcca-info.org

Contributors for Research Compliance Professional's Handbook, 3rd Edition

HCCA would like to thank all who helped produce this book.

LEAD EDITOR

Kelly Willenberg, DBA, RN, CCRP, CHRC, CHC
Owner
Kelly Willenberg & Associates
Chesnee, SC

AUTHORS

Marti Arvin, JD, CCEP-F, CHC-F, CHPC, CHRC
Vice President, Audit Strategy
CynergisTek
Austin, TX

Tammie Bain, BS, JD
Assistant Director,
Industry Contracts
Emory University, Office of
Technology Transfer
Atlanta, GA

L. Steven Brown, MS, CPH
Biostatistician
Parkland Health and
Hospital System
Dallas, TX

Draco Forte, MEd, CHRC
Director
Ankura Consulting
Chicago, IL

Stuart Horowitz, PhD, MBA
President, Institutions and
Institutional Services
WIRB-Copernicus Group
Princeton, NJ

Daniel Kavenaugh, Ph.D.
Senior Scientific Advisor,
Gene Therapy
WIRB-Copernicus Group
Princeton, NJ

Carole Klove, RN, JD
General Counsel / Chief
Nursing Office
Elemeno Health
San Francisco, CA

Heather Kopeck, CHRC
Director of Development Policy and
Advancement Relations
University of California, Office of
the President
Oakland, CA

Darshan Kulkarni, Pharm.D, MS, Esq.
Vice President of Regulatory
Strategy and Policy
Synchrogenix
Philadelphia, PA

Jennifer Laporte, MPA, CRA
Sponsored Programs Manager
Morgridge Institute for Research
Madison, WI

Scott J. Lipkin, DPM, CIP
Managing Director
Ankura Consulting
Orlando, FL

Ryan Meade, JD, CHC-F
Senior Managing Director
Ankura Consulting
Chicago, IL

F. Lisa Murtha, JD, CHC, CHRC
Senior Managing Director
Ankura Consulting
Philadelphia, PA

Susan Partridge, BSN, MBA, CCRC
Vice President, Research
Administration
Parkland Health and
Hospital System
Dallas, TX

Kelé Piper, MS, CIP, CHRC
Director, Research Compliance
Beth Israel Deaconess
Medical Center
Boston, MA

Kathleen Price, RN, MBA, CIP
Director, Office of Human Subjects'
Protection
St. Jude Children's
Research Hospital
Memphis, TN

Wendy Schroeder, BSN, RN, CCRC
Director of Research and
Regulatory Programs
VisionGate, Inc.
Seattle, WA

Juliann Tenney, JD, CHRC
Chief Privacy Officer
University of North Carolina
Chapel Hill, NC

Debbie Troklus, CCEP-F, CHC-F, CCEP-I, CHPC, CHRC
SeniorManaging Director
Ankura Consulting
Louisville, KY

Sheryl Vacca, CHC-F, CCEP-F, CCEP-I, CHPC, CHRC
Senior Vice President, Chief
Risk Officer
Providence St Joseph Health
Providence, RI

Nicole Visyak, MS, MA, CCRC
Director
Ankura Consulting
Boston, MA

David Vulcano, LCSW, MBA, CIP, RAC
Vice President, Research
Compliance and Integrity
HCA Healthcare
Nashville, TN

Kristin West, CHRC, JD, MS
Chief Compliance Officer
Emory University
Atlanta, GA

Table of Contents

1 Research Compliance 101 1

2 Options for Identifying and Managing Financial Conflicts of Interest in Research: Flexible Compliance with the PHS Final Rule................. 29

3 Scientific and Research Misconduct 41

4 Biosecurity, Biosafety, and Biorisk Management 47

5 The Regulation of Research Using Animals...................... 53

6 The Regulation of Research with Human Subjects 63

7 FDA-Regulated Clinical Research............................. 75

8 Research Privacy and Security: Myths, Facts, and Practical Approaches 93

9 Research Records Management 119

10 Data and Safety Monitoring.................................. 127

11 Clinical Research Billing Compliance 139

12 Grant Management... 157

13 Research Auditing and Monitoring............................ 169

14 What are Export Controls?................................... 173

15 Integrating Research Compliance into the Corporate Compliance Program... 179

1
Research Compliance 101

By F. Lisa Murtha, JD, CHC, CHRC, and Debbie Troklus, CCEP-F, CHC-F, CCEP-I, CHPC, CHRC
As updated by: Nicole Visyak, MS, MA, CCRC and Draco Forte, MEd, CHRC[1]

Introduction

Clinical research compliance has become a major focus area of compliance professionals in recent years. Clinical research is highly regulated and as such, the role of a compliance professional is vital to maintaining compliance with NIH, FDA, ORI CMS and OMB requirements. The laws and regulations related to human subject protections, grant and trial accounting, effort reporting, scientific misconduct, privacy and security and clinical trial billing are highly complex and always evolving. This chapter will outline some of the key compliance issues important in research today.

Informed Consent and Human Subject Protections

Informed consent is one of the most coveted rights in healthcare today. Informed consent for treatment by a provider of healthcare services is well known and understood by most people. Informed consent in a research context has been a topic of much debate and reasonable academic minds have differed with regard to how informed consent for research should be administered to a prospective research subject. Informed consent for research is defined in the Belmont Report[2] and is required to be: informed, understood and voluntary. The federal rules for informed consent are outlined in 45 CFR Part 46.116 and 21 CFR Part 50. The rules state that informed consent must contain the following elements:

- Introduction with "this is research"—it must be clear to the subject that they are embarking on a research study and that it is not considered to be "therapy"
- Purpose of the study—what is being studied in the research?
- Description of study procedures—this is "experimental"
- Duration of subject involvement—the length of the study
- Potential risks or discomforts of participation
- Potential benefits of participation—although many institutions include a statement that makes it clear that the individual will be treated appropriately regardless of whether they participate in the research study
- Alternatives—other courses of treatment and/or other research studies that might be appropriate to the disease condition of the participant (if any)
- Confidentiality of records—this statement may include HIPAA language after the HIPAA Privacy Rule Compliance Date (April 14, 2003)
- Compensation for injury statement (for greater than minimal risk studies)
- Contact persons—individuals involved with the study including the name of the Principal Investigator and key study staff
- Statement of voluntary participation—it must be clear that the subject has the right NOT to participate

- One of two statements for research that involves the collection of identifiable private information or identifiable biospecimens (Revised Common Rule provision):
    - Identifiers might be removed from information or biospecimens for distribution or use in future research with additional informed consent
    - Information or biospecimens will not be distributed or used for future research
    - A statement that biospecimens may be used for commercial profit and whether or not subjects will share in the profit (Revised Common Rule provision)
- Unforeseen risks
- Reasons for involuntary termination of participation
- Expected or additional costs to participate or withdraw and information regarding whether there are likely clinical outcomes if the protocol is interrupted
- New findings statement
- A statement regarding whether clinically relevant research results, including individual results will be disclosed to subjects (Revised Common Rule provision)
- Statement that the project may include whole genome sequencing (Revised Common Rule provision)
- Number of subjects projected for accrual
- Payments (incentives)—some individuals believe that it is appropriate to include information related to how much money the Site/Investigator is receiving from the sponsor for each study subject and even a breakdown of costs for each component of care.

The seminal rule of the informed consent document is that it must include all relevant information about the study in language that is understandable to the "reasonable" study subject. Some investigators/sites interpret this rule to mean that the form should be written in language that is understandable to a child with no more than an eighth grade education. It is often the case that research subjects speak languages other than English as their primary language and as such, the forms should be translated into those commonly spoken languages in that geographic region with additional help interpreting them if necessary. While the informed consent document is a useful tool in delivering informed consent to potential subjects, it is merely a tool. Informed consent is, however, not a tool but a PROCESS. The process includes a variety of tools including subject recruitment materials (including advertising/marketing materials), verbal instructions delivered to the subject and his/her familysubject, written materials, and question/answer sessions. It must also include agreement and volunteerism of the subject as documented by signature.

The form that is signed by the potential subject serves as documentation that the informed consent was "informed" as defined by the Belmont Report, but how does one measure "comprehension" and "volunteerism"? Many of us were brought up to consider our physicians to be between an "angel" and "God." As such, we will do whatever our doctors recommend and many patients will do so to please their physicians. Moreover, when we are sick, we feel vulnerable and will latch onto any treatment pathway that may have a chance to make us feel better, or possibly cure us. In cases of serious illness and possible imminent death, it is hard to imagine what would go through your head, much less, what you really understand when your doctor explains a protocol to you. As such, it is incumbent on the investigator and the study site to use diligence in assuring that their subjects truly understand what they are getting into. One way to accomplish this goal is to incorporate a "monitor" into the informed consent process. Another method is to have the consent process "audited" periodically.

In some respects, informed consent really begins with the recruitment methods utilized by the investigator. Some of the common recruitment methods include: formal referrals and informal word of mouth, health workshops, screenings, health fairs, the internet, direct advertising, community meeting places, computerized databases (although HIPAA may change this in the future), and chart/record reviews. Direct advertising is a common mode of recruitment, which includes flyers, posters, newspaper ads, press releases, television spots, as well as radio ads and websites. Direct advertising must be reviewed by the Institutional Review Board for form, content, and mode of communication; it must not state or imply favorable outcomes; it must not be coercive or use undue pressure and must not be misleading to subjects. Finally, it must not use claims of safety, efficacy, equivalence, or superiority. Remember that patients and their families are savvy and they search on the internet and seek out clinical trial sites as well.

A recruitment payment to subjects is a hotly contested topic these days. The Institutional Review Board must approve all payment strategies. The amount of the payment must NOT be an undue inducement of a person to participate. It is very common for potential subjects to be told that their reasonable costs of participation will be reimbursed. These costs typically include parking, lunch, transportation costs, etc. To the extent that reimbursement is offered to subjects, it is recommended that the reimbursement be made when the expenses are incurred, as opposed to lump sum payments that could be construed as "suspicious," or as a way to offer payment of a co-payment. Government investigators carefully scrutinize these payments, and as such, recruitment payments should be carefully considered and specific to the cost being covered.

Many study sites have incorporated research compliance programs into their repertoire of compliance activities. These programs include a regimen of training, periodic reporting, anonymous ways of reporting issues, discipline, prompt follow up, and auditing and monitoring. In the past, the areas that were typically monitored in research were issues related to funding and grants management of federal grants, and time and effort reporting. Given some of the federal investigations and lawsuits in prestigious institutions around the country, auditing and monitoring of human subject protections is a necessary part of the compliance process. In fact, representatives of the Federal Office for Human Research Protections (OHRP) have publicly stated that investigators and study sites should be proactive in monitoring the area of human subject protections on an ongoing basis.

Implementing an informed consent monitoring process is an easy and low-cost way to evaluate how the investigators and study coordinators are doing. The "monitor" could be the compliance officer, an internal auditor, a peer investigator or peer study coordinator, or frankly almost any individual who is independent of the research study. That individual would begin by reviewing the form used to deliver the informed consent to ensure that it contains all the necessary elements as required by the federal rules. Presumably, this will already have been done in detail by the Institutional Review Board as part of the review of the protocol, but it does not hurt to verify the elements of a consent process. In the spirit of full disclosure, the potential subject should be queried as to whether he/she will allow a "monitor" to sit in on the informed consent discussion. Confidential information as well as "protected health information" as defined by HIPAA will be discussed, and you will want to make sure that the subject is comfortable with having a "third party" involved in those discussions. The subject's agreement should be documented in the participant's medical record stating that the subject understands and agrees to the consent elements such as protocol treatment and financial costs.

The monitor could begin by assessing the nature of the recruitment of the potential subjects. The "monitor" would document the time and circumstances of obtaining the informed consent (*i.e.*, it is being obtained while the patient is being admitted to the Emergency Department with a life-threatening illness or otherwise potentially under "duress"). To the extent that the potential subject speaks a language other than English, the monitor would ensure that the informed consent document used is translated into the language of the subjects and/or a translator is available. To the extent that the subject or his/her family members ask questions, the monitor would document not only the questions but the answers as well. As a final step, the monitor may ask the subject certain follow-up questions designed to test the subject's understanding of the material delivered to them.

While monitoring the informed consent process is not foolproof in making sure that the subjects truly understand what will happen if they participate in the research and what will happen if they do not participate in the research, it certainly would demonstrate and document the diligence taken by the investigator/study site. The costs for implementing this process either could be borne by the study site, or could be built into the study costs/budget. As for the number of studies to be reviewed and the number of subjects to be monitored, that would be a factor of what resources are available to the study site/investigator. There is no right or wrong answer—any monitoring is better than no monitoring.

FDA and the IRB Waiver

OHRP regulations at 45 CFR Part 46.116 allow an IRB to waive informed consent requirements if research:

- involves no more than minimal risk to subjects,
- the waiver or alteration will not adversely affect the rights and welfare of the subjects,
- the research could not practicably be carried out without the waiver, and
- when appropriate, the subjects will be provided additional information after participation.

However, FDA regulations only allowed exemptions from informed consent requirements only in life-threatening situations or when requirements for emergency research were met (FDA regulations at 21 CFR Part 50.23-50.24). Upon passage of the 21st Century Cures Act, the FDA was granted the authority to permit exceptions from informed consent requirements. In July 2017 the FDA released its final guidance for the informed consent exceptions for minimal risk clinical investigations. The FDA has yet to promulgate its own regulations for waiver or alteration of informed consent; but through the guidance document, FDA will not object to an IRB adopting the OHRP requirements for waiver or alteration of consent for FDA regulated research.

Revisions to the Common Rule

The ethical principles (*i.e.*, respect of persons, beneficence and justice) that form the foundation of human subjects protections in the US were codified in OHRP regulations in 1991 with The Federal Policy for the Protection of Human Subjects, also known as the Common Rule. Although enforcement agencies have published supplemental guidance to clarify the rules, advancements in technology, electronic health data, and biological specimen collection/storage, among other changes, have grown beyond the regulations. In January 2017, OHRP revised the Common Rule (45 CFR Part 46, subpart A) so that it better comports with how human subjects research is conducted in today's world and how it will be conducted in the future.

Key provisions of the revised regulations include: revised informed consent requirements, introduction of broad consent, limited IRB review, reliance on external IRBs, the elimination of waiver of informed consent for recruiting, and the elimination of the requirement for IRBs to review grant applications.

The Common Rule revisions include new additional consent elements that must be included as applicable:

- a statement regarding whether identifiers may be removed from private information or biospecimens and used in future research,
- a statement that biospecimens may be used for commercial profit and whether or not subjects will share in the profit,
- a statement regarding whether clinically relevant research results, including individual results, will be disclosed to subjects, and
- a statement that the project may include whole genome sequencing.

The revised common rule allows for the use of broad consent in lieu of informed consent (for unspecified future research) for storage, maintenance and secondary research use of identifiable private information and identifiable biospecimens. Broad consent must provide a general description of the types of research that may be conducted, it must describe the identifiable private information or biospecimens that might be used, it must provide the period of time that information or specimens may be stored, maintained, and used (which could be indefinite), it must include details as to whether subjects will be informed of the research that may use the subject information or biospecimens, it must describe whether subjects will be informed of the results of the future research, and it must provide a contact person for questions about subjects' information, biospecimens and subjects rights.

Under the revised Common Rule there are now eight (8) exempt categories in 45 CFR Part 46.104(d)(1-8). Only category 6 remains unchanged from the pre-2018 Common Rule. All others have been either revised, replaced or are brand new. The exempt categories are:

EXEMPT CATEGORY	CHANGES
Category 1: Research conducted in established or commonly accepted educational settings that involve normal educational practices	This has been revised to include a statement to clarify educational practices "that are not likely to adversely impact students' opportunity to learn"
Category 2: Research that only includes interactions involving educational tests, surveys, interviews or observations of public behavior	This has been revised so that research is exempt if one of three criteria is met (not identifiable, does not pose a risk if disclosed, no risk if there is limited IRB review); also, the revised category now includes visual or auditory recording
Category 3: Research involving benign behavioral interventions in conjunction with the collection of information from adult subjects	This is a new category that defines benign behavioral interventions as, "brief in duration, harmless, painless, not physically invasive, not likely to have a significant adverse lasting impact on the subjects, and the investigator has no reason to think the subjects will find the interventions offensive or embarrassing"
Category 4: Secondary research for which consent is not required	This has been revised to clarify that the use of identifiable private information or biospecimens does not require informed consent if: a) the identifiable information or biospecimens are publicly available, b) if the information is recorded by the investigator in such a way that subject identity cannot readily be ascertained, c) research use of identifiable health information is in accordance with HIPAA, d) research is conducted by or on behalf of a federal department or agency
Category 5: Research and demonstration projects conducted or supported by a federal department or agency	This has been revised to allow research supported by a federal agency to qualify for this exemption
Category 6: taste and food quality evaluation and consumer acceptance studies	This criterion is unchanged
Category 7: Storage or maintenance for secondary research for which broad consent is required	This is a new category
Category 8: Secondary research for which broad consent is required	This is a new category

Other revisions include the limited IRB review provision that removes the requirement for continuing review for studies that received expedited initial review and for intervention studies that have completed intervention and are only analyzing data or observational follow-up. The new rule introduces the requirement for the use of a single IRB for cooperative research in the US. Note that this does not apply when more than a single IRB is required by law (tribal law) or when federal sponsor documents that use of a single IRB is not appropriate. The revised Common Rule eliminates the requirement for the IRB to grant a waiver of informed consent to obtain information or biospecimens for screening, recruiting or determining eligibility. Another revision of note is the elimination of the requirement that IRBs review federal grant applications or funding proposals related to the research.

The Department of Health and Human Services delayed the effective and compliance date of the Revised Common Rule until January 21, 2019. However, the single IRB provisions compliance date is January 20, 2020.

Good Clinical Practice

Good Clinical Practice (GCP) is an international ethical and scientific quality standard for human subjects research, which was published by the International Council for Harmonisation of Technical Requirements for Pharmaceuticals for Human Use (ICH). The ICH GCP Guideline provides a unified standard for the conduct of clinical research that engenders public assurance that the rights, safety, and well-being of human subjects are protected and that the clinical trial data are credible.[3] The first Guideline for Good Clinical Practice, ICH E6(R1) was approved in 1996. The Integrated Addendum to ICH E6(R1): Guideline for Good Clinical Practice E6(R2) was published in 2016 to reflect the implications that advancements in technology and electronic data capture have had on clinical trials. ICH E6(R2) provides a unified standard for increased clinical trial quality and efficacy using electronic records while continuing to ensure the protection of human subjects and reliability of clinical trial data. ICH E6(R2) has been adopted by regulatory agencies in the EU, Japan, the United States, Canada, and Switzerland to facilitate mutual acceptance of clinical trials data. The core GCP regulations in the United States are codified in both OHRP regulations at 45 CFR 46, as well as FDA regulations at 21 CFR 11, 50, 54, 56, 312, and 812. Effective January 1, 2017, all NIH-funded clinical investigators and clinical trial staff are required to complete GCP training and training should be refreshed at least every three years.[4]

Clinical investigators and staff engaged in human subjects research must be educated on GCP requirements and maintain proof of training documentation. GCP training may be offered through a course, academic training program, or a certification from a professional clinical research organization. US regulations do not require a specific GCP training program, however the NIH does offer online GCP training modules that fulfill their training requirements for NIH-funded research. Additionally, many pharmaceutical and device sponsors offer GCP training as part of their clinical trial training initiatives. Clinical investigators who design their own clinical trials, *i.e.*, investigator initiated clinical trials, must be trained on all GCP requirements, including sponsor requirements.

GCP Guidelines consist of the eight sections listed below. The full GCP Guidelines can be found on the ICH website.[5]

1. Glossary
2. The Principles of ICH GCP
3. Institutional Review Board/Independent Ethics Committee (IRB/ IEC)
4. Investigator
5. Sponsor
6. Clinical Trial Protocol and Protocol Amendment(s)
7. Investigator Brochure
8. Essential Documents for the Conduct of a Clinical Trial

Scientific Misconduct

Over the course of the last twenty years, we have witnessed a number of prominent enforcement initiatives pursued by the DHHS Office of Inspector General (OIG) and the Department of Justice (DOJ). These initiatives have ranged from the Physicians at Teaching Hospitals (PATH) projects, the clinical laboratory bundling/unbundling scandals, the pharmaceutical company compliance cases, and much, much more. Research compliance cases have received a great deal of attention as well. These cases include the "double billing" cases (*e.g.*, billing Medicare and charging costs against a research grant or clinical trial), conflict of interest cases, and of course, scientific misconduct cases. While the concerns over misconduct in science are not necessarily new, some cases have stood out.

One legendary case is entitled, *United States of America v. Paul H. Kornak, Criminal Action No. 03-CR-436 (FJS)*. A Plea and Cooperation Agreement was signed in January 2005. The defendant was a research assistant at the Stratton VA Medical Center in Albany, New York. The defendant helped manage studies in which payments were made by sponsors based upon enrollment. In the course of his work, the defendant sent case report forms to a sponsor falsely indicating that subjects met the inclusion criteria for the study. One subject who did not meet the inclusion criteria for the study was wrongly enrolled and passed away. The defendant was prosecuted under criminal and civil proceedings, resulting in a 71-month prison sentence, an order to pay $639,000 in restitution, and lifetime debarment from federally funded research.[6]

There have been many other reported instances of misconduct in science. Cases of plagiarism, fabrication and falsification are well reported on ORI's website. The motivations for these actions are varied and always fascinating. In some cases, the motivation amounts simply to the fact that the respondents are overworked and lack resources to pursue the research projects appropriately. Providing insufficient resources can be a serious institutional compliance risk—in other words, if research organizations do not devote sufficient resources to conduct research appropriately, then any problems or issues will amount to significant exposure for the research organization. As such, research organizations are well advised to ensure that the organization has effective scientific misconduct policies and procedures in place to deal with allegations of fraud in science.

Given the increased focus on misconduct in science, ORI updated its regulations in 2005. These regulations, Public Health Service Policies on Research Misconduct, can be found at 42 CFR Parts 50 and 93. Research misconduct is defined as: "Fabrication, falsification, or plagiarism (or "FFP") in proposing, performing, or reviewing research or in reporting research results. Research misconduct does not include honest error or differences of opinion" (42 CFR Pt. 93.103). "Fabrication is making up data or results and recording or reporting them. Falsification is manipulating research materials, equipment, or processes, or changing or omitting data or results such that the research is not accurately represented in the research record. Plagiarism is the appropriation of another person's ideas, processes, results, or words without giving appropriate credit" (42 CFR Pt. 93.103). In contrast to the previous rule, this regulation requires that FFP be a "significant departure" from accepted practices as opposed to the "serious deviation" standard in the previous regulation.

The regulations expand the type of PHS support beyond grants and cooperative agreements to include support provided through contracts and through direct funding of PHS intramural research programs. The Final Rule also extends the rules related to plagiarism to include plagiarism during the journal peer review process as well. The statute of limitations for raising an allegation of scientific misconduct is six (6) years from the date that the alleged misconduct actually occurred.

The ORI regulations state that it is the responsibility of each PHS awardee to have policies and procedures in place for investigating and reporting instances of scientific misconduct. Moreover, each institution that applies for and receives PHS funds for research must file an assurance with ORI that affirms that the applicant has established a process for reviewing, investigating, and reporting allegations of misconduct in research. Therefore, when conducting a compliance assessment into organizational compliance with the ORI regulations, one must start with ensuring that an appropriate assurance is in place and that the organization in fact has the required policies and procedures in place for dealing with allegations of misconduct in science.

An institutional or HHS finding of research misconduct must be proved by a preponderance of the evidence and the institution or HHS has the burden of proof for making a finding of research misconduct. The destruction, absence of, or respondent's failure to provide research records documenting the questioned research is evidence of research misconduct where the institution or HHS establishes by a preponderance of the evidence that the respondent intentionally, knowingly, or recklessly had research records and destroyed them, had the opportunity to maintain the records and did not do so, or maintained the records and failed to produce them in a timely manner. The respondent's conduct in this case constitutes a significant departure from accepted practices of the relevant research community. The respondent in turn has the burden of proving any affirmative defenses or mitigating factors by a preponderance of the evidence standard.

The ORI regulations outline the specific process to be followed for investigating an allegation of scientific misconduct. The process can be broken down into four general phases:

- Inquiry
- Investigation
- Reporting
- Appeals

Inquiry

An inquiry is a means of gathering and initial fact finding to determine whether an allegation or apparent instance of misconduct warrants an investigation (42 CFR Part 212 and 93.307). At the time of or before the beginning of an inquiry, an institution must make a good faith effort to notify in writing the presumed respondent. The institution must also, on or before the date on which the respondent is notified, take all reasonable and practical steps to obtain custody of all research records and evidence needed to conduct the inquiry, inventory the records in evidence, and sequester them in a secure manner. An inquiry does not require a full review of all evidence collected, but rather, to review sufficient evidence to determine whether an investigation is warranted. The institution must complete its inquiry within sixty (60) calendar days of its initiation unless circumstances clearly warrant a longer period. Any time extensions must be documented in writing. The institution must provide the respondent an opportunity to review and comment on the inquiry report and attach any comments received to the report.

In the event that the results of the inquiry indicate that the allegation of scientific misconduct has merit, the institution will (within thirty (30) days) provide ORI with the written finding by the responsible institutional official. The written inquiry report must include:

- The name and position of the respondent
- A description of the allegations of research misconduct
- The PHS support, including, for example, grant numbers, applications, contracts, and publications listing PHS support
- The basis for recommending that the alleged actions warrant an investigation
- Any comments on the report by the respondent and complainant.

ORI may further request that the institution provide information related to:

- The institutional policies and procedures under which the inquiry was conducted
- The research records and evidence reviewed, transcripts, or recordings of any interviews, and copies of all relevant documents
- The charges for the investigation to consider.

In the event that the institution deems that insufficient evidence exists to support an allegation of scientific misconduct, it must keep complete documentation to support this conclusion in its files. ORI may request a review of these documents at any time.

Investigation

If the results of the inquiry reflect a likelihood of scientific misconduct, the institution will begin an investigation within thirty (30) days of the completion of the inquiry. The institutional official must contact the ORI director of the decision to begin an investigation on or before the date that the investigation begins (42 CFR Part 93.310 (b)). The respondent must also be notified in writing of the allegations within a reasonable period of time after determining that the investigation is going to begin, but before the investigation actually begins. The investigation must be fair and complete. Interviews will be conducted at this stage and all leads must be pursued. The institution must complete the investigation within one hundred twenty (120) days of beginning it. This period includes all time required to prepare the investigation report (42 CFR Part 93.311). Extensions may be granted by ORI if a request is made in writing and if circumstances warrant it. The respondent has the right to review and comment on the report within thirty (30) days after receiving the investigation report. The institution may also provide the complainant a copy of the report.

The investigation report must include the following information:

- The allegations of research misconduct
- PHS support information including grant numbers, etc.
- The specific allegations of research misconduct subject to the investigation
- If not already provided, copies of the institutional policies and procedures
- The research records and evidence reviewed, and identify any evidence taken into custody and not reviewed
- Statement of findings
- Whether the misconduct was falsification, fabrication, or plagiarism and if it was intentional, knowing, or in reckless disregard
- The facts which support the conclusion
- Whether any publications need correction
- The person responsible for the misconduct
- Any current support or known applications or proposals for support that the respondent has pending with non-PHS federal agencies
- Any comments made by the respondent and complainant
- All relevant research records and records of the investigation (including interview notes, etc.) (42CFR Part 93.313).

The institution must give ORI the following information:

- The investigational report
- Final institutional action
- A statement as to whether the institution accepts the investigation's findings
- A description of any institutional administrative actions (42 CFR Part 93.315).

Reporting

Once ORI has completed its review, it may either close the case without a finding of scientific misconduct, or it may make a finding of research misconduct and obtain HHS approval of administrative actions based on the record. ORI may also recommend that HHS seek to settle the case (42CFR Part 93.405). Some of the possible outcomes of a finding of scientific misconduct include debarment, suspension, letters of reprimand, restriction on research activities, special review of all requests for PHS funding, imposition of supervision requirements, termination of grants, certification or attribution of all requests for support and reports to the PHS, and more (42 CFR Part93.407). Moreover, HHS may seek to recover PHS funds spent in support of activities that involved research misconduct. HHS will consider whether the actions were knowing or reckless, whether the actions were part of a pattern or practice of wrongdoing, the impact of the misconduct, the respondent's acceptance of responsibility, and other mitigating circumstances.

Appeals

Clearly the ramifications of engaging in scientific misconduct are grave for those individuals involved. Respondents have appeal rights (even appeals to District Court); however, the process can be extremely costly and time intensive. Perhaps even more problematic is the damage to reputation and career that can result from an allegation of scientific misconduct. In addition, institutions that do not develop and implement the required process for dealing with allegations of scientific misconduct have great exposure. ORI can pursue various enforcement actions against research institutions, including letters of reprimand, refer the matter to HHS, and place the institution on special review status, debarment or suspension of the institution and much more (42 CFR Part 93.413).

Given what is at stake today, research institutions should strongly consider developing and implementing a research compliance program. This effort should include (at a minimum) comprehensive training and education for all administrative staff, investigators and coordinators, and detailed auditing and monitoring. Being proactive and having an effective offense, is always the best defense.

Conflicts of Interest

On December 12, 2005, the *Wall Street Journal* prominently featured an article titled, "How a famed hospital invests in device it uses and promotes."[7] Its writer, David Armstrong, systematically detailed the financial ties between ArtiCure, Inc. and the Cleveland Clinic Foundation (hereinafter 'the clinic'), a venture capital partnership it founded (Foundation Medical Partners or FMP), its chief executive officer, board of trustees and surgeons. Armstrong's article focused upon the clinic's usage—in 1,247 of its patients, including 16 who were enrolled in then underway clinical trials—and wholesale advocacy of ArtiCure's atrial-fibrillation medical device and procedure by the clinic and its officers.

ArtiCure applications for heart use had been rejected by the Food and Drug Administration (FDA) on three separate occasions and the clinic's usage of the device was on an off-label basis. In June 2005, ArtiCure, when filing with the SEC to go public, stated in its prospectus, "serious complications...including death... [had] been encountered in connection" with the minimally invasive procedure. ArtiCure's Chief Executive, David Drachman, acknowledged in the *Wall Street Journal* article that there were four deaths related—if not attributable—to the procedure.

The financial relationship between the clinic and ArtiCure, Inc. was a fairly complex one, although largely unknown to and undisclosed even among the clinic's researchers and its patient population. FMP's equity holdings in ArtiCure, Inc. amounted to 4.1% of its stock, with an estimated value of $7million; as FMP's largest investor, the clinic's pro-rata share of its profits amounted to 38%. Heart surgeon Dr. Delos "Toby" Cosgrove, the chief executive officer of the Cleveland Clinic, was not only a general partner managing FMP, but also a personal investor in the fund until October 2005, and a member of ArtiCure's board of directors until March 2005. Dr. Cosgrove had also developed a medical device for ArtiCure entitling him to receipt of royalties from the company.

Clinic surgeons performing the ArtiCure procedure—Drs. Marc Gillinov and Patrick McCarthy—continued to serve as consultants. Each had been offered $25,000 in stock options in the company, though the former declined the same and limited his consulting fee to $10,000 annually in order to comply with clinic guidelines, while Dr. McCarthy left the clinic for Northwest Memorial Hospital.

The Cleveland Clinic Foundation's laxity in its acknowledging or monitoring its institutional and individual conflicts of interest provides a cautionary tale of the risks posed by a failure to methodically and transparently manage such conflicts. The media coverage and consequent damage to the clinic's reputation and the credibility of its research program underscore only one possible outcome of a cavalier approach to the ethical and practical dilemmas posed by the competing objectives of research integrity and financial profitability. Other foreseeable results of unchecked conflicts of interest include deterrence of the public's participation in future research, harm to human subject s and related civil litigation and, in some instances, criminal liability. Institutions neglectful of managing conflicts of interest also risk the suspension or discontinuance of federally funded research support. There are many other examples of conflict of interest investigations at places such as the University of Pennsylvania (in the matter of Jesse Gelsinger) and at Emory University (related to Dr. Nemeroff) and the list grows with each passing day.

Identifying Conflicts of Interest

The U.S. Department Health and Human Services (DHHS) requires medical centers and universities to assess the impact of institutional and individual financial ties and develop a plan to "manage, reduce or eliminate" actual or potential conflicts of interest.[8] Specifically, 42 CFR Part 50, Subpart F, (as amended in 2011) mandates disclosure of any "significant financial interest" in entities whose financial interests might be affected by the research, and require the institution to designate an "institutional official(s)" to solicit and review the financial disclosure statements made by investigators. The above referenced regulatory subsection defines a "significant financial interest" as: Income (salary, royalties and other payments) which, when aggregated for the investigator, an investigator's spouse or dependent children, exceeds $5,000 over twelve months, or [an] equity interest (including spouse and dependent children) in excess of $5,000 or 5% ownership in a single entity.

PHS regulations do not mandate a methodology an institution should employ to identify or manage conflicts of interest. However, they do require that institutions maintain written policies on financial conflicts of interest, ensure that investigators complete conflict of interest training at least every four years (when working on PHS funded research), and "take reasonable steps" to ensure that subrecipient investigators comply with PHS financial conflict of interest regulations. Also, the PHS regulations stipulate that institutions designate officials to review conflict of interest disclosures. Developing and enforcing policies and procedures to manage conflicts of interest is left largely to the discretion of medical centers and academic institutions. In order to accomplish this Herculean task, a workable definition of what constitutes a conflict of interest (something more tangible than the unease or intuitive recognition signaled by Supreme Court Justice Potter Stewart's famous attempt to define obscenity: "I know it when I see it...") is a vital first step. Should an institution determine that an individual has an actual or perceived conflict of interest, it must self-report to the "PHS awarding component—such as the National Institutes of Health (NIH)—and explain whether the conflict has been managed, reduced or eliminated." Upon request, institutions must also make publicly available certain information regarding significant financial interests held by senior/key personnel.

Generally, a conflict of interest arises when financial or other personal considerations have the potential to compromise or bias professional judgment and objectivity. Conflicts of interest inevitably involve the use of an individual's authority for personal and/or financial gain.

However, financial relationships between industry and hospitals/universities may introduce conflicts at the institutional level. When an institution or its senior officials own a financial interest in a company that holds a patent to a new drug or device, a conflict or a perception of a conflict can arise. If the interests of an institution either affect or appear to affect institutional processes such as the conduct, review, or oversight of human research, then an actual or perceived institutional conflict of interest exists. Institutions with equity or intellectual property interests should evaluate whether it would be appropriate to conduct research at their facilities and, if yes, then determine what measures and controls ensure a firewall to separate such research and its results from any financial considerations. Conflicted senior officers, trustees and board members should generally be viewed as requiring attention and management on both an individual and institutional basis.

The NIH Grant Policy Statement lists the following as examples of ways to manage actual or perceived conflicts of interest:

- Public disclosure of "significant financial interests" and/or disclosure directly to research subjects
- Monitoring of research by independent, external reviewers
- Modification of the research plan
- Change of personnel, personnel responsibilities or disqualification from participation in all or part of the research
- Reduction or divestiture of significant financial interests
- Severance of relationships that create actual or potential conflicts.

FDA regulations at 21 CFR Part 54 require that applicants who submit a marketing application must submit the financial interests and arrangements of any clinical investigator conducting the studies. Under 21 CFR Part 54, an investigator must disclose any potentially conflicting financial interest of the investigator, the investigator's spouse and dependent children when:

- There is compensation to the investigator by the sponsor that may be affected by the study outcome.
- It is an equity interest in a publicly traded corporation in excess of $50,000 during the timeframe the study is ongoing and for one (1) year following its completion.
- It is a proprietary interest in the test product (including patent, trademark, copyright, or licensing agreement).
- It is a significant payment of other sorts ("SPOOS") valued at more than $25,000, exclusive of costs of conducting the study, during the project and for one year after its completion.

Institutional Review Board (IRB) conflict of interest issues are regulated pursuant to 45 CFR 46.107(e) and 21 CFR 56.107(e). Under these regulations, "No IRB member may participate in initial or continuing research in which they have a conflicting interest except to provide information requested by the IRB." In the event of an IRB member being conflicted, the IRB member must recuse him or herself. Both the PHS and FDA regulations demand reporting of financial interests only and neither require any recusal by conflicted researchers with a conflict of interest or notification to human research subjects.

Naturally, when an academic institution or medical center has an IRB, conducts FDA-regulated research and receives PHS (including but not limited to NIH) funding, it must follow all three sets of regulations.

Identifying and managing conflicts of interest is a multifaceted process. Conflict of interest policies and procedures must be designed to protect the implementing institution and its human research subjects. Academic institutions and medical centers must diligently track and monitor any and all individual and institutional financial relationships that create the potential for actual or perceived conflicts of interest.

Once an institution defines what constitutes a financial conflict of interest, it must then make determinations as to the threshold amounts or situations that require management. What are, for instance, allowable or *de minimis* amounts of investments, fees and honoraria, consulting fees, intellectual property rights, enrollment bonuses, payments coupled to results and spouse/dependent finances? Does remuneration in excess of $25,000 or $50,000 warrant additional supervision and/or necessitate an investigator's recusal or the introduction of independent controls? How should institutions decide whether to continue research when conflicted? Should there be a "rebuttable presumption," where research is to be discontinued unless "compelling circumstances" exist, such as the existence of unique facilities and expertise or special patient populations at a specific academic or medical institution?

Institutions must also establish and communicate enforcement mechanisms and sanctions for noncompliance with conflict of interest management protocol. Cultural and contextual considerations will play a role in deciding how aggressively an academic institution or medical center regulates conflicts of interest. For instance, an extremely entrepreneurial institution may be more inclined to view disclosure as an effective means of managing conflicts of interest in lieu of mandating complete divestiture.

The linchpin in managing conflicts of interest is annual disclosure from research faculty and others who are in a position to influence the application, conduct or reporting of research, make business decisions, teach, or deliver healthcare services or information, regarding real or perceived conflicts of interest. Therefore, developing policies and co-extensive processes to collect and review relevant information as to the financial interests of research faculty and personnel is critical. Without a systemic means of soliciting and evaluating disclosures, no academic institution or medical center is equipped to determine whether conflicts of interest exist or how to appropriately manage them.

Some general guidelines as to disclosure process—whether tailored to paper or electronic system—may include the following:

1. Required annual disclosure with an ongoing obligation to provide incidental self-disclosure should new relationships with any entity pose or result in a real or perceived conflict of interest.
2. A comprehensive list of research faculty and personnel, which identifies individuals institutionally exempted for reasons such as long-term disability, leave of absence or retirement.
3. Communication between the vice-dean for research, department chairs and supervisors.
4. Consultation, as needed, with a Conflict of Interest Committees, Office of Research Administration and Institutional Review Board.
5. A means to direct non-financial conflicts related to commitment, purchasing or nepotism to the appropriate operational units in the Compliance Office, Procurement Office, and/or Office of Human Resources.
6. Clear-cut deadlines for disclosure, complete with reminders and consequences for noncompliance.

In order to be complete, a disclosure form should request detailed information as to all of an individual's (including spouse and dependent children) financial relationships and interests that are research related. Therefore, disclosure forms should request the enumeration of equity interests in privately held and publicly traded entities, royalties, consulting fees, honoraria when a research sponsor is involved or, alternatively, when federally funded research could be impacted by such financial interests.

Responses to financial questions posed in disclosure forms should enable conflict of interest administrative staff persons or, should it exist, conflict of interest management software to make preliminary decisions as to the individuals and relationships requiring additional review for actual or perceived conflicts of interest. Therefore, research faculty or personnel with either no or *de minimis* financial relationships may be deferred until the next annual disclosure period unless a change occurs in the interim. The speed and efficacy of this initial phase of review hinges entirely upon how clearly an institution's policies and procedures are enunciated and can be applied.

The second phase of review consists of issuing, tracking and monitoring management plans. The ensuing analysis of disclosure forms entails a review of more specifics into the type of financial relationship that results in an actual or perceived conflict of interest. "Simple" or straightforward conflicts of interest will trigger the administrative issuance of a standard management plan requiring disclosure in all publications, presentations, informed consent documents, consulting activities, and grant applications involving related research. Such situations will not require Conflict of Interest Committee deliberation and may be added to an informal "consent agenda." More complex conflicts of interest require committee input and the issuance of a "custom" management plan with provisions tailored to address any concerns peculiar to the situation.

Please find below, for your reference, a detailed approach to the issuance of management plans (Simple and Custom):

1. A management plan is sent via e-mail to:
    a. individual with the conflict;
    b. the chair of the department if individual is faculty;
    c. immediate supervisor if individual is non-faculty;
    d. the ORA if the individual is listed on a federally funded grant or grant application in the last two years;
    e. the IRB if the individual also conducts human subject research.
2. The management plan is logged into a "plan tracker" database
3. Individual acknowledges management plan via electronic or actual signature
4. Management plan is tracked and monitored:
    a. Plan tracker sets ticklers for communication and reminders to individuals
    b. Requests and reminders sent to individuals to forward samples of disclosures or other documents related to compliance with management plans
5. Compliance and/or noncompliance with management plan noted in plan tracker database
6. Noncompliance notice sent to:
    a. individual
    b. original recipients of management plan
    c. compliance officer

Periodic, randomized internal audits of research staff and personnel with management plans are one way of assessing, if not assuring, compliance. Retention and maintenance of records of conflict of interest disclosures and management plans are essential and require the allocation of institutional resources—specifically, space (physical or electronic) and personnel. Such records are the only tangible way for a compliance auditor—institutional or federal—to assess whether a university or medical center are satisfactorily managing conflicts of interest.

The failure to monitor or manage conflicts of interest poses myriad risks. Financial considerations may compromise or appear to compromise human research subjects' safety. A research institution, its reputation and credibility are damaged among peer institutions and the public-at-large when details regarding unaddressed conflicts of interest surface. Unchecked conflicts of interest undermine public's faith in research findings and its willingness to participate in clinical research studies. Suspension or discontinuance of research funding and support by the NIH may also result from neglect or mismanagement of conflicts of interest.

Sunshine Act

In addition to tracking conflicts of interest pursuant to an organization's conflicts of interest policy and procedures, organizations will need to focus attention on disclosures of payments made to physicians by "manufacturers" as required by the Physician Sunshine Provisions of the Patient Protection and Affordable Care Act. Section 6002- Transparency Reports and Reporting Physician Ownership or Investment Interests, or "Sunshine Provisions," require manufacturers of drugs, devices and biologics, to track and report (on public websites) any payments of $10 or more made by them to physicians. This provision applies to pharmaceutical companies, biotech firms and medical device manufacturers that have products which are eligible for payment by Medicare, Medicaid or the Children's Health Insurance Program (CHIP). The final Sunshine provisions were published in early 2013 and they require certain types of information to be reported including but not limited to consulting fees, honoraria, gifts, food, charitable contributions, ownership or investment interests, and compensation for serving as faculty or speaker for medical education programs. This means that the information that is disclosed by a physician on his/her FDA Form 3455, and the information he/she discloses on the annual institutional conflict of interest disclosure must be consistent with the information that is reported by the manufacturers. The Patient Protection and Affordable Care Act Sunshine Provisions impose civil and monetary penalties for non-compliance. Failure to report may result in a civil monetary penalty of not less than $100 but not more than $10,000 for each payment or transfer of value not reported (not to exceed $150,000). A "Knowing Failure to Report" may result in a civil monetary penalty of not less than $10,000 but not more than $100,000 for each payment or transfer of value not reported (not to exceed $1,000,000).

Effort Reporting

As we cheer the incredible scientific advances of the past decade, it is hard not to notice how these advances have changed the research landscape. As is often the case, progress comes at a price. With clinical research, this price has come in the form of increased scrutiny by the government, public exposure of transgressions and large fines and penalties. As we have repeatedly seen, the government through Congress and various federal initiatives has taken swift and aggressive action to tighten the reins on research. Whether you believe that the government has gone too far in their enforcement efforts, or you believe the additional scrutiny is overdue, the fact remains: research compliance has entered a new era. The challenge facing the investigator, his/her institution and those charged with assuring compliance is to find a way to meet the requirements of the new regulations without impeding the progress of research.

It is likely Sir Isaac Newton did not consider the impact of research compliance violations on government regulators when he postulated one of his Laws of Nature. Had he done so, the law might more correctly read, "For every inaction, there is a swift and ominous reaction." To the research community, this has certainly been the case during the recent past in the area of time and effort reporting. Following the recent tragic cases of failure to uphold acceptable standards of human subject protections, the federal government has begun to focus its attention on time and effort reporting and other mechanisms by which dollars flow from the federal government to investigators and research institutions. For example, in the recent past, there have been four widely publicized cases of time and effort infractions. Two cases were civil actions and two were criminal cases. Perhaps the most highly publicized cases involved Northwestern University, in which the suit resulted in a $5.5 million-dollar settlement. This case was filed under the *qui tam* provisions of the Civil False Claims Act. The case specifically related to a review of 1995-2001-faculty effort. One of the reasons cited for failure to comply with federal time and effort rules was the fact that the university lacked a system to reconcile proposed effort and the reports filed on a periodic basis. The government was able to claim that these transgressions resulted in false statements made to the government.

Getting Started

Given the government's aggressive enforcement agenda related to time and effort reporting, it should be clear that research (and time and effort reporting) deserves heightened attention of compliance professionals. It is recommended that each institution conduct its own strategic time and effort reporting compliance risk assessment. If an assessment is conducted, it is important to consider involving legal counsel to ensure that the assessment is covered under the attorney-client and/or work product privileges. The most important thing is that investigators be educated regarding the rules related to time and effort reporting, and that research organizations develop and implement firm policies, procedures and ongoing monitoring to ensure that time and effort reporting remains compliant.

Education

A time and effort education program must, at a minimum, include the following topics:

- Cost Principles
- Definition of Effort Reporting
- Effort Report Scope
- Reporting Basis
- Certification
- Cost Sharing
- External Activities
- Use EXAMPLES!

Cost principles outlined in the Code of Federal Regulations (CFR) and the Office of Management and Budget (OMB) Circulars set forth the minimum requirements for compliant effort reporting. For example, 48 CFR Part 31 outlines the requirements for "for-profit" organizations; OMB Circular A-21 deals with universities—"every term" reporting; OMB Circular A-122 focuses on "non-profits;" and 45 CFR Part 74, Appendix E contains the requirements for hospitals involved in research—"every month" reporting.

These provisions define effort reporting as a means of verifying that the percent of effort expended by research personnel on various activities is commensurate with the percentage of salaries and wages charged to those accounts. Effort reporting further verifies that cost sharing commitments were met, total effort commitments were met and that costs were appropriately treated in the indirect cost rate.

It is critical that investigators understand the scope of effort reporting so that they can effectively track and report their time and efforts expended on the many activities they are involved in on a daily basis. Effort reports must reflect all compensated activities, including those efforts not federally funded, such as instruction, governance, and academic teaching. Moreover, OMB Circular A-21 J 8 a makes clear that "compensation for personal services covers all amounts paid currently or accrued by the institution for services of employees rendered during the period of performance under sponsored agreements." Hence, principal investigators and other "key" employees involved in the research must be accounted for in time and effort reports.

Effort reports should be prepared on a percentage basis so as to assure consistency with award terms and utilize flexibility by regulation. OMB Circular A-21 J (2) (b) states: "These reports will reflect an after the fact reporting of the percentage distribution of activity of employees." Section J 8 (l) (c) goes on to clarify that "...it is recognized that research, service, and administration are often inextricably intermingled. A precise assessment of factors that contribute to costs is not always feasible." Since these principles are subject to interpretation, it is helpful to include numerous examples in the training session. This will allow investigators to learn how to distinguish between those activities that require reporting and those that do not.

Certification of effort is perhaps the most important concept for investigators to learn and understand. Effort reports must be certified by an individual with full knowledge of all aspects of the employee's effort. Reports should be certified by the employee whenever possible, but may be approved by the principal investigator or chair of the department in the employee's absence. From a monitoring perspective, research institutions should conduct periodic assessments of payroll and effort consistency, permitting variations between effort and payroll by reporting period and to permit accuracy in reporting and certification.

Another important concept for investigators is to understand the link between effort reports and cost sharing. Effort reports play a pivotal role in documenting cost sharing commitments; in particular, the fact that only cost sharing that has been committed to the sponsor needs to be reported in the effort reports. Research institution policies and procedures should be developed to address the type of cost sharing that is allowed and the institutional reporting policy.

External activities must be accounted for within the auspices of time and effort reporting. OMB Circular A-21 states that "charges to sponsored agreements may include reasonable amounts for activities contributing and intimately related to work under the agreements, such as delivering special lectures about specific aspects of the ongoing activity, writing reports and articles, participating in legitimate seminars, consulting with colleagues and graduate students, and attending meetings and conferences." Research institutions are well served to develop and implement time-keeping mechanisms that make it easy for investigators to track their time on various activities on a real-time basis. Most of these systems are electronic in nature and allow time to "roll-up" into the time and effort reporting forms.

One of the common questions asked by investigators (which must be incorporated into active training) is what they should do if the efforts expended during a single reporting period are "different" from what was promised at the time that the grant was awarded. There is no single, easy answer to this question. Research institutions must develop policy to address this issue and must perform ongoing monitoring to ensure that effort reports are accurate.

Policies, Procedures and Forms

As organizations develop research compliance programs, they will likely incorporate policies, procedures and templates/forms for use in accurate and compliant time and effort reporting. Examples of topics typically covered in policies and procedures are:

- Duty to Accurately Report Time and Effort/Certification Obligations
- Cost Sharing, Cost Transfers, etc.
- Reporting External/Extramural Activities
- Changes in Time and Effort Between Reporting Periods
- University vs. Hospital Reporting Obligations (if applicable and if investigators share time between two different research organizations)—these policies will likely define terms for faculty and research staff and make reporting terms consistent
- Requirement for Written Agreements Between Universities and Hospitals (for shared research grants)
- Ongoing Requirement for Monitoring Time and Effort Reporting.

In addition to these recommended policies, corresponding procedures must be implemented in order to standardize time and effort reporting practices. Successful research organizations have actually conducted pilot programs in certain departments to test the procedures prior to implementing them across the entire research enterprise. That way, the "bugs" in the system can be worked out and subjects in the pilot project can be positive "spokespersons" for the new time and effort reporting initiative.

Perhaps most importantly, research organizations should develop standardized effort reporting forms—preferably automated programs that collect and assimilate the data. Using an automated program reduces administrative and monitoring workload by automating tasks and will provide consistency in reporting, validation and error checking. These programs enhance compliance by delegating responsible effort certifiers. Finally, one of the ancillary benefits of an automated process is that they help capture costs that can be recovered through the indirect cost rate.

Monitoring

As mentioned many times, ongoing monitoring is a critical component of a research compliance program for effort reporting. Whether the auditing and monitoring is performed by the Internal Audit Department, external auditors, the compliance officer, or someone in research administration, is not important. The crucial factor is that auditing and monitoring is conducted on a regular basis and where errors or inconsistencies are found, they are immediately corrected. If organizations are diligent in their actions related to timely and accurate effort reporting, they are much more positively scrutinized in the event that problems occur that result in government intervention. The old adage "an ounce of prevention is worth a pound of cure" is true when it comes to time and effort reporting compliance.

Clinical Research Billing

Clinical Research Billing ("CRB") compliance is at the forefront of healthcare compliance for academic medical centers ("AMC"), hospitals, and research institutions who are engaged in humans subjects research. Clinical trial billing processes are oftentimes subject to high interest due to the complexities involved in doing it correctly, and the regulatory requirements that may adversely impact providers should they submit a claim incorrectly. Since 2005, there have been several institutions that have been penalized by the government due to improper billing of Medicare for clinical research items and services (Rush University Medical Center: $1 million; Tenet USC Norris Cancer Hospital: $1.9 million, Emory University: $1.5 million).[9] Despite these challenges, the very fact that clinical research items and services can be billed to third-party payers has allowed many subjects to take part in cutting edge research which not only has the potential to benefit the health and well-being of the general population, but that of the subjects themselves.

CMS finalized the Clinical Trial Policy ("CTP")[10] in 2008 which is the driver for clinical research billing compliance in the United States. The CTP sets forth CMS' requirements for coverage for certain "routine care services" that are provided as part of a research study. Importantly, not every routine service that is billable outside of a research study, is necessarily billable as part of a research study. Alternatively, the CTP allows for certain additional provisions in the context of a research study that may not otherwise be considered a "routine care service" outside of the study. Therefore, research sites must do their homework in order to avoid potential false claims allegations and double billing concerns, while also remaining fiscally responsible.

Most research organizations were created as clinical and treatment-focused organizations. They were neither constructed with a view toward research, nor were their billing systems created with research in mind. Hence, most organizations have developed "work-arounds" to ensure that billing is completed. It is typically not, however, a foolproof solution. There needs to be adequate checks and balances, a system of oversight, coordination, advanced planning and internal controls to really make things work. The following sets forth one such methodology to create a compliant process to ensure that tests or services performed that are "standard of care" are appropriately billed to the insurer or participant, and those tests or services that are "research only" get billed against the clinical trial budget. That sounds easy, right? Hardly! Where does one even begin?

Many organizations begin this process by reviewing the "current state of things." In other words, they select a sample of active clinical trials and review the process to see what works well and what is not working so that it can be corrected. There is great value in analyzing current procedures, as it gives you insights into what is and what is possible from a clinical, budgeting, registration, information systems and billing perspective. In some cases, a particular investigator or clinical trial coordinator has developed a compliant "work-around" process that can be emulated across the entire organization. That may be a step in the right direction, but it is likely not an enterprise-wide solution. Most organizations find that they inevitably need to start from scratch and build new procedures. Affected individuals will ultimately need to be trained on those new policies and procedures.

As a starting place, one needs to consider the affected constituencies who should be involved in the process. At a minimum, they are as follows:

- Investigators
- Office of Contracting and/or Technology Transfer
- Research Finance and/or Research Billing
- Clinical Trial Coordinators and/or Research Nurses
- Registration staff (both inpatient and outpatient)
- Information Systems staff
- Clinical Trials Office (if applicable/available)
- Health Information Management staff
- Pharmacy and Laboratory support
- Compliance Officer and Legal Resources
- Hospital Administration
- Hospital/Physician Practice Billing Office
- Coding staff

Clinical Research Billing Life Cycle

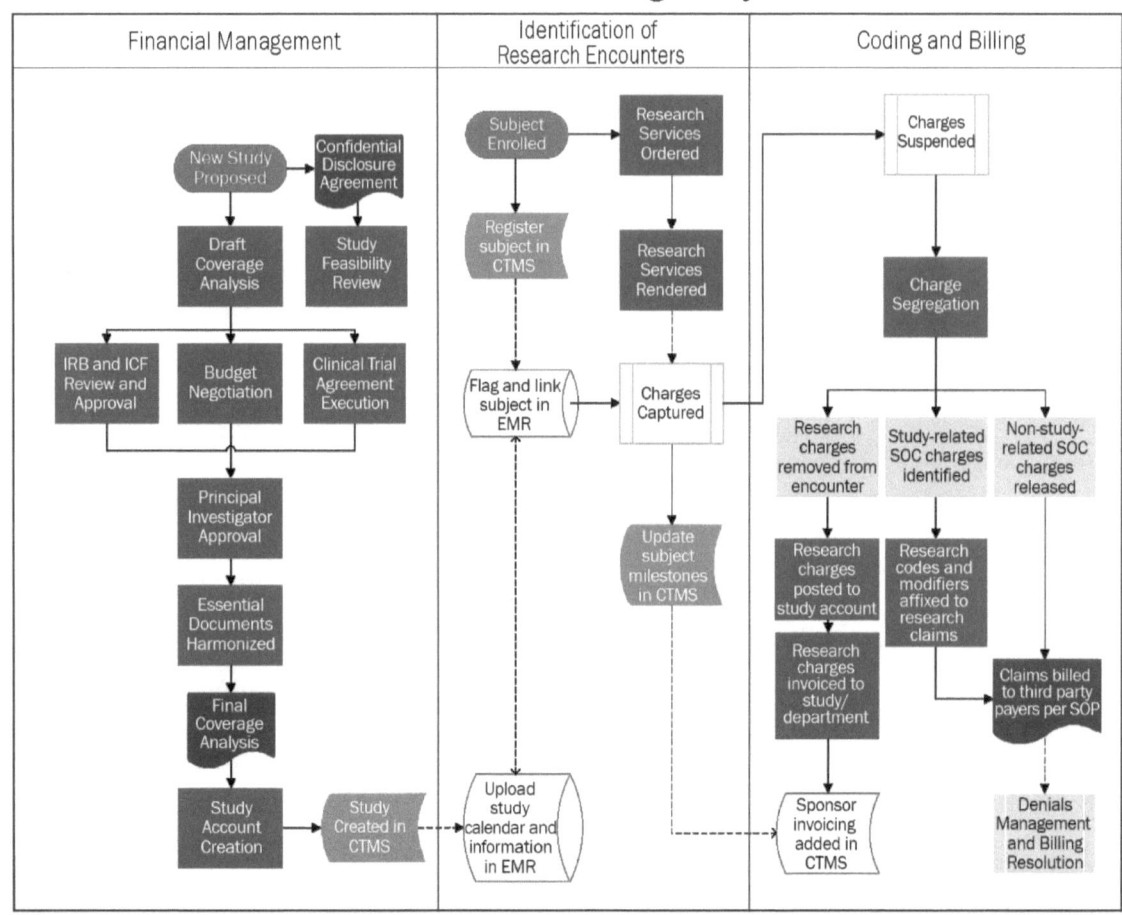

Financial Management

New Study Proposed → Confidential Disclosure Agreement

Draft Coverage Analysis → Study Feasibility Review

IRB and ICF Review and Approval, Budget Negotiation, Clinical Trial Agreement Execution

Principal Investigator Approval

Essential Documents Harmonized

Final Coverage Analysis

Study Account Creation → Study Created in CTMS

Identification of Research Encounters

Subject Enrolled → Research Services Ordered

Register subject in CTMS

Research Services Rendered

Flag and link subject in EMR → Charges Captured

Update subject milestones in CTMS

Upload study calendar and information in EMR

Coding and Billing

Charges Suspended

Charge Segregation

- Research charges removed from encounter
- Study-related SOC charges identified
- Non-study-related SOC charges released

Research charges posted to study account

Research codes and modifiers affixed to research claims

Research charges invoiced to study/department

Claims billed to third party payers per SOP

Sponsor invoicing added in CTMS

Denials Management and Billing Resolution

Clinical Research Billing compliance requires institutional coordination and support of several complex processes that extend throughout the institution. These processes can be summarized into the following three categories: (1) Financial Management; (2) Identification of Research Encounters; and (3) Coding and Billing. In addition to understanding how these processes are effectuated, organizations must also evaluate how structure and governance affects CRB, including staffing resources, information technology solutions, policies and procedures, and education and training. Furthermore, it is critical to understand what routine auditing and monitoring activities, if any, are in place to support clinical research billing compliance.

The diagram on page 20 illustrates the typical Clinical Research Billing Life Cycle and demonstrates the intricacies of what is required to effectuate compliant research billing.

Financial Management
- Coverage Analysis
- Budget Development and Clinical Trial Agreement Execution
- Sponsor Invoicing
- Research Account Reconciliation and Close-out

Clinical Research Billing compliance begins with the Coverage Analysis ("CA"). Coverage analysis is a formal method for determining the parties responsible for payment of hospital and professional fees during clinical research studies. It evolved out of the RUSH University Medical Center settlement with the United States Attorney's Office of the Northern District of Illinois and the Department of Health and Human Services Office of Inspector General in 2005. Coverage analysis utilizes essential documents that drive the clinical research billing including: study protocol, research informed consent form ("ICF"), clinical trial agreement ("CTA"), sponsor proposed budget, Food and Drug Administration ("FDA") documentation, Medicare coverage decisions, along with national treatment guidelines. The CA process involves evaluation of the essential documents in the context of the Medicare Clinical Trial Policy. The result is a document that memorializes the tools and information used to determine whether the research qualifies for reimbursement from Medicare (and other third party insurers) and which of the patient care items can be billed. If a provider institution is unaware of the items that are allowable, it risks improperly billing Medicare. Improper billing of Medicare could result in repayments, negative press, and in its most egregious circumstances, could be considered a false claim violation subject to fines and criminal penalties. Conducting a proper Coverage Analysis is therefore an essential element of clinical research billing compliance.

The development of proper clinical research budgets is key to ensuring that the provider institution is made whole for its costs for the conduct of research. Proper budgeting prevents the institution from underwriting research that should be paid by pharmaceutical and medical device manufacturers. It also ensures that any compensation provided by manufacturers is in accordance with applicable laws and regulations regarding financial relationships between manufacturers and providers. The CA should be used in developing study budgets so that research sites can ensure that they are receiving payment from sponsors for those items and services that are determined to be for research purposes only and therefore not billable to Medicare. This stage contemplates active communication with affected departments including the Laboratory, Pharmacy, Radiology and possibly other clinical specialties required for your research. In some cases, it may be prudent to meet in person with certain affected departments, particularly in the early stages of the new process, or if the study in question has unique qualities.

Many organizations have developed standardized budget templates and other standardized communication documents that make the process much more streamlined. Those templates can be developed to include administration and other overhead expenses, to ensure that those line items will not be forgotten. In addition, it will be necessary for institutions to always keep an updated list of hospital charges, known as a research charge description master ("CDM") so they can be sure that they are including the correct amounts of money for each test/visit/procedure performed on the study. That will help eliminate under-budgeting that occurs from time to time. The budget is negotiated with study sponsors and becomes fully executed as part of the CTA which is a legal contract between the research site and the study sponsor. It is imperative to ensure that all studies have a funding source, even if that funding source is the investigator's clinical department.

Invoicing the sponsor for completed research items is the manner through which the institution receives compensation. Billing milestones should be developed to ensure that submitting invoices to a sponsor is done on a timely basis, and completely. Monthly or weekly billing is recommended. If there is a problem, it is much easier to correct in a monthly or weekly cycle as opposed to waiting until the entire study is completed. Disruptions in invoicing, whether failure to send invoices or inability to account for a remittance can result in funding deficits and misappropriation of research funds. Therefore, it is essential that institutions have a reliable way to produce and account for clinical research receivables. Many institutions utilize a Clinical Trials Management System ("CTMS") to automate sponsor invoicing and payments, but organizations who do not use a CTMS must design manual methods to track when sponsor invoices must be sent, and subsequently track and document payments received from sponsors.

Research financial accounts must be maintained on an on-going basis and reconciled at the completion of all study activity to ensure that funds were appropriately allocated in accordance with regulatory and grant/contract requirements. Additionally, accounts should be reviewed before study close-out to ensure that all patient billing has been reconciled.

Identification of Research Encounters
- Study Account Creation
- Flagging Research Participants
- Registration of Research Visits

It is critical for institutions that bill the Medicare program for routine costs in clinical trials to develop processes to properly identify, or "flag," research participants in the billing system in a timely manner so that research and routine costs and conventional care charges can be segregated. Claims for research encounters must be scrubbed, reviewed for accuracy, and coded with the CMS or other commercial payer required codes and modifiers. A study account number must first be created in the billing system so that research participants may be linked to the proper study billing code. Institutions effectuate identification of research participants in the billing system(s) in different ways depending upon the IT/software resources available. Additionally, many institutions initiate a "bill-hold" for all encounters for flagged research subjects to ensure that the research claims are scrubbed, and codes and modifiers are appended to claims before they are dropped to Medicare and other third-party payers.

Coding and Billing
- Charge Capture
- Charge Review and Segregation
- CMS Required Elements
- Medicare Advantage Plan
- Billing inquiries and Resolution
- Denials Management

Medicare's Clinical Trials Policy provides the most defined standards for clinical research billing and represents the most significant compliance risk to providers. As such, it is the industry best practice to use the Medicare research billing rules as the standard for all third-party payers. The process of coverage analysis relies on the use of Medicare coverage rules and routine care guidelines as the basis for making billing decisions, and for ensuring that claims that are to be sent to insurers are only for the routine care delivered during a clinical trial.

Per the Clinical Trial Policy, also known as National Coverage Determination 310.1 (NCD 310.1), Medicare will cover the *routine costs* of *qualifying clinical trials*. Routine costs and Qualifying Clinical Trials (QCT) are both defined terms in NCD 310.1. Institutions must ensure that studies meet the QCT criteria before any items and services rendered in the context of a clinical trial are billed to participants and/or third-party payers.

Qualifying Clinical Trials are clinical research studies that meet the following three criteria, and must also be "deemed":

- Must evaluate an item or service that falls within a Medicare benefit category and is not statutorily excluded
- Must have therapeutic intent
- Must enroll participants with diagnosed disease

The CTP states that "The three requirements above are insufficient by themselves to qualify a clinical trial for Medicare coverage of routine costs. Clinical trials should also have the following desirable characteristics; however, some trials, as described below, are presumed to meet these characteristics and are automatically ('deemed') qualified to receive Medicare coverage:"

1. The principal purpose of the trial is to test whether the intervention potentially improves the subjects' health outcomes;
2. The trial is well-supported by available scientific and medical information or it is intended to clarify or establish the health outcomes of interventions already in common clinical use;
3. The trial does not unjustifiably duplicate existing studies;
4. The trial design is appropriate to answer the research question being asked in the trial;
5. The trial is sponsored by a credible organization or individual capable of executing the proposed trial successfully;
6. The trial is in compliance with federal regulations relating to the protection of human subjects; and
7. All aspects of the trial are conducted according to the appropriate standards of scientific integrity.

A study is automatically "deemed" if it meets one of the following four criteria:

1. Trials funded by NIH, CDC, AHRQ, CMS, DOD, and VA;
2. Trials supported by centers or cooperative groups that are funded by the NIH, CDC, AHRQ, CMS, DOD, and VA;
3. Trials conducted under an investigational new drug application (IND) reviewed by the FDA; and
4. Drug trials that are exempt from having an IND under 21 CFR 312.2(b)(1)

If a study does not meet the initial three requirements and it is not "deemed," institutions may not bill Medicare for any study items/services required by the protocol (with some very limited exceptions).

CMS NCD 310.1 defines Routine Costs as:

- Items and services that are typically provided absent a clinical trial (conventional care)
- Items and services required solely for the provision of the investigational item or service (*e.g.*, administration of a non-covered chemotherapeutic agent)
- Items and services provided for the clinically appropriate monitoring of the effects of or prevention of complications from the investigational item
- Items or services needed for reasonable and necessary care arising from the provision of an investigational item or service—in particular, for the diagnosis or treatment of complications.

The rule also explicitly states that the following are not considered routine costs:

- Items which are statutorily excluded or for which there is a non-coverage decision

- The investigational item or service itself, unless otherwise covered outside of the clinical trial
- Items and services provided solely to satisfy data collection and analysis needs
- Items and services that are not used in the direct clinical management of the participant
- Items and services customarily provided by the research sponsors free of charge for any enrollee in the trial

Coverage for investigational devices ("IDE") and associated services fall under different Medicare rules.[11] These determinations are made by CMS upon receipt of an application from the research sponsor or device manufacturer. However, having all items and services identified in the CA is essential to compliance with Medicare coding and documentation requirements for research charges.

Research participant care charges must be sorted and released as prescribed by the CA with appropriate codes and modifiers on the claims. "Back end" processes for the accurate identification of research charges, removing them from the claim, and affixing the proper CMS required elements is just as essential to research billing compliance as preparing a proper CA and flagging research participants.

CMS rules require that providers include the following information in the beneficiary's medical record:[12]

- Trial Name
- Sponsor
- Sponsor assigned protocol number
- Informed Consent Form

Providers must include the following information on the claims of Medicare beneficiaries:

- HCPCS modifier Q0 (number zero) for the investigational clinical service provided in the clinical study
- HCPCS modifier Q1 (number one) for routine clinical services provided in the clinical study
- Condition code 30 (hospital claims only)
- ICD-10 diagnosis code of Z00.6 (or ICD-9 diagnosis code V70.7)
- ClinicalTrials.gov registration or 'NCT' number
- Category B IDE device HCPCS code if applicable
- Condition Code 53 when the investigational device is furnished to the hospital at no cost (outpatient hospital claims only).

Needless to say, the above processes require substantial coordination and communication across the research enterprise. This will represent dramatic changes for investigators, clinical trial coordinators, research administration, registration staff, and billing staff in institutions who are designing or re-designing new CRB systems and processes. Therefore, it will be necessary to plan and execute significant training on these new procedures. There are some likely challenges that will arise in the course of planning a new and more streamlined process. Those challenges will vary a bit from one organization to the next, but nevertheless it is important to anticipate some of those challenges early on. For example, the development and implementation of standardized budgeting and CA templates will go a long way but can be detrimental if a complete billing process throughout operations is implemented.

Other critical billing issues include who can be billed for research-related injuries (which may trigger the CMS Medicare as Secondary Payer Rule "MSP") and how billing should be accomplished for Medicare Advantage beneficiaries. For example, CMS' MSP rule states that when a beneficiary has insurance that is supplemental to Medicare coverage, their other insurance must be billed first and then Medicare stands in the secondary payment position. In the research context, this is triggered when there is language in a clinical trial agreement that indicates that the sponsor will be billed for research-related injury if and when insurance denies the claim. CMS has determined that in that context, the sponsor becomes the primary guarantor and places the sponsor in the first payment position. Hence, it is critical for research sites to carefully negotiate clinical trial agreements to ensure that everyone is on the same page with respect to billing obligations.

Medicare Advantage billing is also quite complicated. The rules require that protocol-scheduled services be billed to Medicare prime as opposed to the Advantage "plan" in drug clinical trials and any services that are unrelated to the research protocol be billed to Medicare Advantage. In large part this is done so that CMS can track the amount it is paying to support research and because many Medicare Advantage plans do not have the claims processing capability to handle required modifiers used to denote "research," such as a Z00.6 code placed in the secondary diagnosis position or a Q1 or Q0 modifier to denote either a standard of care service (e.g., Q1) or a research related service (e.g., Q0).

Unfortunately, there is no single perfect process for clinical trial billing. Every research organization has its own unique challenges. The important thing in today's complex and highly charged regulatory environment is to have an effective process in place to ensure that there is oversight, coordination and compliance. When there is a problem, the compliance staff must contemplate ways to remediate. That will go a long way to keeping your organization on the right track.

Research Privacy and Security

The primary laws and regulations that cover research privacy and security are found in the Health Insurance Portability and Accountability Act ("HIPAA) and the HITECH provisions dealing with data breaches. The final HIPAA Omnibus Rule was published in January 2013 and in research-related issues, it essentially modified the rules related to authorizations to use or disclose protected health information ("PHI") for research purposes. In the past, a HIPAA authorization was required to be specific to a single research study. Under the final HIPAA Omnibus Rule, an authorization may be "compounded"—meaning that it may include authorization for multiple studies or uses and disclosures for multiple purposes. In addition, the final HIPAA Omnibus Rule now allows for authorizations for future research (which were not possible under the previous HIPAA Privacy Rule). In addition, the final HIPAA Omnibus Rule requires training on privacy and security requirements (for those who handle or use PHI for research purposes) as well as auditing and monitoring of compliance with the rules.

Basically, HIPAA provides that PHI may be used for research purposes:

1. with an authorization signed by the subject or his/her legal representative; or
2. with a waiver of authorization from an IRB or Privacy Board; or
3. with a limited data set and a data use agreement; or
4. if the data is fully de-identified; or
5. if the data is on a decedent.

Much like the other research risk issues described herein, compliance with the HIPAA Privacy, HITECH and Security Rules is critical for ongoing compliance and is likely to be the subject of enforcement issues in the coming years.

Oversight of Clinical Research

The myriad regulatory schema, oversight agencies and enforcement all reinforce the importance of an effective clinical research compliance program. A strong clinical research compliance program should be multifaceted. To be effective, it must safeguard the integrity of the research, steward resources, shore up the reputation of the organization and individuals conducting research. Another priority is ensuring that subjects volunteering to participate in clinical research are fully informed of the risks and benefits of the research study in which they are participating. Developing and maintaining a robust compliance program may not be easy, but it is an essential component of clinical research.

Clinical research is an organized attempt to confirm hypotheses, test theories and use a scientific approach to learning more about the human physiology. It holds out great hope for people, but is also fraught with many dangers. While clinical research findings can be used for tremendous good, such as eradicating disease and improving lives, its potential for untold barbarism, malevolent ends, egoism and control necessitates vigilance in oversight. A study's purpose must not only have value and a constructive end, but the actual conduct of research must demonstrate integrity in dealings with subjects and other ethical arenas. History confirms that clinical research can be abused and that safeguards must be established to preserve both the higher goals of and the confidence in clinical research held by society.

While clinical research in the United States does have a highly regulated framework governing its conduct, it is often the compliance professional embedded within an organization who shoulders the responsibility for reconciling laws, policies, procedures and ethical principles with practical demands and budgetary constraints. These individuals play a vital role in assuring the operational and administrative well-being of their organization's research enterprise. Consequently, they are also instrumental in guaranteeing society the at-large benefits from clinical research. Everyday, clinical research compliance programs should exemplify the maxim, "the ends do not justify the means."

Clinical Trials Registration and Results Information Submission

Title VIII of the Food and Drug Administration Amendments Act of 2007 (FDAAA) requires certain clinical trials to be registered on the clinicaltrials.gov database to increase patient access to clinical trials and to improve transparency in clinical trial design and results reporting. The database is managed by the National Library of Medicine at the National Institute of Health.

The final rule (42 CFR 11) was effective January 18, 2017 and details the requirements of the responsible party for submitting clinical trials and results information to clinicaltrials.gov. The "responsible party" is the sponsor of the clinical trial, unless the sponsor designates a qualified principal investigator as the responsible party.

The FDA requires submission of Form FDA 3674 with certain human drug, biological product, and device applications and submissions to FDA, including:[13]

- Investigational New Drug Application (IND)
- New Clinical Protocol Submitted to an IND
- New Drug Application (NDA)
- Efficacy Supplement to an Approved NDA
- Biologics License Application (BLA)
- Efficacy Supplement to an Approved BLA
- Abbreviated New Drug Application (ANDA)
- Premarket Approval Application (PMA)
- PMA Panel Track Supplement
- Humanitarian Device Exemption (HDE)
- 510(k) submissions that refer to, relate to, or include information on a clinical trial.

It is important for research organizations, especially with a large portfolio of investigator-initiated clinical trials, to assign oversight of this regulatory requirement to an office or individual to ensure that the institution is in compliance with clinicaltrials.gov regulations.

Chapter 1 Endnotes

1. **F. Lisa Murtha, JD, CHC, CHRC**, is Senior Managing Director for Ankura Consulting in Philadelphia, PA; **Debbie Troklus, CCEP-F, CHC-F, CCEP-I, CHPC, CHRC** is Senior Managing Director for Ankura Consulting, in Louisville, KY; **Nicole Visyak, MS, MA, CCRC**, is Director for Ankura Consulting in Boston, MA; and **Draco Forte, MEd, CHRC**, is Director for Ankura Consulting in Chicago, IL.
2. Office of the Secretary, U.S. Dep't of Health, Education and Welfare, "Protection of Human Subjects; Belmont Report: Ethical Principles and Guidelines for the Protection of Human Subjects of Research, Report of the National Commission for the Protection of Human Subjects of Biomedical and Behavioral Research" (18 April 1979), 44 Fed. Reg. 44: 23191–7, https://www.hhs.gov/ohrp/regulations-and-policy/belmont-report/read-the-belmont-report/index.html#xinform.
3. International Council for Harmonisation of Technical Requirements for Pharmaceuticals for Human Use, GUIDELINE FOR GOOD CLINICAL PRACTICE E6(R2), (November 9, 2016), https://www.ich.org/fileadmin/Public_Web_Site/ICH_Products/Guidelines/Efficacy/E6/E6_R2__Step_4_2016_1109.pdf.
4. Notice Number: NOT- OD- 16-148: Policy on Good Clinical Practice Training for NIH Awardees Involved in NIH- funded Clinical Trials (https://grants.nih.gov/grants/guide/notice-files/NOT-OD-16-148.html).
5. See *supra* note 2.
6. U.S. Dep't of Health and Human Services, Office of Research Integrity, Case Summary: Kornak, Paul H., https://ori.hhs.gov/case-summary-kornak-paul-h.
7. David Armstrong, "How a famed hospital invests in device it uses and promotes." *Wall Street Journal*, December 12, 2005.
8. Public Health Service (PHS) Regulations: 42 CFR Part 50, Subpart F.
9. Rush University Medical Center News Release December 8, 2005 http://www.hcca-info.org/Portals/0/PDFs/Resources/Conference_Handouts/Compliance_Institute/2006/510handout1.pdf; DHHS and DOJ Health Care Fraud and Abuse Control Program Annual Report FY 2010 http://thehill.com/images/stories/blogs/fraudreport.pdf; DOJ US Attorney's Office Northern District of Georgia Press Release August 28, 2013 https://www.justice.gov/usao-ndga/pr/emory-university-pay-15-million-settle-false-claims-act-investigation.
10. https://www.cms.gov/medicare-coverage-database/details/ncd-details.aspx?NCAId=248&NcaName=Intensive+Behavioral+Therapy+for+Cardiovascular+Disease&ExpandComments=y&ver=2&NCDId=1&ncdver=2&bc=BEAAAAAAEEAAAA%3D%3D&.
11. U.S. Dep't of Health and Human Services, Centers for Medicare and Medicaid Services, Medicare Benefit Policy Manual, "Chapter 14 - Medical Devices," (Rev. 198, November 6, 2014) https://www.cms.gov/Regulations-and-Guidance/Guidance/Manuals/downloads/bp102c14.pdf.
12. U.S. Dep't of Health and Human Services, Centers for Medicare and Medicaid Services, Medicare Benefit Policy Manual, Medicare Claims Processing Manual, "Chapter 32 - Billing Requirements for Special Services" (Rev. 4111, August 10, 2018), https://www.cms.gov/Regulations-and-Guidance/Guidance/Manuals/downloads/clm104c32.pdf.
13. U.S. Food and Drug Administration, "FDA's Role: ClinicalTrials.gov Information," https://www.fda.gov/scienceresearch/specialtopics/runningclinicaltrials/fdasroleclinicaltrials.govinformation/default.htm.

2
Options for Identifying and Managing Financial Conflicts of Interest in Research: Flexible Compliance with the PHS Final Rule

By Stuart Horowitz, PhD, MBA[1]

Introduction

Merriam-Webster Online defines conflict of interest ("COI") as: *"a conflict between the private interests and the official responsibilities of a person in a position of trust."*

Simply put, a COI arises when two different interests are at odds with one another. It is actually a conflict of interests. There can be no conflict unless there are at least two interests; thus, the term "conflict of interest" is illogical, because there is no conflict unless there is more than one interest. Nevertheless, the term conflict of interest has entered the vernacular, and the even-more illogical term: conflicts of interest (COIs), is also in common usage. For these reasons and until or unless common usage harmonizes with English grammar, this chapter reverts to the vernacular terms: conflict(s) of interest.

There is no wrongdoing in the existence of a COI. These conflicts are part of human existence. For example, nearly all parents who have routinely read bedtime stories to their children have experienced a situation where, on the one hand, they recognized the importance and value of reading to a child at night. But on the other hand, invariably, a night arrived where they also recognized how tired they felt, and how important their own sleep was to them. At that moment, they had a bona fide COI. Note that both interests are important and legitimate... and in conflict. That particular COI might be managed differently depending on the day. For example, spouses might take on the task of reading some nights. On other nights, children might have to be told that mommy or daddy is too tired to read.

In conducting research, a problem arises when a COI leads to bias. It's not just actual bias, however, that presents a problem for researchers. The appearance of bias is also a concern. In the realm of COI, it is sometimes said that perception is reality. This is an important concept to bear in mind whenever considering COI in research. The goals are to eliminate bias (because bias is not acceptable in research), and to either eliminate or manage the appearance of bias.

This chapter is focused on financial COI (FCOI) only. However, not all COI involves money. For example, nepotism is a form of COI that is not necessarily financial. There are also conflicts that arise because of (real or perceived) scientific bias. That is, many researchers have strong beliefs—built on a pet theory, for example. These beliefs can influence research design, analysis and reporting. There may also be beliefs related to religion and faith that have potential to lead to research bias. This chapter does not address any of these conflicts, however, because federal regulations do not address non-financial COI.

The focus of this chapter is on FCOIs that investigators (individual people doing research) may have. Please note that there are also FCOIs that are harbored by institutions. For example, a university, or academic medical center, or hospital may have a significant financial interest in a new technology, drug, or device (by virtue of a patent, for example), and may choose to pursue a research project related to that technology, or drug, or device. Such a situation creates an institutional FCOI. That FCOI may be unacceptable to the public. To date, however, there are no federal regulations that address this issue, and likewise, it is not addressed in this chapter.

Financial Conflict of Interest in Federally-Funded Research

Visit the National Institutes of Health (NIH) home page for financial conflict of interest and you'll find a notable quote from the current Director of the NIH, Dr. Francis Collins, stating: "The public trust in what we do is just essential, and we cannot afford to take any chances with the integrity of the research process."[2] The interpretation of this quote gets to the heart of some of the greatest challenges faced by research compliance professionals with responsibility for identifying and handling financial conflicts of interest at institutions conducting research. As Director of the NIH and one of the country's strongest advocates for research, Dr. Collins was acutely aware of the risks to the public trust—and the associated public funding of the NIH's intramural and extramural research programs.

Reduction of research funding is not the only immediate concern over the public's perception of the loss of integrity in research. Another short-term pain point is the public scrutiny faced by the NIH, research institutions, and investigators at congressional hearings and by the popular and science press. The longer-term consequences are especially troubling: When too many people lose faith in the integrity of research, progress itself will be slowed.

In the aftermath of a series of high-profile cases questioning the integrity of research conducted by investigators at some of the finest research institutions in the US from 2008 to 2011,[3] two new/revised rules were enacted. One addresses *giving*: i.e., transfers-of-value (essentially payments) from corporate entities to physicians, including payments to physician-researchers. The other addresses *receiving*: income received by researchers given by outside entities, or ownership of outside interests by researchers. Although these seem, superficially, like two sides of a coin, they're actually more like two sides of two partially-overlapping coins. The first set of rules were incorporated into the Physician Payment "Sunshine" Provisions of the Affordable Care Act,[4] which describe the obligations of pharmaceutical companies and medical manufacturers to publicly report all transfers of value made to healthcare providers. Some of these are payments made to physician-researchers, and to healthcare organizations conducting research. But many of these payments are unrelated to research or researchers. This chapter does not address the Sunshine Provisions of the Affordable Care Act, which is covered in Chapter 1.

The second rule was published on August 25, 2011, and is known as the *Final Rule on Financial Conflict of Interest Regulations—Responsibility of Applicants for Promoting Objectivity in Research for Which Public Health Service Funding is Sought and Responsible Prospective Contractors.*[5] It is a revision of an older, less-prescriptive rule and is meant to increase transparency and to clarify perceived ambiguities in the older rule. At the time of its publication, the Federal Register notice provided applicable organizations (primarily those which received, are receiving, or have applied to receive PHS research support) up to one year to implement the rule. Note that the rule applies to all PHS-funded research, investigators and their institutions, regardless of whether they are also healthcare providers. Although the rule required compliance by no later than August 26, 2012, it is still referred to as the "Final Rule," and still the topic of much discussion.

Because applicable organizations are now required to comply with the Final Rule, this chapter neither compares nor contrasts it with the older rule. Also, because the published rule can easily be referenced, we do not rehash it here (with the exception of a few small elements). Similarly, there are no model policies or procedures to be found here. For these, the reader is referred to The Institute on Medicine as a Profession, which has a public website compendium and searchable database of COI policies and processes from various organizations and organization types.[6] Instead, this chapter focuses on the major options inherent in the rule and the flexibility it allows, including applicability and standards, disclosure and disclosure thresholds, tolerance and management, transparency, and technology.

Applicability and Standards

Who is required to follow the Final Rule? The rule is clear in stating that it applies to institutions that have PHS research support (or who have recently had it, or seek it), and to the investigator(s) receiving that support. Note that the terms "research" and "investigator" have clear, broad, and non-obvious definitions embedded in the rule. But even when it is crystal clear when and to whom the rule must apply, the institution has the option of widening the scope of the rule and applying it to others.

Why apply the PHS Final Rule where it is not required? The issue comes down to standards. That is, does the institution have a single standard for FCOI that it applies fairly to investigators across the board, or does it have a double-standard—one for PHS-funded investigators, and one for those who are not PHS-funded? Or does it have multiple standards? For example, one for PHS-funded investigators, one for National Science Foundation (NSF)-funded investigators,[7] another for another agency, and perhaps one for state-funded investigators?[8] The choice of whether to apply one standard or more can be made on the basis of three considerations: ethics, fairness, and practicality.

Ethics: If we accept the notion that bias in research as a result of a FCOI is bad, and that the FCOI rules are designed to reduce or eliminate bias, it may seem ethically unsupportable to set anything but a single standard. Whether or not research is funded by PHS, we would not want to accept bias in that research. For example, it is not unusual for a single investigator to have research projects funded by multiple sources. The idea that even the appearance of bias in the investigator's non-PHS-supported research would be acceptable, but disallowed for a PHS-funded project, seems unfathomable. For this reason, some institutions have adopted a single standard. Note that this approach may require harmonizing multiple regulatory requirements to "set the bar" high enough so that all hurdles are overcome together in one process (this issue is also addressed below under "practicality").

On the other hand, an institution might adopt a single ethical standard and believe that the different requirements of various federal, state, and local agencies and private sources are nuanced, regulatory in nature, and though they require compliance, are not ethically relevant. In this case, it is possible to set the ethical bar and as long as the differences in requirements do not allow any research to go under the bar, multiple regulatory standards are acceptable.

Fairness: The FCOI rules are often viewed by investigators as intrusive because considerable information about their personal finances is disclosed. The disclosure requirements under the Final Rule—and the ensuing administrative processes—are burdensome. In a university, academic medical center, or research hospital environment, no investigator wants to feel singled out for financial disclosure, for any reason. For this reason, some institutions have chosen to apply the same set of rules (and tools for analysis, such as disclosure forms) to all investigators, regardless of funding source. This levels the playing field and fairly distributes the burden among all investigators.

On the other hand, this approach might be viewed as "collective punishment." For example, some investigators may *never* seek or receive PHS funding, simply because their research is outside of PHS's mission (as in the case of most faculty of chemistry, physics, engineering, or mathematics). Is it really "fair" to burden them with all the complexities and requirements of the PHS Final Rule? Perhaps it would be more appropriate to acknowledge that the rules simply don't apply to them? With this perspective in mind, some institutions with mature programs, including research faculty in diverse disciplines, have chosen to apply the PHS Final Rule strictly when required, but no more.

The issue of fairness can also be linked to the alignment of incentives and the growth of the research institution. As described above, a mature organization may feel it is unfair to burden non-biomedical faculty with PHS requirements. But the opposite can be true in other institutions. For example, organizations seeking to establish/grow a PHS-funded portfolio of research may struggle to appropriately encourage the submission of grant applications. In this circumstance, those investigators aligned with organizational goals and who seek or obtain PHS support can interpret the situation as "no good deed goes unpunished," because they are burdened with disclosures and processes, while their less-productive colleagues are undisturbed. Thus, in the institution focused on research growth, the issue of fairness can be analyzed differently.

Practicality: What could be more practical and straightforward than a single policy with a single set of processes, one disclosure form, one set of analytical tools and standard operating procedures? From a utilitarian perspective, this approach may be more practicable than adopting two or more processes, forms, SOPs, etc. However, depending on the type of institution, its resources and its goals, there are circumstances where a single, consistent process is more challenging to implement, and multiple processes may actually be more practicable. For example, in a research hospital environment, where there may be only five PHS-funded investigators, but a cadre of 95 clinical investigators doing corporate-sponsored clinical trials, applying the PHS Final Rule to all investigators may generate much more work than the hospital is able to manage, especially if it uses manual workflows and document management, rather than dedicated electronic COI (eCOI) software (discussed further below).

Disclosure and Disclosure Thresholds

All investigators—as widely defined here—must provide annual and prompt ongoing disclosures. Look carefully at the definition for investigator in the PHS Final Rule:

> Investigator means the project director or principal Investigator and any other person, regardless of title or position, who is responsible for the design, conduct, or reporting of research funded by the PHS, or proposed for such funding, which may include, for example, collaborators or consultants.[9]

Not only that, but for each investigator, note the following disclosure requirement:

> A financial interest consisting of one or more of the following interests of the Investigator (and those of the Investigator's spouse and dependent children) that reasonably appears to be related to the Investigator's institutional responsibilities...[10]

Note that the disclosure requirements are limited to the investigator's spouse and dependent children. However, there is nothing in the Final

Rule preventing an institution from widening the disclosure requirement to include others related to the investigator in other ways. Although some may feel it is appropriate or even "better" to expand the family circle of disclosure to siblings, parents, and others, this option is not recommended for two reasons. First, the collection of payment and ownership information is intrusive enough for the investigator, spouse and dependent children. To expand this may be overly-burdensome. Second, it is impracticable. The investigator typically has no access to such information and might not be able to obtain it. The likelihood of obtaining a complete and accurate disclosure from a wider circle of family members is small, and thus the value of the information, if it can be collected at all, is questionable.

The PHS Final Rule sets required thresholds for investigator disclosure of ownership in, and remuneration by publicly-traded entities ($5,000 combined annual from a single entity) and remuneration by non-publicly-held entities ($5,000 annual from a single entity). Investigator ownership of any amount in a non-publicly-traded entity must also be disclosed. Although this seems straightforward, investigator disclosure can be a significant point of confusion and resulting noncompliance. Confusion can stem from the annual look-back period, the value of an equity holding, changes in stock value, stock vesting schedules, whether a payment or ownership is "related" to the investigator's institutional obligations or to his or her research project(s), whether payments come from separate subsidiaries or a single entity, memory lapses, spouse's income or equity holdings, how and when to add payments, non-financial compensation (such as airfare), payments made indirectly through the institution, and other sources.

Fortunately, PHS allows some flexibility in disclosure. The institution can take two steps to help establish a full and accurate record of the investigator's outside financial interests. First, it can set the annual disclosure due date at or near April 15, and open the window for annual disclosures in the second week of February. This timing makes it likely that the investigator will have received all investment and income statements, including Form 1099s, for the previous year and be able to use them to assist in the disclosure process. Second, it can set a zero-dollar threshold for disclosure, and instead, ask the investigator to transcribe the amounts from his or her statements. This avoids math errors by the investigator, and places the burden on the institution. If an e-COI system is deployed, the math can be done automatically, assisting the institution in determining if the financial interest meets the "significant" threshold.

The excerpted section from the regulation on disclosure notes the concept in the Final Rule of a requirement to disclose financial interests relating to the investigator's institutional responsibilities. There are three approaches to take in order to capture this information. The first is to make sure investigators understand their institutional responsibilities, and to use their best judgment in this regard. The second is to require investigators to list everything except that which is obviously unrelated to their institutional responsibilities (for example, a biomedical researcher need not disclose ownership of 20% of a movie theater). The third, and perhaps the most conservative approach, is to ask them to list all outside financial interests (except those excluded in the regulations, like mutual funds), and for the institution to determine relatedness.

Finally, the regulation requires investigator disclosure of outside payments. Some payments that originate from outside entities—such as royalty payments and, in larger institutions, clinical trial reimbursements—are paid to the institution, not directly to the investigator. Yet some institutions ask investigators to list those amounts in their disclosure forms. To the extent possible, it is recommended that institutions do not burden investigators with a requirement to disclose information that the institution already has. For example, if an institution has a policy that requires it to consider royalty payments paid first to the institution and then shared (in part) with the investigator, it already has such information and should not require the investigator to provide this information again.

Tolerance and Management

Although the Final Rule is highly prescriptive, it is rather flexible in the key area of how FCOIs are managed.[11] As noted in the introduction to this chapter, the mere existence of an FCOI is not a statement of bias or wrongdoing. Thus, the institution's goal should not be to eliminate FCOI, but rather to address FCOIs in a manner that avoids bias in the research, or the *appearance of bias*. Whether or not an FCOI appears to lead to bias is a matter of opinion, however. The term "reasonable" appears a dozen times in the Final Rule, and reasonable people can have different opinions on the appearance of bias. In light of these reasonable (and predictable) differences in opinion, the rule gives the institution a great deal of discretion on how it manages FCOIs. Discretion, however, can be perceived as arbitrary, and if not managed carefully, unfair if it is inconsistently applied. Therefore, discretion should be exercised thoughtfully, systematically, and consistently.

The basis for discretion should be rooted in institutional culture. There are basically two, non-exclusive approaches. Some institutions emphasize that each circumstance is unique and each deserves special consideration. Ideally, these institutions develop a clear set of written principles, and apply these principles to deliberate on each FCOI. Typically, the investigator's peers sit on a committee that consider the FCOI. This *principles-based* approach can be applied fairly if the principles upon which each decision is made are documented and understandable to the investigator. A principles-based approach is generally time-consuming, as each situation is analyzed and evaluated. It is important, as each case is decided, to memorialize the circumstances and the outcome, so that the principles are applied consistently, and so that any change in how the principles are applied over time are understood and documented.

Alternatively, some institutions embrace the notion that many FCOIs are alike and can be managed using a *rules-based* approach. Typically, a clear set of rules (based on principles) are developed, permitting many (or most) FCOIs to be analyzed, categorized, and managed or eliminated. The benefits of utilizing a rules-based system for managing FCOIs are that it is rapid, fair and consistent, and easily understandable to the investigator. Ideally, the investigator community has an opportunity to participate in the creation of the institution's rules. The weakness of this approach is that it is inadequate for complex situations. Thus, even institutions that employ rules-and-tools (analytical processes, described below), actually take a hybrid approach, deliberating carefully in those cases when the rules do not readily apply.

When taking a hybrid approach (favored by this author), the flexibility utilized when managing FCOIs should be informed by the institution's tolerance for risk. That is: What is the organization's appetite for dealing with allegations that it failed to identify or manage an FCOI related to research? In the world of COI, it is useful to remember the adage: *perception is reality*. What institutions need to consider is the question: *Whose* perception is paramount? It is *a given* that each institution must comply with applicable regulations and therefore is concerned with the regulators' determinations. However, it is possible to comply with all regulations and still be haunted by the press, Congress-members, and the public, whenever conflicts are alleged. Institutions need to consider not only what it takes to follow the rules, but also what they need to do to avoid news stories that exceed their tolerance for negative press. However, this need not necessarily mean adopting a zero-tolerance approach across-the-board.

A convenient paradigm with which to establish a set of rules consistent with institutional tolerance for risk is to categorize FCOIs in three ways. FCOIs may be thought of as: show-stoppers, garden-variety manageable, complex and custom. The first two categories are managed by rules-and-tools. The third requires deliberation based on principles.

Show-stoppers are FCOIs that the institution will not tolerate under any circumstances. A show-stopper is an FCOI that the institution feels cannot be managed or is not worth the risk of management. For these, either the FCOI is eliminated, or the research is disallowed. It goes without saying that any circumstance in which there is *actual bias* cannot be allowed. But these situations are few and far between, and much of the time, it boils down to whether the institution believes the *appearance of bias* is so strong and obvious, that it is not worth the risk to try to manage it. These need not necessarily be lucrative opportunities for investigators. For example, many academic medical centers have decided that none of their faculty may participate on speakers' bureaus—panels of paid experts who deliver public presentations on behalf of a pharmaceutical or medical device company.

The rules for show stoppers typically consist of a list of prohibited FCOIs. In addition to the speakers' bureau rule, this list might include situations where:

- The value of the investigator's remuneration or ownership is linked to the outcome of a study in which the investigator is participating.
- The investigator receives payment from the research sponsor while being unduly restricted from publishing the results of the research.
- The investigator has sole responsibility for data analysis for a study sponsored by a company in which he or she has a significant financial interest (as defined in the Final Rule or at a lower threshold if set by institutional policy).
- The investigator has sole responsibility for obtaining informed consent from research volunteers in a study involving a technology in which he or she has a significant financial interest.
- The investigator is the PI of a multi-center clinical trial at the institution, and is also a consultant to the sponsor, receiving $250,000 per year for providing services/advice.

There may be other FCOIs that an institution chooses to prohibit under all circumstances. In addition to listing them in the institution's policies and procedures, it is useful to develop a set of SOPs that include flowcharts used as tools, instructing staff on how to determine if an FCOI falls into this category. It may also be possible to develop logic within software to assist in this process (see "Technology," below).

An FCOI can be categorized as *garden-variety manageable* if it meets a set of predetermined criteria. A garden-variety manageable FCOI is one that meets two broad criteria. First, it is typical or unremarkable. Second, it is one that the organization believes can be managed with a formal and (ideally) standard management plan. Note that an institution may adopt a policy that not every garden-variety FCOI can be managed—as in the case of the speakers' bureau example. Membership on speakers' bureaus is certainly typical and unremarkable (although these days, perhaps less so at academic medical centers). However, in some institutions, it does not meet the criteria for being manageable.

Some examples of garden-variety manageable FCOIs:

- Consulting for a company related to the investigator's laboratory research but remunerated in an amount predetermined to be acceptable. For example, the institution can set policy that a consulting arrangement valued at no greater than $20,000 per year is an FCOI that can be managed.
- Conducting a clinical trial with a pharmaceutical company in which the investigator

owns $25,000 in publicly-traded stock. The institution can set a policy that ownership of up to $25,000 is an FCOI that can be managed.
- Advising a medical device company about the design of product in a multicenter clinical trial that the investigator is leading at one site. The institution can set a policy that payment to the investigator of up to $30,000 is an FCOI that can be managed.

In these examples, the upper limit of value may seem arbitrary. Ideally, however, the institution sets values reflecting its belief that they are acceptable because the appearance of bias is small, based partly on the amount, the investigator's overall compensation, and the fact that the investigator is following a specific management plan. As suggested above, the institution can develop a small library of standardized, formal management plans for each garden-variety manageable FCOI. Each FCOI categorized in this way can be issued the appropriate standard management plan. For example, the investigator holding the stock may be issued a plan requiring that the prospective participant is informed of the ownership interest verbally and in writing, that all public presentations or publications emanating from the research include a predetermined ownership disclosure statement, and that the person obtaining informed consent is not the investigator.

As with show-stoppers, garden-variety manageable FCOIs can be identified and managed without committee deliberation. A clear set of standard operating procedures and flowcharts, managed by competent administrative staff or in smaller institutions, can be used by one staff member. It is also possible to automate a significant part of the process using dedicated eCOI software. This approach, backed up by quality assurance, can handle the bulk of FCOIs that require management plans.

An FCOI may be considered to be *complex and custom* if it does not fall into either of the two categories already discussed. These conflicts are atypical and require not only careful analyses in order to be fully understood, but also careful deliberation and if the FCOI is allowed, a customized management plan. Examples in this category:

- Investigator has founding shares of a new company launched to develop a medical device, and wishes to conduct a feasibility study in a group of patients at your hospital.
- Investigator is paid $50,000 per year for serving on the board of directors of a pharmaceutical company, and wishes to "donate" all the money to his or her division's fellowship program.
- Investigator has developed a new drug and is named as an inventor in a pending patent application filed by the institution. The investigator seeks to conduct the first-in-human studies at your institution.

Such scenarios do not lend themselves to standard treatment, and deserve the institution's investment in time and effort to determine the most appropriate course of action, consistent with the institution's policies and the principles underlying those policies. Although there is no regulatory requirement to organize and convene a COI Committee, this approach is strongly recommended when the "rules and tools" are not adequate for FCOI analysis, decision-making, or management plan assignment. Rather than asking an institution-wide COI Committee to address these circumstances, some institutions distribute the decision-making across the organization, *e.g.*, to department chairs, division chiefs, or deans. The primary weakness of this approach (whether used only for complex and custom FCOIs, or for all FCOIs in an organization that chooses the principles-based approach) is that it often results in inconsistent outcomes. A well-trained committee charged with the task is more likely to be consistent and to develop fair and appropriate decisions.

Transparency

The concept of transparency means that the process used on the inside is visible and understandable to people on the outside. The regulations are focused on the public and establishing sufficient transparency to address the public's desire to understand how an institution deals with FCOIs. They should disclose what FCOIs have been identified and how it is managing those conflicts. But for many institutions, this is only one group. For some institutions, there are actually two groups who expect and are entitled to transparency. The first is the public; the second is the community of investigators who demand an understanding of how their disclosures are analyzed and how decisions are made.

Again, although not a regulatory requirement, transparency for investigators in your organization is important to the institution's ability to comply with the regulations. The system relies substantially on the completeness and veracity of the financial disclosures received from investigators. Informal observations suggest that the worst (and most frequent) complaint from investigators is that their financial disclosures enter a "black box," with unpredictable and inconsistent outcomes. To promote complete and accurate disclosures and to engender the community of investigators, institutions should consider the following:

- Involve investigators in policy, process, and SOP development
- Make all policies, processes, and SOPs available and easy-to-find on your intranet for your investigators
- Include links to policies, processes, and SOPs in all correspondences with investigators
- Encourage active dialogue with investigators

Transparency for the public requires that all institutions with a website (these days, few if any do not have a website), publish their FCOI policies online. This is easily achieved. There is no obligation to post processes or SOPs.

Transparency also requires that the institution either post and update key information about all FCOIs in the organization, or if it chooses not to post this information, that it responds promptly—within five business days—to all formal inquiries of FCOI at the institution. How each institution chooses to comply depends on its size, organizational culture, and in some cases, its adoption of eCOI technology. There are two schools of thought on whether to proactively post FCOIs on the institution's public-facing website vs. responding reactively to specific requests for information. Those advocating responding to requests note that the transparency requirement does not require public posting—and therefore abstain. A related point is that their investigators wish to keep these matters out of the public eye, unless absolutely required. Some also note that the challenge of keeping the posted information accurate and up-to-date, is more than they can manage routinely.

The other point of view is that by posting FCOI information, the institution "controls the message" that the public will get. Remember that the Sunshine Provisions of the Affordable Care Act require that pharmaceutical companies and medical manufacturers publicly post information about payments or "transfer of value" to all healthcare providers, including investigators. This information will be publicly available, and will generally not include meaningful detail (beyond the amounts). A curious reader may learn how much the investigator at an institution is paid by a particular company, but the underlying details justifying the payment will not be evident. In contrast, the FCOI information published by the institution can include sufficient information to inform the reader that the payment was appropriate for activities or services that were rendered by the investigator. To the extent such payments yield FCOIs, the institution can acknowledge them, and describe how they are managed. Depending on the size of the institution, it may be difficult to make this information readily available without the use of eCOI software.

Technology

Any system of effectively identifying and handling FCOIs includes three components: Disclosure, Analysis, and Management. Today, there are commercially-available as well as university-developed eCOI software applications that can handle one, two, or all three of these. This section offers a brief overview of eCOI software, and a cautionary note: Technology is not a panacea for an inadequate or dysfunctional system of identifying and managing FCOI. The adoption of an eCOI solution provides a way to improve a system by making it more efficient and reducing the time people need to spend. However, technology by itself does not make a process more effective. In fact, there is potential for an eCOI system to facilitate noncompliance, if it is configured with inadequate processes. Likewise, compliant processes that are paper-based are unlikely to be optimized for eCOI implementation; to configure a technology solution with a paper-based process is equivalent to "paving the cow path," rather than designing an efficient highway. For these reasons, it is highly recommended that organizations either develop a set of work flows and SOPs that can be readily adopted by an eCOI solution before configuring the system, or that their system for identifying and handling FCOIs be redesigned at the time of configuration. When evaluating eCOI solutions, it is worthwhile to budget not only for the software license, but also for the full cost of implementation, including revising/developing work flows and SOPs that exploit the features of the software you choose.

The minimum functionality for eCOI software is that it should facilitate the complete disclosure of outside financial interests. Ideally, it utilizes a relational database and document management system so that investigators do not need to enter information more than once if that information does not change. For disclosure, some software solutions utilize "smart forms," so-called because they cascade with new pages and questions only as needed based on the answers to earlier questions. They are the alternative to a single form asking all possible questions. Smart forms are seductive for good reason: they save time for the respondent and the analyst, but be sure to take the time to design them correctly.

Some eCOI software utilizes logic that can analyze the answers to questions and determine if an investigator's outside interests are related to their institutional commitments, reach a level determined to be "significant," and are of a nature that might be considered "garden variety-manageable" or complex and custom. Each institution considering a technology solution, depending on its organizational culture, policy, size, faculty/staff composition, core competencies, and budget, can determine if it is more valuable for software to manage these issues, or if it wishes to analyze them with people's time.

As noted earlier, every significant financial interest determined to be a FCOI requires a formal and written management plan. Software can assist with the assignment of these plans, their documentation, and their communication to investigators. According to your SOPs, it can also communicate with other key individuals in the institution. The eCOI solution can also help to track management plans and when appropriate, document and facilitate their sunset.

Depending on the organization, there may be a desire to integrate eCOI software with other technology solutions already in place (or planned) for research administration. There are two approaches to take: The most obvious is to adopt an integrated suite of software solutions that meet the entirety of institutional needs. For example, some institutions adopt a single software platform to facilitate not only FCOI, but also IRB, IACUC, grants management, and IBC. Others choose a best-of-breed approach, and find solutions that work best for each need, and integrate them through interfaces or data-exchange processes. There are hybrid approaches as well.

Whatever approach you take, consider that there is a PHS requirement to either post information about FCOIs online, or to have it available so that it can be provided promptly in the event of a query. In the first case, eCOI software can conveniently "serve up" accurate and up-to-date information to your external website. On the other hand, if you choose not to post such information routinely, a good eCOI application can help locate and report the information at the touch of a button. In either case, all but the smallest of institutions should consider adopting an eCOI solution.

Chapter 2 Endnotes

1. **Stuart Horowitz, PhD, MBA** is President, Institutions and Institutional Services for WIRB-Copernicus Group in Princeton, NJ.
2. U.S. Dep't of Health and Human Services, National Institutes of Health, Office of Extramural Research, "Financial Conflicts of Interest," (updated August 15, 2018), http://grants.nih.gov/grants/policy/coi/.
3. News stories and US Senate actions spearheaded by Sen. Charles Grassley are summarized in Grassley's May 29, 2012 letter to the NIH, located at https://www.grassley.senate.gov/sites/default/files/about/upload/2012-05-29-CEG-to-NIH-Dr-Nemeroff-grant.pdf.
4. SSA § 1128G(a)(1), which can be found at:http://www.ssa.gov/OP_Home/ssact/title11/1128G.htm.
5. 76 Fed. Reg. No. 165, 53256-53293 (August 25, 2011), http://grants.nih.gov/grants/policy/coi/fcoi_final_rule.pdf.
6. The Institute on Medicine as a Profession, "COI Policy Database," http://imapny.org/conflicts-of-interest/conflicts-of-interest-2/.
7. NSF does not currently follow the PHS Final Rule for extramurally-funded investigators. The NSF rules can be found in the Grants Policy Manual NSF 05-131 July 2005 Chapter V - Grantee Standards, located at https://www.nsf.gov/pubs/manuals/gpm05_131/gpm5.jsp.
8. In many states, the receipt of state funding for research, or the conduct of research in a state-funded institution is subject to that state's COI rules.
9. 76 Fed. Reg. No. 165, 53256-53293 (August 25, 2011), http://grants.nih.gov/grants/policy/coi/fcoi_final_rule.pdf.
10. Ibid.
11. An FCOI must either be eliminated or managed. Elimination is achieved by prohibiting certain conflicted activities (such as complete divestiture, or disallowing the research) or reducing the amount of the financial interest to a level below the threshold. An FCOI requires a written management plan.

3
Scientific and Research Misconduct

By Juliann Tenney, JD, CHRC[1]

Scientific and research misconduct may present the most vexing of challenges for the compliance officer. Lines of inquiry that have been supported by human and animal subjects (and sacrifice), as well as significant financial investment, can be wholly discredited and rendered worthless if misconduct has occurred. Careers may be ruined and institutions shamed. Settlements, fines and awards deplete resources and imprisonment may await those who would perpetrate fraud upon the government. Investigators may be excluded from participating in Public Health Service (including National Institutes of Health) and National Science Foundation supported research. In addition, private causes of action from defamation to conversion (theft) may be available to victims.

Most areas of compliance address developing an institution-wide approach to ensuring that behaviors, practices and systems are consistent with laws and regulations. If an electronic medical record has been improperly accessed, providers have programs that will detect such a breach. The fact of the breach and its electronic detection does not have a personality. Conversely, allegations of scientific or research misconduct may arise among colleagues who work together or out of a position of trust (peer review of grant proposals; work overseen by a dissertation advisor). The real or apparent violation takes on a life of its own as those who used to go about their business in peaceful co-existence take sides and prepare for battle. Institutional anxiety runs high as those not directly involved seek to avoid the fall-out.

This chapter will review governing regulations and provide examples of scientific misconduct. A distinction is drawn between scientific misconduct and regulatory misconduct. The latter is conduct inconsistent with regulations and standards that govern the process of research, and that are found, for example, in the Common Rule, the Health Insurance Portability and Accountability Act (HIPAA), and regulations regarding the use of animals. Scientific misconduct may, indeed, include elements of some or all of these, and can be found in other sections of this compendium; however, this chapter will focus on the standards enunciated in 42 CFR Part 93 (Department of Health and Human Services) and 45 CFR Part 689 (National Science Foundation) that address institutional responsibilities regarding "fabrication, falsification, plagiarism, or other practices that seriously deviate from those that are commonly accepted within the scientific community for proposing, conducting, or reporting research." The essence of this chapter and its body of rules is to support the integrity of the public investment in "biomedical and behavioral research, research training or activities related to that research ...".[2] It should be noted that compliance with the section is required upon application for support and is not contingent upon success in securing funding.

Institutions that seek Public Health Service (PHS) funding are required to have in place an "assurance." This assurance certifies that the institution has adopted and implemented policies and procedures to address allegations of fabrication, falsification or plagiarism, including the identification of an appropriate institutional official to carry out the intent of such provisions, a research integrity officer (RIO). Prior to 1996, institutions filed an "initial assurance form;" however, beginning in 1996, signing the face page of a grant application constitutes/is deemed assurance. In addition, there is an annual reporting obligation that describes the status of activities that have taken place during the course of the preceding year. Failure to file a timely annual report could expose the institution to heightened scrutiny, as well as the need to pursue reinstatement of its assurance status in order to become eligible for Public Health Service (PHS) funding.

The regulations are prescriptive regarding the steps that must be taken when an allegation is received or misconduct suspected. The clarity and detail lend themselves to institutions adopting the process outlined 42 CFR Part 93 in applying its provisions to misconduct allegations that are expressed beyond the scope of behavioral or biomedical fields. The PHS approach, then, becomes imbedded and actually may serve to raise the standard of review universally.

Definitions (42 and 45 CFR)

Research misconduct means fabrication, falsification, or plagiarism in proposing, performing, or reviewing research, or in reporting research results.

a. **Fabrication** is making up data or results and recording or reporting them.
b. **Falsification** is manipulating research materials, equipment, or processes, or changing or omitting data or results such that the research is not accurately represented in the research record.
c. **Plagiarism** is the appropriation of another person's ideas, processes, results, or words without giving appropriate credit.
d. **Research misconduct** does not include honest error or differences of opinion.

Requirements for findings of research misconduct

A finding of research misconduct made under either of these sections requires that:

a. There be a significant departure from accepted practices of the relevant research community; and
b. The misconduct be committed intentionally, knowingly, or recklessly; and
c. The allegation be proved by a preponderance of the evidence.

Response to an allegation of misconduct takes on a life of its own. It is logical to consider this process as a series of stages. At the first stage, the "notice" or allegation stage, the RIO or compliance officer (CO) becomes aware of the possibility of misconduct. The method of discovery could be direct, from someone who has specific knowledge of a transgression. The Office of Research Integrity may advise that it has received a report. Such communications can be transmitted through anonymous or confidential "hotlines." Indirect knowledge could be obtained through an intermediary, such as an administrator in a department, or a non-involved researcher who reports "something she has heard from a lab technician ..." In any event, having received such notice, the official is compelled to examine the situation with the information available and to consider advancing the process to the second stage, initiating an inquiry.

Consider the following scenario:

The phone rings... The voice on the other end of the line asks if he can be assured of confidentiality.

You (the compliance official) say, "I will protect your confidentiality as completely as allowed by law." The caller then declines to identify himself, but says that the pressure to enroll subjects into a clinical trial that he supports is enormous. If patients don't meet inclusion criteria detailed in the protocol, the staff is "encouraged" to "check those values again," and reminded that jobs are dependent upon grant support. The caller says that he doesn't want you to do anything, he just had to tell someone—he does not identify the study or the investigator. Weeks later you receive an anonymous call from a person describing herself as a monitor for a sponsor. She advises you that she believes subject records she has reviewed have been altered to satisfy study inclusion criteria.

The first caller was likely expressing frustration over the stress abundant in a grants-dependent work environment. The second call, however, should lead the listener to begin developing strategies to begin the second stage, or pre-inquiry review. In addition, caution is urged regarding a representation to anyone that their communications can be kept completely confidential. Institutional officials, except for professional ombudsmen or an official appointed to investigate, generally have an "obligation to report" that could be considered a breach of confidentiality. Counsel should be consulted regarding limitations in these matters.

The standard for moving forward states: "An inquiry is warranted if the allegation ... (3) is sufficiently credible and specific so that potential evidence of research misconduct may be identified".[3] Your plan should include the following steps:

- Develop a written record of all the facts, including a complete statement from the complainant;
- Identify others who may be involved with the challenged conduct;
- Identify others who may "be aware" of the situation;
- Review relevant grant proposals, protocols, monitoring/ audit records, journal articles;
- Assess the course the complainant wishes to follow—review concepts of anonymity and confidentiality as well as institutional policies on research integrity and nonretaliation.

Steps that must be taken to protect the records and evidence over which the (now) respondent has physical control, for example, in the laboratory, will likely produce turmoil and anxiety. Section §93.307 provides substantial detail regarding the kinds of evidence that should be protected, as well as provision of notice to the respondent. The appearance of institutional officials to take custody of the evidence may be the first opportunity for the respondent to be made aware that a misconduct allegation has been lodged. Although the notion of lack of advance notice may seem harsh, this element of surprise could be critical so that there is no opportunity to destroy or remove evidence that must be available throughout the course of the investigation and possibly beyond. Counsel and appropriate institutional officials should be advised of what actions will be taken (they, too, should be reminded of the need for confidentiality). In addition, the researcher's work will need to be supported until resolution, which will likely include locating new laboratory space (if applicable).

The compliance or integrity officer should remember that he/she must maintain a posture of equipoise—it is her responsibility to manage a process that is fair. The rights of both the complainant and respondent must be protected. He/she should not provide legal advice. Institutional counsel should notify the respondent that retaining his or her own counsel should be considered.

"An inquiry's purpose is to decide if an allegation warrants an investigation. An investigation is warranted if there is—(1) A reasonable basis for concluding that the allegation falls within the definition of research misconduct ... and (2) Preliminary information-gathering and preliminary fact-finding from the inquiry indicates that the allegation may have substance".[4]

The institution is required to prepare an "inquiry report" to which the respondent is entitled to respond. The respondent's comments should be attached to the report and be made part of the inquiry record. The regulation directs that the inquiry should be completed within sixty days of its initiation. Upon completion of the inquiry, the respondent must be notified whether an investigation will be undertaken and provided with a copy of the report. Note that the complainant may be notified and may be provided with relevant portions of the report. Though this is not required, anticipate that the complainant will likely be interested—it would be wise to review at the beginning of the process what the institution is able to accommodate. Consider that other laws and regulations may be invoked, such as HIPAA or those that protect the privacy of personnel records.

It may be that the institution determines not to investigate. Perhaps the allegation was found not to have substance. The institution should be prepared to restore the accused to his pre-allegation stature. Records supporting the decision not to investigate are directed to be maintained for seven years. If an investigation is warranted, it must be initiated within thirty days of conclusion of the inquiry and the Office of Research Integrity provided with the report and findings. Section §93.309 outlines the information that must be included in this communication.

After a determination that the allegation likely has substance, the investigation stage begins and should be concluded within one-hundred twenty (120) days. Review of the evidence, examination of witnesses, including experts in the relevant discipline and perhaps forensics, should be thorough and rigorous. Witnesses should have the opportunity to review their statements for accuracy. Again, the regulation, in section §93.310, is prescriptive and detailed. Succeeding sections address the development of the investigation report, requiring that there be a "[s]tatement of findings. For each separate allegation of research misconduct identified during the investigation, provide a finding as to whether research misconduct did or did not occur, and if so—(1) Identify whether the research misconduct was falsification, fabrication, or plagiarism, and if it was intentional, knowing, or in reckless disregard".[5] The potential "public nature" of this process becomes clear through (4): "Identify whether any publications need correction or retraction." In addition, all instances of Federal support must be identified.

The institution's policies and procedures regarding research misconduct must be included with both the inquiry report and the investigation report. For instance, the regulations may not address whether the institution should terminate the respondent's employment relationship. Rather, the institution's policies should provide guidance on consequences for engaging in misconduct.

Sections 93.316–93.318 address steps that must be taken to conclude the process, including notifications and opportunity for appeal. Note that ORI may assert itself into the process, provided it has jurisdiction, at any time. Remember, too, that complainants may take their concerns directly to the agency rather than through the institution that is the site of the grievance.

Institutional policies should recognize that consequences of research misconduct extend well beyond those assessed against the person responsible for engaging in the reprehensible behavior. Fines, settlements, exclusion from federal funding (debarment), civil actions for damages and the prospect of imprisonment appear not to be sufficient to discourage some. For an institution, the conduct of an inquiry and/or investigation will represent a significant drain on resources, including time and possibly space, and expert witness fees, for example. Junior researchers, students and colleagues may be unaware of the corrupt premise upon which their futures depend, and could fall. In order for our research to blossom into products, processes and services of benefit to us all, there must be mechanisms in place for anyone to advance a good faith concern about circumstances that jeopardize this objective.

Increasingly, federally funded researchers are required to submit peer reviewed articles and research to depositories so that the public and other researchers may have access to the products of our national research investment. NIH-funded, peer reviewed articles must comply with that agency's Public Access Policy.[6] Clinical trials, too, must be timely registered or continuation funding may be jeopardized.[7]

Scientific efficacy is demonstrated by the ability of researchers who do not have an interest in a research outcome to achieve the same results as reported by the original team. "Replicability" of research findings is increasingly a subject of concern and will likely be a source for allegations of misconduct. Access to original data is critical in order to prove or disprove a finding or theory. Inability of successor researchers to achieve the same findings or theories may raise questions about the integrity of the data or data analysis. Those who urge rigorous, unbiased review of findings and therapeutic "breakthroughs" support requiring that original data be made available so that it can be tested and scrutinized to ensure that conclusions are correct. In addition, as inquiry becomes more complex, biostatisticians will need to join research teams to ensure analysis is reliable. Though whistleblowers, as identified in the earlier example, may serve as the primary source of misconduct allegations, peer researchers may increasingly lodge challenges if they are able to access and challenge data or data analysis.

Note that the Health and Human Services Office of Research Integrity (ORI) is responsible for oversight of misconduct for Public Health Service Agencies, including the NIH. The National Science Foundation Office of Inspector General is responsible for NSF-funded research. Additionally, all personnel, except for principal investigators, supported through NSF-funded research, are required to be trained in the Responsible Conduct of Research, for which employing institutions are responsible.

Finally, in addition to the above cited regulation, excellent resources are available. The Office of Research Integrity offers an excellent, web-available, Handbook for Institutional Integrity Officers[8] as well as a quarterly newsletter that provides news of investigations.[9]

Chapter 3 Endnotes

1. **Juliann Tenney, JD, CHRC**, is Chief Privacy Officer for The University of North Carolina at Chapel Hill.
2. 50 CFR 93.102(a).
3. 42 CFR §93.307.
4. 42 CFR §93.307.
5. 42 CFR §93.313(f)(1).
6. US Dep't of Health and Human Services, National Institutes of Health Public Access Policy, http://publicaccess.nih.gov/policy.htm.
7. See http://clinicaltrials.gov.
8. US Dep't of Health and Human Services, Office of Research Integrity, ORI Handbook for Institutional Research Integrity Officers, http://ori.hhs.gov/rio-handbook.
9. See http://ori.hhs.gov/newsletters.

4
Biosecurity, Biosafety, and Biorisk Management

By Daniel Kavanagh, Ph.D.[1]

Introduction

Historically, the terms *biosafety* and *biosecurity* have had closely related and sometimes overlapping definitions. Today, a useful way to think about the two terms is that the goal of *biosafety* is to manage the risk of accidental release or unintended effects of potentially hazardous biological materials; whereas the goal of *biosecurity* is to manage the risk of intentional or malicious misuse of hazardous biological materials. Biosafety and biosecurity are important considerations in a broad range of endeavors from plant and animal agriculture to environmental protection; however this chapter is specifically focused on implications for human clinical research and human health.

At clinical research institutions, biosafety programs must be prepared to manage risks associated with several types of products, including:

- **Infectious agents and toxins from natural sources or clinical isolates;** this includes genetically unmodified microbial cultures used for research or diagnostic purposes, as well as human tissue samples.
- **Biological toxins manufactured for clinical or research purposes.** Examples include botulinum toxin used in the clinic (as Botox), as well as a wide variety of neurotoxins and immunotoxins used for basic laboratory research.
- **Recombinant and synthetic nucleic acid molecules.**
- **Genetically-modified microbes or animals** for use in preclinical or basic science laboratory research.
- **Human Gene Transfer products,** such as viral vectors made with recombinant DNA technology, intended for use in human gene transfer and gene therapy research and in clinical trials.

Every institution where these products are administered, handled or stored should have biosafety protocols in place, preferably as part of a formal biosafety program. At various institutions, the biosafety program may constitute an independent department, or may be incorporated into other departments such as Environmental Health and Safety, or Infection Control. Biosafety programs should be developed under the guidance of a **biosafety professional**—*i.e.*, a biosafety expert with significant training and experience. Some but not all biosafety professionals will have professional credentials certified by an organization such as the American Biological Safety Association (ABSA) International[2]. For institutions with complex biosafety needs, a key staff position is that of **Biological Safety Officer (BSO)**. The BSO is a biosafety professional who is familiar with the facilities, procedures and training at the institution and who provides advice and supervision related to safe handling and storage of biohazardous products. If an institution is subject to the *NIH Guidelines For Research Involving Recombinant and Synthetic Nucleic Acid Molecules (NIH Guidelines)*, that institution is required to employ a BSO if the institution engages in research with Biosafety Level 3 or 4 containment (see below).

The primary goal of any well-designed biosafety program is to manage the risks associated with activities involving biohazardous products. These activities include acquiring or manufacturing, tracking, transporting, labeling, storage, handling, and disposal of biological samples and biohazardous products. In the case of human gene transfer research, it also involves dosing and administration of the gene transfer product to the research subject. An important goal is to *contain* the biohazardous materials under conditions that minimize the risk to persons and the environment. To develop a biosafety protocol for each of these activities, it is necessary to assess the risk posed by accidental loss of containment, and by the relative potential for harm to persons or the environment by accidental exposure or release.

Implementing a biosafety protocol involves ensuring that packages containing biohazardous materials are properly labeled and that areas where these materials are handled have proper signage and security measures to prevent unauthorized persons from accidentally or intentionally interfering with biocontainment. Supervisors in charge of these areas must ensure that only trained personnel handle the biohazardous materials, and that personnel always use appropriate personal protective equipment (PPE). Depending on the product and activities under study, appropriate PPE may include, gloves, gown, shoe covers, eye protection, and a mask or respirator. The protocol must also describe the biohazard waste stream, including how all waste materials that have come into contact with biohazardous materials should be disposed of. Biohazard waste management requires coordination with the building facilities team and with appropriately certified waste haulers, as well as careful attention to local and national environmental regulations. Each protocol should also include emergency procedures in case of loss of containment. These include plans to provide first aid and medical care to exposed persons, spill clean-up, and coordination with first responders and emergency personnel.

For many biosafety protocols, a key piece of equipment is the **biosafety cabinet (BSC)**. A BSC provides a hood with a partially enclosed work area having directed airflow such that air is constantly pulled into the BSC and away from the researcher, who can sit or stand outside the BSC and manipulate experimental materials. The directed airflow ensures that most airborne contaminants are pulled away from the lab worker and into the hood for capture by a high-efficiency filter. BSCs are only useful if installed, maintained, and operated by properly trained personnel. BSCs are a key piece of equipment for most protocols at Biosafety Levels 2, 3, and 4.

In the US, there are several federal agencies that provide guidance and regulatory oversight affecting biosafety and research activities. The Department of Transportation (DOT) imposes a variety of rules regarding proper labeling and shipment of hazardous substances, including specific training requirements for persons who ship or receive such materials. The Occupational Health and Safety Administration (OSHA) sets standards for worker safety that can have a significant impact on design and implementation of biosafety programs. The two federal agencies that have the greatest day-to-day impact on biosafety programs at research institutions in the US are the Centers for Disease Control (CDC) in Atlanta, GA, and the National Institutes of Health (NIH) in Bethesda, MD. Between them, these two agencies publish the most important biosafety guidance documents for research: *Biosafety in Microbiological and Biomedical Laboratories (BMBL)*[3] , a joint publication of CDC and the NIH; and the *NIH Guidelines For Research Involving Recombinant and Synthetic Nucleic Acid Molecules (NIH Guidelines)*[4] .

The *BMBL* has been "the cornerstone of biosafety practice and policy in the United States" since the publication of the first edition in 1984. The *BMBL* is compiled by a team of dozens of scientific editors from government, academic, and industry settings and includes the work of hundreds of scientific contributors.

The *BMBL* includes sections on topics such as risk assessment, principles of biosafety, and principles of laboratory biosecurity, as well as summary statements on specific considerations for handling of specific categories and species of agents (viruses, fungi, bacteria, parasites, biological toxins, etc). Appendices address issues such as biological safety cabinets (BSCs), decontamination, transportation, and pest management, among others.

The historical origins of the *NIH Guidelines* are rooted in the 1975 Asilomar Conference on Recombinant DNA, organized in response to growing concern over potential implications of recombinant DNA technology. The *NIH Guidelines* were first issued in 1976 and subsequently amended many times. At presstime, new revisions due in the final months of 2018 had not been released.[5] The main body of the *NIH Guidelines* includes sections on scope, safety considerations, specific types of experiments, and roles and responsibilities of investigators, institutions, and the NIH. The guidelines also incorporate several appendices with technical information related to research with specific biological agents, plants and animals.[6]

All research involving recombinant and synthetic nucleic acid molecules is subject to *NIH Guidelines* if conducted at institutions that receive relevant NIH funding; furthermore all human gene transfer research involving relevant NIH funding is also subject to *NIH Guidelines* at every clinical trial site. Additionally, the *NIH Guidelines* recommend voluntary compliance for research involving recombinant and synthetic nucleic acid molecules even if NIH funding is not involved. Finally *NIH Guidelines* compliance may be required by local government regulations or by various funding agencies other than NIH itself.

The *NIH Guidelines* apply to many categories of basic science, preclinical, and clinical research involving microbes, plants, animals and human subjects. A notable research category defined by the *NIH Guidelines*, Section III-C[7] is **Human Gene Transfer (HGT)** research. HGT research is the deliberate transfer into a human research subject of an investigational product that includes genetically modified components including those derived from recombinant or synthetic DNA or RNA, with the exception of certain very short or molecularly inert nucleic acid molecules. Notably, HGT research includes "gene therapy", as well as a broad range of other applications using genetically modified probiotics, stem cells, vaccines, or viral vectors.

In the past, an NIH committee known as the **Recombinant DNA Advisory Committee (RAC)** played an important role in review and approval of HGT protocols; however in August 2018 the Director of the NIH announced that the role of the RAC would be greatly reduced, such that the RAC no longer has any routine oversight role for HGT research[8].

For each institution subject to *NIH Guidelines*, a key component of compliance is registration of an **Institutional Biosafety Committee (IBC)** with the NIH. Currently there are over 1,200 IBCs registered with NIH. The IBC membership at each institution must include both scientific experts with relevant experience and also members of the public to serve as the voice of the local community. The primary roles of the IBC as mandated by the *NIH Guidelines* are to assure institutional compliance and approve research involving recombinant and synthetic DNA and RNA and genetically modified organisms and viruses. An especially high-profile aspect of this oversight is review and approval of clinical trials involving HGT research. Under the *NIH Guidelines*, HGT research at an institution must be approved by the IBC prior to enrollment of any subjects. The requirement for IBC approval is separate from and in addition to requirements for review by other entities such as the FDA and the Institutional Review Board (IRB).

Another important role of the IBC is to serve as an advisory body to the institution on all aspects of biological safety. Because of the expertise of the committee membership, many institutions choose to rely on their IBCs to approve a range of research activities that involve infectious agents or biohazards, even if the research does not include genetically modified agents (and thus falls outside of the *NIH Guidelines* mandate).

As a substitute for—or in addition to—administering its own IBC, an institution has the option of engaging an **externally-administered IBC**, which is operated on behalf of the research site by an external service provider. About a third of all IBCs registered with NIH are externally administered on behalf of research sites. For research such as *multicenter clinical trials* that extends to multiple sites and institutions, it is important to note that, in general, activities at each site must be approved by an IBC registered for that site. In other words, a clinical trial subject to the *NIH Guidelines* conducted at twelve clinical trial sites must have twelve IBC approvals. Many clinical trial sponsors find that it is most efficient to work with a single provider of externally-administered IBC services at all twelve sites (importantly, it is up to each site to decide whether or not to defer to an externally-administered IBC).

Each new biosafety protocol should be designed in consultation with a biosafety expert, and at institutions subject to the *NIH Guidelines* the protocol must be approved by the IBC (except for certain minimal risk activities that are exempt). Among other considerations, each protocol will describe the containment measures required for safe handling of materials under study. This description will include assignment of a **Biological Safety Level (BSL)** on a scale of BSL-1 (lowest containment) to BSL-4 (highest containment). Research at BSL-1 usually requires simple PPE and usually does not usually require use of a BSC. Research at BSL-2 involves higher-risk infectious agents and generally involves use of a BSC, along with more stringent training. Research at BSL-3 and BSL-4 requires very complex and sophisticated containment facilities, training, and security as well as direct supervision by highly trained biosafety professionals.

Biosecurity, Select Agents Research, and Dual Use Research of Concern

Most scientific activities at institutions engaged in clinical research involve minimal to moderate biohazards that do not pose catastrophic risks to public health or economic activity. The US federal government has identified a limited subset of biological agents and toxins that have "the potential to pose a severe threat to public health and safety, to animal or plant health, or to animal or plant products." These agents and toxins are identified as **Select Agents**. The current list of sixty-three select agents can be accessed on the Federal Select Agent Program website[9]. Research with select agents is subject to very stringent permitting and security measures overseen by the federal government and no such research should be undertaken without consulting the Federal Select Agent Program[10]. Institutions that receive federal funding for life sciences research and that conduct research involving any of fifteen specified select agents are also subject to the *Policy for Institutional Oversight of Life Sciences Dual Use Research of Concern (DURC)*. This policy requires investigators and institutions to take special measures to evaluate potential risks associated with the results of such research, including information and publications that could be used for malicious or terroristic purposes[11].

In conclusion, the accelerating development of new technologies in genetic engineering, synthetic biology, precision medicine, and gene transfer will require that more and more research activities engage with products and techniques with biosafety implications. Institutions can benefit from proactive engagement with biosafety experts in order to ensure that research is conducted safely and in compliance with government regulations and best practices.

Chapter 4 Endnotes

1. **Daniel Kavenaugh, Ph.D.** is Senior Scientific Advisor, Gene Therapy, for WIRB-Copernicus Group in Princeton, NJ.
2. Professional Credentials in Biosafety offered by ABSA International: https://absa.org/credentials/.
3. US Centers for Disease Control and Prevetion, *Biosafety in Microbiological and Biomedical Laboratories (BMBL) 5th Edition*, https://www.cdc.gov/biosafety/publications/bmbl5/index.htm.
4. National Institutes of Health, Office of Science Policy, *NIH Guidelines for Research Involving Recombinant or Synthetic Nucleic Acid Molecules*, https://osp.od.nih.gov/biotechnology/nih-guidelines/.
5. As of January 15, 2019, the 2018 revisions were not finalized. Visit https://osp.od.nih.gov/biotechnology/biosafety-and-recombinant-dna-activities/ to see their current status.
6. Previously, one particular appendix, Appendix M, mandated an extensive set of reporting requirements specifically for human gene transfer (HGT) research. In August 2018, the NIH Director announced that all of the previous registration and reporting requirements would be immediately discontinued. The requirement for IBC approval of HGT research was not changed.
7. National Institutes of Health, Office of Science Policy, *NIH Guidelines for Research Involving Recombinant or Synthetic Nucleic Acid Molecules*, Section III-C-1: "Experiments Involving the Deliberate Transfer of Recombinant or Synthetic Nucleic Acid Molecules, or DNA or RNA Derived from Recombinant or Synthetic Nucleic Acid Molecules, into One or More Human Research Participants," https://osp.od.nih.gov/wp-content/uploads/NIH_Guidelines.html#_Toc446948323.
8. National Institutes of Health, "Statement on modernizing human gene therapy oversight," https://www.nih.gov/about-nih/who-we-are/nih-director/statements/statement-modernizing-human-gene-therapy-oversight.
9. Centers for Disease Control and Prevention, Federal Select Agent Program, "Select Agents and Toxins FAQs," https://www.selectagents.gov/faq-general.html.
10. To contact the Centers for Disease Control and Prevention, Division of Select Agents and Toxins, email LRSAT@cdc.gov.
11. US Department of Health and Human Services, Public Health Emergency website, "Implementation of the U.S. Government Policy for Institutional Oversight of Life Sciences DURC: Frequently Asked Questions," http://www.phe.gov/s3/dualuse/Documents/durc-faqs.pdf.

5
The Regulation of Research Using Animals

By Kristin H. West, JD, MS[1]

Overview

The area of animal research presents a myriad of regulatory and ethical issues. Currently, clinical trials in animals are required as a condition to approval of new drugs by the U.S. Food and Drug Administration (FDA),[2] and thus, animal research plays an important role in pharmaceutical innovation. Accordingly, research compliance officers should be familiar with the regulatory requirements governing animal research. This chapter will provide an overview of the regulatory structure that governs animal research and includes a discussion of the following topics:

- Primary principles, laws and regulatory agencies governing animal research
- Major players in animal research programs and their roles and responsibilities
- Additional compliance considerations unique to animal research

Within each of these areas, focus areas for effective compliance programs are identified.

Primary Principles, Laws and Regulatory Agencies Governing Animal Research

The overarching set of ethical principles that govern animal research conducted or regulated by the federal government is the U.S. Government Principles for the Utilization and Care of Vertebrate Animals Used in Testing, Research and Training (the "Principles.")[3] The principles set forth the premises that should be followed in designing and conducting animal research, and they form the basis of all other laws regulating animal research.

The principles are based on the "3 Rs" of animal research: **R**educe the number of animals used in research; **R**efine experiments to minimize pain and discomfort to animals; and **R**eplace animal experiments with alternatives when feasible. Research compliance programs should ensure that personnel who staff animal care and use programs are familiar with the principles' main tenets:

- Avoid using animals needlessly. Design and perform research procedures in a way that ensures the research is relevant to advancing human/animal health or important knowledge.
- Use an appropriate animal species and the minimum number of animals necessary to obtain valid research results.
- Research should be designed to prevent or minimize discomfort, pain, and distress in animals. If a procedure would hurt a human, it should be assumed to hurt an animal, unless specific knowledge to the contrary has been established.
- Research that causes more than momentary or slight pain or distress in an animal should incorporate the use of anesthetics, analgesics or tranquilizers ("AAT Drugs").
- Animals that suffer severe or chronic pain or distress that cannot be relieved should be euthanized.
- Research animals must have appropriate living conditions and receive care that is directed by a qualified veterinarian.

- Research must be conducted by qualified investigators who are trained in the use of research animals.
- Animal research must be conducted in accordance with all applicable federal regulations, and any exceptions to the regulations must be pre-approved by an Institutional Animal Care and Use Committee (IACUC).

The principles' influence is readily apparent in the two main sets of federal laws that govern animal research in the United States: (a) the Public Health Service *Policy on Humane Care and Use of Laboratory Animals,*[4] and (b) the Animal Welfare Act[5] and its implementing Animal Welfare Regulations,[6] referred to collectively as the "AWA." Each of these laws is discussed more fully below. As with any area in which multiple laws and regulations apply, the strictest of the applicable laws or regulations should always be followed.

Public Health Service Policy and the Office of Laboratory Animal Welfare

The Public Health Service *Policy on Humane Care and Use of Laboratory Animals* ("PHS Policy") applies to live, vertebrate animals of all types (whether warm or cold blooded) that are used in research, research training or experimentation that is supported by funding from the United States Public Health Service (PHS) or one of its components (*e.g.*, National Institutes of Health [NIH], FDA, Centers for Disease Control and Prevention, etc.). The PHS Policy covers PHS-funded activities that take place both inside or outside of the United States, and it applies to both traditional lab-based research and field work in the animals' natural setting.

The PHS Policy is administered and enforced by the federal Office for Laboratory Animal Welfare (OLAW). The PHS Policy requires that individuals who receive PHS-funding for animal research be affiliated with an institution that assumes responsibility for complying with the PHS Policy. The PHS Policy requires that the institution comply with the *Guide for the Care and Use of Laboratory Animals* (the "Guide")[7] and that euthanasia methods conform to the *American Veterinary Medical Association Guidelines for the Euthanasia of Animals.*[8] Additionally, the PHS Policy requires inclusion of the following information in PHS grant applications for animal research: rationale for use of animals; appropriateness of species to be used; number of animals to be used; description of proposed use; description of methods used to minimize pain and discomfort; and euthanasia methods.

Prior to the receipt of any PHS funds for animal research, and every four years thereafter, institutions must file an Animal Welfare Assurance ("assurance") with OLAW.[9] The assurance mandates, among other things, that institutions adhere to the following requirements:

- Compliance with the Principles, AWA, PHS Policy and the Guide.
- Establishment of an institutional animal care and use program with appropriate lines of responsibility and participation by qualified veterinarians.
- Establishment of an IACUC.
- Maintenance of specific assurance, IACUC and animal care and use program records.

The assurance document must provide an accurate description of the research institution's animal care and use program, and the research compliance officer should be very familiar with the assurance's contents. If the institution makes any changes to its animal care and use program that affect the assurance, an amended assurance must be filed with OLAW at the time of the change.

The assurance must include a description of all of the institution's facilities in which animals and used or housed, and include the species and number of animals that are used. The assurance requires designation of an institutional official who has top-level authority within the organization for oversight of the animal care and use program. A description of the program's specific lines of authority and approval also is required. The assurance must describe the membership of the IACUC and its procedures, including those for reporting and reviewing concerns about the care and use of animals at the institution. Finally, the assurance must describe the training required for animal users and caretakers, as well as the occupational health program in place for all persons who work with animals at the institution. Research compliance officers should ensure that appropriate institutional health and safety officials are involved in the development and implementation of the occupational health program to ensure compliance with any workers compensation and/or state or federal occupational health and safety requirements.

In addition to filing the assurance, each research institution also must file an annual report with OLAW. This annual report must describe any changes in the animal care and use program, including any change in an institution's accreditation status if accredited by AAALAC (see accreditation discussion below). The report also must include an assurance that all IACUC inspections and program evaluations have been conducted, as well as any minority view voiced by an IACUC member who disagreed with the IACUC's conclusions regarding facility or program reviews.

The Guide for the Care and Use of Laboratory Animals

As noted above, the PHS Policy and Assurance require that institutions performing PHS-funded animal research follow the requirements of the *Guide for the Care and Use of Laboratory Animals*, or the "Guide." The Guide sets forth very detailed standards for the administration and operation of animal care and use programs, including IACUC operations; engineering standards for animal environment, housing and management; veterinary care; physical plant; and emergency and disaster planning. Research compliance programs should undertake a detailed review of the Guide and determine its specific application to their institutions' facilities and programs. Working with the IACUC, the compliance officer should develop appropriate checklists to ensure that Guide requirements are being addressed.

Animal Welfare Act and the U.S. Department of Agriculture

The Animal Welfare Act and its implementing regulations (referred to collectively as the "AWA") governs live or dead warm-blooded animals that are intended for use in research, teaching, testing, experimentation, exhibition or as pets. The AWA is enforced by the U.S Department of Agriculture (USDA) through its Animal and Plant Health Inspection Service (APHIS). The AWA applies to research using all species of live or dead warm-blooded animals ("covered species") with a very important exception: research with mice, rats and birds is not covered.

Under the AWA, organizations or individuals must register with the USDA as "research facilities" if they plan to use a covered species in research and the research is federally-funded, or the animals were purchased in commerce. A new registration must be filed with the USDA every three years, and each registration or renewal requires the facility to certify that it is in full compliance with the AWA. Research compliance officers should be aware that their facilities additionally will need to apply to the USDA for an animal dealer's license if they also sell or trade some of their research animals to other research facilities.

Each registered research facility will be annually inspected by a USDA inspector. The inspector generally arrives at the facility unannounced and visually inspects all facilities in which covered species are used, housed or transported. In addition, the USDA inspector will review program records, as well as records maintained by the IACUC. Deficiencies noted during inspections must be corrected within the timeframe specified by the USDA, and serious or uncorrected deficiencies may result in citations and fines.

In addition to registration, each research facility must file an annual report that the USDA posts on its website. The annual report lists the number and type of each covered species held by the research facility, along with the USDA pain and distress class to which the animal has been assigned. The pain and distress classes are as follows:

Class B: The animal is being held but has not yet been used for research.

Class C: The animal is used in research that does not involve any pain or distress and does not use any analgesics, anesthetics or tranquilizers (collectively referred to as "AAT Drugs")

Class D: The animal is used in research that causes pain and/or distress but AAT Drugs are used.

Class E: The animal is used in research that causes pain and/or distress and AAT Drugs are not used because their use would have an adverse impact on the research. For animal used in Class E research, the annual report must include a description of the procedures that the animals undergo and the scientific justification for withholding AAT Drugs.

The annual report is a very important document because it is posted on the USDA website to permit public scrutiny of the number of animals being held in various pain and distress classes, with particular attention being paid to animals used in Class E research. Research compliance officers should work closely with their animal care and use programs to ensure that there are solid processes in place for maintaining accurate animal counts and that rigorous scientific justification is required for any animals being used in Class E research.

Other Pertinent Laws and Regulations

Although the PHS Policy, Guide and the AWA form the backbone of animal research regulation in the United States, other federal laws and state and local laws also must be considered. For example, if the research involves capturing animals in their natural setting, state or local laws may require that certain capture permits be obtained. Similarly, if the research requires the collection and/or transport of certain animal specimens, U.S. Fish and Wildlife regulations may apply and/or certain USDA permits may need to be obtained. Attention also must be paid to the species of animals involved, in order to determine if there are any species-specific regulatory research requirements or prohibitions. For instance, research involving species of animals protected by the U.S. Endangered Species Act, the Convention on International Trade in Endangered Species of Wild Flora and Fauna (CITES), or other similar laws may require special permits, or in some cases, be prohibited altogether. Accordingly, in all cases involving the collection, transport or use of wild animals or animal specimens, the research compliance officer should consult with counsel's office for assistance in identifying all applicable legal and regulatory requirements.

Major Players in Animal Research Programs and Their Roles and Responsibilities

A team of highly skilled individuals is required to properly administer and operate an animal research facility. These persons may act individually, such as by serving as the attending veterinarian, or they may act as members of the IACUC, the institutional committee charged with primary responsibility for animal research oversight. Set forth below is a description of the roles and responsibilities of each of the major players in a research facility's animal care and use program. Research compliance officers should identify the persons within their organizations who serve in these roles and be familiar with their various responsibilities.

Institutional Official

The institutional official is the individual at a research facility who has administrative and operational authority over the animal care and use program. The institutional official must be a top-level administrative who has the authority within the institution to ensure compliance with the AWA, PHS Policy and PHS Assurance. This authority must include the ability to commit institutional resources to support the institution's animal care and use program. In this regard, the institutional official must ensure that the program is properly resourced with staff, facilities, materials and funding because lack of resources can never serve as an excuse or mitigating factor for non-compliance with the AWA, PHS Policy or the Guide.

The institutional official is named on and signs the PHS Assurance on behalf of the research institution. He/she is responsible for reporting to USDA and/or OLAW any IACUC suspensions of protocols or instances of serious or continuing non-compliance or serious deviations from the requirements of the Guide. Although, the institutional official may halt animal research, only the IACUC can officially suspend a research protocol. Further, if the IACUC disapproves an animal research protocol, the institutional official cannot overrule the IACUC's disapproval.

Attending Veterinarian

The attending veterinarian is the veterinarian at the research facility who is in charge of seeing that all research animal receive adequate veterinary care. The attending veterinarian must have appropriate training and experience in the veterinary oversight of animal research programs, and he/she must have extensive knowledge of the requirements of the AWA, PHS Policy, and most especially, the Guide. Like the institutional official, the attending veterinarian must have appropriate lines of authority within the institution to ensure that the health and welfare of research animals is always protected. As a part of this authority, the attending veterinarian must have the power within the institution to prevent or end an animal's participation in a research protocol and/or to euthanize the animal if necessary, even if the principal investigator in charge of the protocol disagrees. The attending veterinarian is required to be a voting member of the IACUC, and will ensure that veterinary review and oversight is provided for research protocols.

Institutional Animal Care and Use Committee (IACUC)

Membership: A research facility's establishment of an IACUC is required by the AWA and the PHS Policy, but the two laws have different requirements for the IACUC's composition. These requirements are summarized in the table below, and for IACUCs subject to both the AWA and the PHS Policy, the stricter of the two requirements apply.

AWA IAUC Requirements	PHS Policy IACUC Requirements
Minimum of 3 members.	Minimum of 5 members.
Members appointed by institution's CEO or his/her designee.	Members appointed by institution's CEO or his/her designee.
Membership must include at least one veterinarian with training/experience in lab animal care and program responsibility (*i.e.*, the attending veterinarian).	Membership must include at least one veterinarian with training/experience in lab animal care and program responsibility (*i.e.*, the attending veterinarian).
One member must not be affiliated with the research facility. If the IACUC has more than 3 members, then no more than 3 members may be from the same administrative unit in the facility.	One or more persons with the following qualifications must be members, however, a single person may fulfill more than one qualification, provided there are 5 members: ■ 1 person unaffiliated with the facility ■ 1 practicing scientist with experience in animal research ■ 1 non-scientist
Quorum consists of 50% of the IACUC membership +1. Individuals with specific qualifications are not necessary to constitute quorum, but if these individuals do not regularly attend IACUC meetings, the IACUC will not be considered properly constituted.	Quorum consists of 50% of the IACUC membership +1. Individuals with specific qualifications are not necessary to constitute quorum, but if these individuals do not regularly attend IACUC meetings, the IACUC will not be considered properly constituted.

Meetings and Protocol Review: The IACUC must have regular convened meetings at which quorum is present in order to carry out its' responsibilities. Detailed minutes must be kept of each IACUC meeting, including a record of each vote taken.

One of the IACUC's primary responsibilities is to perform initial and continuing review of animal research protocols that are conducted at the research facility. The IACUC must initially approve a protocol before it can be conducted, and this approval is required before any federal funds can be expended for the research. Significant modifications to a protocol also require IACUC approval. The IACUC must conduct continuing review of research protocols involving AWA covered species at least annually, while continuing review of research that is regulated by PHS must be conducted at least every three years. Members who have conflicts of interest that prevent them from being able to participate in a particular protocol's review (*e.g.*, they are part of the research team conducting the protocol) must recuse themselves from the IACUC meeting while the protocol is discussed, and review cannot continue if their absence causes the IACUC to lose quorum.

Research compliance officers frequently attend IACUC meetings as "ex officio" members, and they need to have a thorough knowledge of the IACUC protocol review requirements and the types of IACUC review that may be used. IACUCs may review research protocols by one of two methods: review by the full IACUC committee ("full committee review" or "FCR"); or review by or by one or more designated members of the IACUC appointed by the IACUC chair ("designated member review" or "DMR"). IACUCs may have procedures that require FCR for certain types of research, *e.g.*, research involving animals in the pain and distress Class E, or research involving non-human primates. Further, before DMR can be used, the IACUC must have fulfilled the following conditions:

- All members of the IACUC must be provided an opportunity to request FCR for each individual protocol or pursuant to a written procedure in place to which all IACUC members previously have agreed.
- If no member requests FCR, then the protocol may be reviewed by DMR.
- If DMR is performed by more than one designated reviewer, the reviewers must be unanimous in their decisions regarding the protocol, including any decisions regarding required modifications.
- DMR may not be used to withhold approval from a protocol. Disapproval may only be carried out the full IACUC.

DMR also may be used to review protocols that previously have been reviewed by FCR but require additional modifications to secure approval. In order to use DMR in this manner, the IACUC must fulfill the following conditions:

- If all members of the IACUC are present at the convened meeting, then the IACUC may vote to require modifications to the protocol to secure approval and to have the revised protocol reviewed and approved by DMR, as opposed to returning to the IACUC for FCR.
- If all members of the IACUC are not present, then in order for DMR to be used to approve a protocol that FCR has determined requires modifications for approval: (a) the use of DMR for this purpose must be included in the institution's Assurance; (b) all IACUC members must have agreed in advance in writing that a quorum of member present at a convened meeting may decide by unanimous vote to use DMR to review a protocol that requires modifications for approval; and (c) any member of the IACUC may, at any time, request to see the revised protocol and/or require FCR.[10]

Approval Criteria: In order to approve a research protocol, the IACUC must determine that specific criteria have been met. First, the investigator must have provided evidence that he/she has considered alternatives to the use of animal research and that his/her research does not unnecessarily duplicate prior experiments. Second, the research procedures that are used must minimize pain, discomfort and distress and either utilize appropriate AAT drugs, or provide rigorous scientific justification as to why such drugs must be withheld to conduct the research. In addition, the research may not involve the use of paralyzing agents without the concurrent use of anesthesia, and when appropriate, animals must be euthanized with appropriate agents. Third, the protocol must have been reviewed by a veterinarian who will oversee the animals' living conditions, housing, feeding and veterinary care. Fourth, all personnel involved in the research must be appropriately trained, and medical care must be provided by a qualified veterinarian. Fifth, with the exception of rodents, if surgery is involved, it must use sterile techniques and include appropriate pre- and post-operative care. Finally, in general, no animal may be used in more than one major operative procedure from which it is permitted to recover. IACUC minutes should reflect that approval criteria have been met.

Facility Inspections: In addition to protocol reviews, IACUCs must perform semiannual inspections of the research institution's animal care and use program (*i.e.*, its policies and procedures) and of all physical facilities in which animals are used or held. For covered species, facilities must be inspected by the IACUC if animals are kept there for longer than 12 hours. For non-covered species that are regulated under the PHS Policy, inspection is required if the animals are kept there for more than 24 hours.

Facility inspections are conducted by groups of IACUC members who report back to the full IACUC with their findings. Any member of the

IACUC who requests to attend an inspection must be permitted to participate. IACUC or institution policy generally permits participation by the research compliance officer as well, and participation is a facility inspection is an excellent way for the compliance officer to gauge the status of an animal care and use program. A compliance officer who wants to participate in a facility inspection, however, should be mindful of any animal safety or occupational health and safety requirements that must be met to gain access to animal facilities. For example, training in the use of appropriate personal protective equipment and/or a negative skin test for tuberculosis may be required in order to visit certain animal facilities.

The IACUC inspection team reviews the program and the facility with respect to its compliance with the requirements of the AWA, PHS Policy and the Guide. Physical facilities, personnel training, animal transport mechanisms, surgical suites, animal feed and pharmaceuticals are all subject to inspection. Results of inspections are recorded in reports that are provided first to the IACUC for acceptance, and then to the institutional official. The reports must distinguish between significant deficiencies—deficiencies that are or may be a threat to the health or safety of animals—and minor deficiencies. When deficiencies are noted, they must be accompanied by a plan for their correction within a prescribed time. Failure to correct a significant deficiency affecting a covered species in accordance with the schedule must be reported within 15 business days to the USDA by the institutional official.

Post-Approval Monitoring: In addition to program and facility inspections, many IACUCs have programs in which they monitor the conduct of specific research protocols. Under these post-approval monitoring programs, IACUC employees or members will visit the sites at which the research is conducted and observe the research to verify that the protocol and all applicable laws and IACUC policies are being followed. Post-approval monitoring is an excellent tool for ensuring compliance in the animal care and use program.

Protocols Involving Field Work: Both the AWA and the PHS Policy can apply to animal research that is conducted in an animal's natural setting, but the criteria for application of the AWA and PHS Policy differs. Under the AWA, a field study is a study conducted on "free-living animals in their natural habitat." The AWA does not require IACUC review or site inspection for true "field studies," but if the study involves an invasive procedure or harms or materially alters the behavior of a study animal, then IACUC review, but not site inspection, is required. Under the PHS Policy, however, the IACUC always has oversight over PHS-funded field studies involving vertebrate animals. This oversight requires that the IACUC be aware of the field study's location, as well as the nature of the procedures involved and their impact on the animals. The IACUC, however, is not required to conduct a protocol review unless under the PHS Policy unless the field study research alter or influence the animals' activities (*i.e.*, capture and release of the animals). Similar to the AWA, the PHS Policy does not require IACUC inspection of field sites of free-living wild animals.

Other IACUC Responsibilities: In addition to protocol review and inspections, the IACUC is also responsible for carrying out the following responsibilities:

- Suspension of animal research protocols. Only the IACUC can vote to suspend a protocol at a full committee meeting, although the institutional official can halt research activity until the IACUC can meet and vote on suspension.
- Investigation of concerns and complaints regarding non-compliance with applicable IACUC policies, laws and regulations. In this regard, the AWA specifically prohibits retaliation against persons who report possible violations of the AWA.
- Report to the USDA and/or OLAW via the institutional official any of the following

occurrences: serious or continuing non-compliance with the AWA, PHS Policy, or the Guide; serious deviation from the Guide; failure to correct a program or facility deficiency in accordance with a prescribed plan; or suspension of a research protocol.
- Make any other recommendations to the institutional official regarding the animal care and use program.
- Prepare the annual reports for the USDA and OLAW that are transmitted by the institutional official. The reports must include any minority views expressed by a member of the IACUC who did not agree with the IACUC's conclusions regarding program or facility compliance.

Accrediting Agencies

In addition to the governmental agencies that regulate animal research, research facilities also may voluntarily apply for accreditation by the AAALAC International. Accreditation by AAALAC requires adherence to AAALAC standards, which for facilities within the United States are based primarily on the Guide. Documentation of a site's adherence to AAALAC standards must be set forth in a detailed program description. AAALAC inspectors visit the site and perform a detailed inspection prior to initial accreditation and every three years thereafter. The USDA and OLAW recognize AAALAC accreditation.

Additional Compliance Considerations

The world of animal research is one in which policies and regulations are subject to constant change. Some of this change has been brought about through ethical challenges to animal research and concerns about animal care and use championed by organizations such as the Humane Society of the United States, People for the Ethical Treatment of Animals (PETA) and similar groups.

Organizations advocating against the use of animals in research may use lawful processes to facilitate their activities such as requesting information about government-funded animal research through state open-records and federal Freedom of Information Act requests. Compliance officials should contact their counsel's office for advice about how to respond to any request for records that is received.

In addition, to promoting lawful changes in laws and regulations, some anti-animal research groups may resort to illegal actions to promote their agenda, such as breaking into research facilities to remove animals or threatening animal research personnel. Accordingly, compliance personnel must be cognizant of these potential security threats, and incorporate processes and procedures to respond to these possible emergency situations.

Conclusion

Animal research is a complex area of compliance that is subject to many varied laws and regulations. The research compliance officer working in the area must have a solid understanding of these regulations, and in particular the AWA, PHS Policy and the Guide. In addition, the research compliance officer must know and work closely with personnel in the institution who have primary oversight for animal research programs such as the Institutional Official and the Attending Veterinarian. Finally, and perhaps foremost, the research compliance officer also must be prepared to work closely with the institution's IACUC in its efforts to ensure full regulatory compliance and protection of all research animals' health, safety and welfare.

Chapter 5 Endnotes

1. **Kristin H. West, JD, MS**, is Chief Compliance Officer for Emory University in Atlanta, GA.
2. 21 CFR § 312.23.
3. Available at http://grants.nih.gov/grants/olaw/references/phspol.htm#USGovPrinciples.
4. Dep't of Health and Human Services, National Institutes of Health Office of Laboratory Animal Welfare, PHS Policy on Humane Care and Use of Laboratory Animals (2015) http://grants.nih.gov/grants/olaw/references/phspol.htm).
5. Animal Welfare Act, 7 U.S.C. Chapter 54, §§ 2131-2159.
6. Animal Welfare Regulations , 9 C.F.R. Chapter 1, Subchapter A, Parts 1-4.
7. National Research Council of the National Academies, *Guide for the Care and Use of Laboratory Animals,* 8th Edition, (Washington, DC: National Academies Press), available athttp://grants.nih.gov/grants/olaw/Guide-for-the-Care-and-Use-of-Laboratory-Animals.pdf.
8. American Veterinary Medical Association Panel on Euthanasia, *AVMA Guidelines for the Euthanasia of Animals*, 2013 Edition, available at https://www.avma.org/KB/Policies/Documents/euthanasia.pdf.
9. A sample assurance can be found at https://grants.nih.gov/grants/olaw/sampledoc/assursmp.htm.
10. See OLAW's *Guidance to IACUCs Regarding Use of Designated Member Review (DMR) for Animal Study Proposal Review Subsequent to Full Committee Review (FCR)* athttps://grants.nih.gov/grants/guide/notice-files/NOT-OD-09-035.html.

6
The Regulation of Research with Human Subjects

By Scott J Lipkin, DPM, CIP[1]

Overview:

Research involving human subjects is governed by various federal regulations, state laws, institutional based policies, and whenever applicable, accreditation standards. This chapter will provide an overview of the regulatory framework that governs human research and will:

- Review the framework and applicability of the federal regulations, state laws, and institutional policies that govern human research;
- Provide an overview of the role of a Human Research Protection Program ("HRPP");
- Discuss, in depth, the regulatory requirements that institutional review boards follow; and
- Review ancillary compliance functions that fall within the purview of the HRPP.

The Human Subject Protection Federal Regulatory Framework

The regulations governing human subjects research are based on the three core ethical principles as set forth in the Belmont Report.[2] These principles, *Respect for Persons, Beneficence, and Justice*, collectively form the foundation on which the Department of Health and Human Services ("HHS") Common Rule regulations[3] and the United States Food and Drug Administration's ("FDA") human subject protection regulations[4] are based. Published on April 18, 1979, the Belmont Report was the work product of the National Commission for the Protection of Human Subjects of Biomedical and Behavioral Research. The National Commission was created in 1974, as part of the National Research Act.[5]

Respect for Persons: The principle of respect for persons includes the requirement to treat people as autonomous, self-governing agents and the requirement to protect individuals with diminished autonomy.

Beneficence: The Belmont Report frames beneficence as an obligation to treat individuals ethically by making efforts to secure their well-being. Beneficence should be thought of as an obligation to minimize the potential of harm and to maximize possible benefits.

Justice: In the context of the Belmont Report, justice refers to the concept of ethical distribution of burdens and benefits associated with a research study.

In 1981, with the Belmont Report as a foundational background, HHS and the FDA revised their existing human subjects regulations.[6] In 1991, the core HHS regulations (45 CFR Part 46, Subpart A) were formally adopted by more than a dozen other federal departments and agencies that conduct or fund research involving human subjects as the Federal Policy for the Protection of Human Subjects, or "Common Rule." On January 19, 2017 HHS and 15 other Federal Departments and Agencies issued final revisions to the Common Rule, which after several delays, became fully effective January 21, 2019.[7]

FDA and HHS regulations governing human research are not harmonized with one another.

There exist key differences related to scope, definitions, exemptions, informed consent, and other provisions.[8] Alignment of the two disparate sets of rules is anticipated as a requirement of Section 3023 of the 21st Century Cures Act, which directs the HHS Secretary to harmonize the differences between the HHS and FDA Human Subject Regulations.[9]

Taking a closer look at the federal regulatory framework, the HHS regulations for the protection of human subjects (45 CFR Part 46) includes five subparts; the FDA regulations for the protection of human subjects (21 CFR Part 50) includes four subparts; and the FDA regulations for institutional review boards includes five subparts (21 CFR Part 56).

	45 CFR PART 46	**21 CFR PART 50**	**21 CFR PART 56**
Subpart A	Basic HHS Policy for Protection of Human Research Subjects	General Provisions	General Provisions
Subpart B	Additional Protections for Pregnant Women, Human Fetuses and Neonates Involved in Research	Informed Consent of Human Subjects	Organization and Personnel
Subpart C	Additional Protections Pertaining to Biomedical and Behavioral Research Involving Prisoners as Subjects	Reserved	IRB Functions and Operations
Subpart D	Additional Protections for Children Involved as Subjects in Research	General Provisions	Records and Reports
Subpart E	Registration of Institutional Review Boards	n/a	Administrative Actions for Noncompliance

Applicability of Federal Regulations, State Laws, and Institutional Policies Governing Human Research

It is essential to understand how to determine whether the HHS or FDA regulations apply to a given human subject[10] research[11] study. HHS regulations apply whenever research involving human subjects is conducted, supported, or otherwise subject to regulation by any federal department or agency that takes appropriate administrative action to make the policy applicable to such research.[12] FDA regulations apply to all clinical investigations regulated by the FDA under sections 505(i) and 520(g) of the Federal Food, Drug, and Cosmetic Act, as well as clinical investigations that support applications for research or marketing permits for products regulated by the Food and Drug Administration.[13] At times, a human research study might be subject to the requirements of both the HHS and FDA regulations.[14] When both sets of regulations apply to the same study, institutional review boards ("IRBs") and investigators must apply those specific regulations that offer the greatest protections to participants. Federal regulations do not apply to research that doesn't fall under the jurisdictional oversight of HHS or FDA. However, most institutions that support human research have established policies that require protections, equivalent to those set forth in HHS and FDA regulations for human research studies that are not otherwise subject to federal regulatory requirements.

In addition to federal oversight, several states have enacted into law specific requirements related to human subject research. For example, the California Human Experimentation Act[15] requires that a "experimental subject's bill of rights" be provided to all research subjects in medical experiments and it describes the hierarchy of surrogate decision makers who are able to provide informed consent. Many state-specific laws have direct bearing on the conduct of human research, including for example laws related to the legal age of consent, emancipated minors, genetic testing, diagnosing and treatment of certain sexually transmitted diseases, and others.

The Federalwide Assurance

Before an institution engages in federally funded research, *i.e.*, research that is funded or supported by a Common Rule federal agency, the institution must sign a Federalwide Assurance ("FWA") and submit it to the HHS Office for Human Research Protections ("OHRP"). An FWA is a contract between an institution proposing to conduct federally funded research and the federal government, via HHS, whereby the institution commits to the federal government that the institution (via its employees and agents) will comply with 45 CFR Part 46 when conducting FWA covered research.

The key features of the FWA are the following:

a. Identifying information for the institution filing the FWA, including the human protections administrator ("HPA") at the institution and the institutional official ("IO") signing the FWA;
b. A list of the institution's legal components that operate under different names that will be covered by the FWA and the city and state or country where the component is located. Legal components are generally defined as parts of an institution that may be viewed as separate organizations, but remain part of the legal entity or institution. For example, ABC University can list its XYZ University Hospital, KLM School of Public Health, and EFG Institute for International Studies as components;
c. A statement of ethical principles to be followed in protecting human subjects of research;
d. An applicability statement indicating that the FWA applies whenever the institution becomes engaged in human subjects research conducted or supported by any United States federal department or agency that has adopted the Common Rule, *i.e.*, 45 CFR Part

46, Subpart A, unless the research is exempt from Common Rule requirements or a Common Rule agency or department determines the research will be conducted under a separate assurance of compliance. U.S. institutions may voluntarily extend the Common Rule to all research conducted by the institution regardless of the source of support;

e. An assurance of compliance indicating that the institution will comply with the terms of the FWA;

f. The designation of all internal IRBs that will review the research covered by the FWA. If the institution has no internal IRB, it must designate the external IRB that reviews all research covered by the FWA. If the institution relies upon multiple external IRBs, the institution should designate the external IRB that reviews the largest percentage of the research covered by the FWA. All IRBs designated on an institution's FWA must be registered with OHRP before the FWA can be approved. All IRBs reviewing research covered by an institution's FWA must be registered with OHRP whether or not they are designated on the institution's FWA;

g. Whenever the institution relies upon an IRB operated by another institution or organization for review of research covered by the FWA, the institution must ensure that this arrangement is documented by a written agreement between the institution and the other organization or institution operating the IRB. The agreement must outline their relationship and include a commitment that the IRB will adhere to the requirements of the Institution's FWA. This agreement must be kept on file at both institutions/organizations and made available to OHRP or any U.S. federal department or agency conducting or supporting research covered by the FWA upon request.

An FWA must be signed by a high-level institutional official authorized to represent the institution and the components named in the FWA; this individual is identified on the FWA as the signatory official (better known as the institutional official). Entities that the IO is not authorized to represent may not be covered under the FWA. This person signing an FWA is usually the president, chief executive officer, chief operating officer or chancellor. The IO must assure that human subjects research to which the FWA applies is conducted in accordance with the terms of the assurance.[16]

The intent in requiring that the IO be a high-level individual is two-fold. First, OHRP encourages institutions to promote a culture of conscience for the ethical conduct of human subjects research at the highest level within the institution. Second, the IO should be at a level of responsibility that would allow authorization of necessary administrative or legal action, should that be required. Moreover, OHRP recommends that the IO not be the chair or member of any IRB designated under the FWA.

Human Research Protection Programs

A human research protection program ("HRPP") supports an institution-wide approach to protecting human research participants. This is accomplished through synchronization of resources and business units who play a role in human research. Typically, the IRB Office provides the primary administrative support for the HRPP, including the work of the IRB committee. Other components of the HRPP include investigators, the HIPAA privacy board, the conflicts of interest committee, the Office of General Counsel, the Research Compliance Office, scientific review committees, investigational pharmacy, the Office of Sponsored Programs, and others.

The Institutional Review Board

The IRB is the research ethics review committee whose primary purpose is to provide protections to human research participants. The work of the IRB should always be framed within the context of the applicable regulatory oversight requirements. Under FDA regulations, an IRB is an appropriately constituted group that has been formally designated to review and monitor biomedical research involving human subjects. In accordance with FDA regulations, an IRB has the authority to approve, require modifications in (to secure approval), or disapprove research. This group review serves an important role in the protection of the rights and welfare of human research subjects.[17]

Explicit rules are set forth that describe the requirements of IRB functions including, for example, membership, written policies and procedures, the basis for IRB approval of research, informed consent requirements, IRB meeting minutes requirements, and retention of IRB records. The following sections detail the core functions of an IRB. Additional IRB functions related to FDA-regulated clinical investigations are not covered in this chapter.[18]

IRB Membership

HHS regulations at 45 CFR 46.107(a) and FDA regulations at 21 CFR 56.107(a) provide, among other things, that each IRB shall have at least five members, with varying backgrounds to promote complete and adequate review of research activities commonly conducted by the institution. In addition, the regulations provide that the IRB be sufficiently qualified through the experience and expertise of its members to promote respect for its advice and counsel in safeguarding the rights and welfare of human subjects and be able to ascertain the acceptability of proposed research in terms of institutional commitments and regulations, applicable law, and standards of professional conduct and practice. If an IRB regularly reviews research that involves a vulnerable category of subjects (*i.e.*, children, pregnant women, prisoners), consideration should be given to the inclusion of one or more committee members who are knowledgeable about and experienced in working with these subjects. Each IRB must include at least one member whose primary concerns are in scientific areas and at least one member whose primary concerns are in nonscientific areas. Additionally, each IRB must include at least one member who is not otherwise affiliated with the institution and who is not part of the immediate family of a person who is affiliated with the institution.

IRB Written Procedures

HHS regulations at 45 CFR Part 46.108(a)(3) and (4); and FDA regulations at 21 CFR 56.108 require that IRBs follow written procedures that adequately describe the following activities:

- Conducting initial review of research;
- Conducting continuing review of research;
- Reporting findings and actions to the investigator and the institution;
- Determining which projects require review more often than annually;
- Determining which projects need verification from sources other than the investigators that no material changes have occurred since the previous IRB review;
- Ensuring prompt reporting to the IRB of proposed changes in a research activity, and for ensuring that such changes in approved research, during the period for which IRB approval has already been given, are not initiated without IRB review and approval except when necessary to eliminate apparent immediate hazards to the subject; and
- Ensuring prompt reporting to the IRB, appropriate institutional officials, any department or agency head and OHRP (for research covered by an institution's FWA) and the FDA (for FDA-regulated research) of: (a) any unanticipated problems involving risks to subjects or others ("UPs"); (b) any instance of serious or continuing noncompliance with 45 CFR part 46 and/or applicable FDA regulations or the requirements or determinations of the IRB; and (c) any suspension or termination of IRB approval.

Both OHRP and FDA recommend that IRB written procedures be sufficiently detailed so that the procedures provide IRB members and administrative staff with an understanding of how to carry out their duties consistently and effectively in ways that ensure that the rights and welfare of subjects are protected.[19] Moreover, it is believed that such step-by-step operational details in written procedures will help IRBs operate in compliance with governing regulations. This is why IRB written procedures that simply reiterate the regulations are found insufficient, *i.e.*, such "procedures" do not provide sufficient detail about the IRBs' operations and how those operations satisfy regulatory requirements.

Research Exempt from IRB Review

HHS regulations permit exemptions from IRB review for research where the only involvement of human subjects falls within one of the following categories:[20]

- Educational research
- Interactions: educational tests, surveys, observation of public behavior
- Benign behavioral interventions
- Secondary research when informed consent is not required
- Federal research and demonstration projects
- Taste and food quality evaluation and consumer acceptance studies
- Storage or maintenance when broad consent is required
- Secondary research when broad consent is required

Providing an exempt determination is not a requirement of the IRB. In practice, most exempt determinations are made by an IRB chair, IRB administrator, or experienced IRB staff. Exemptions should be granted by knowledgeable individual(s) who have been granted authority through institutional policy. Some categories of exemption require ***Limited IRB Review***.[21] Limited IRB review must be performed by an IRB member. When conducting limited IRB review, the IRB reviewer must determine that:

- There are adequate provisions to protect the privacy of subjects and to maintain the confidentiality of data;
- For exemptions granted under 45 CFR Part 46.104(d)(7)(8), limited IRB review must also include a determination that broad consent for storage, maintenance, and secondary research use of identifiable private information or identifiable biospecimens must be obtained and documented in accordance with the applicable regulatory requirements.[22]

Limited IRB review can be conducted by the expedited procedure and continuing review is not required for research approved by limited IRB review.

Review by the Expedited Procedure

HHS regulations at 45 CFR Part 46.108(b) and FDA regulations at 21 CFR Part 56.108(c) require that the IRB review proposed research at convened meetings at which a majority of the members of the IRB are present, including at least one member whose primary concerns are in nonscientific areas, except where expedited review is appropriate under HHS regulations at 45 CFR Part 46.110/FDA regulations at 21 CFR Part 56.110. FDA regulations permit the use of expedited review procedures for initial or continuing review to specific research categories published in the Federal Register at 63 FR 60364-60367[23] when the research is determined to involve no more than minimal risk. Expedited review is permitted under HHS regulations for minimal risk[24] research that fits in types of research that appear on the Secretary's list, for minor changes in previously approved research, or for research where limited IRB review was a condition of exemption. An expedited reviewer is authorized to exercise all of the authorities of the IRB except that the reviewer may not disapprove the research. Research may only be disapproved after review has been performed in accordance with the non-expedited procedures by the convened IRB. OHRP recommends that the IRB document—for initial and continuing reviews conducted under an expedited review procedure—the specific permissible categories justifying the expedited review. Continuing review of research approved by the expedited procedure is not required.[25]

IRB Approval Criteria

FDA regulations at 21 CFR Part 56.111 delineate that the following criteria must be satisfied before an IRB can approve research:

- Risks to subjects are minimized;
- Risks to subjects are reasonable in relation to anticipated benefits, if any, to subjects,

and the importance of the knowledge that may reasonably be expected to result;
- Selection of subjects is equitable;
- Informed consent will be sought from each prospective subject or the subject's legally authorized representative, unless waived or altered by the IRB;
- Informed consent will be appropriately documented unless waived or altered by the IRB;
- When appropriate, the research plan makes adequate provision for monitoring the data collected to ensure the safety of subjects;
- When appropriate, there are adequate provisions to protect the privacy of subjects and to maintain the confidentiality of data;
- When some or all subjects are likely to be vulnerable to coercion or undue influence, additional safeguards are included in the study to protect the rights and welfare of such subjects.

In addition to the above, HHS regulations at 45 CFR Part 46.111(a)(8) include an additional approval criterion for research approved using the limited IRB procedure.[26]

Informed Consent

HHS regulations at 45 CFR Part 46.116(a) and FDA regulations at 21 CFR Part 50.20 set forth requirements for legally effective informed consent. In the context of informed consent process, HHS regulations require that:

- Informed consent should only be obtained under circumstances that provide the prospective participant sufficient time to discuss and consider whether or not to participate;
- Informed consent should only be obtained under circumstances that minimize the possibility of coercion or undue influence;
- The information given during the informed consent process must be in language understandable to the subject or the legally authorized representative;
- The prospective subject or the legally authorized representative must be provided with the information that a reasonable person would want to have in order to make an informed decision about whether to participate, and an opportunity to discuss that information;
- Informed consent may include exculpatory language; and
- Informed consent must begin with a concise and focused presentation of the key study-related information (except when broad consent is obtained).

Both HHS and FDA regulations require that when seeking informed consent, certain basic and additional elements/information be provided to each subject[27] unless the IRB approves a consent procedure that waives or alters, some or all of the of the informed consent elements.

Informed consent requirements differ between HHS and FDA regulations. Specifically, FDA regulations do not require that the informed consent process begin with a concise and focused presentation of the key study-related information, nor do they require a reasonable person standard when information is presented to prospective subjects. Moreover, HHS regulations set forth additional requirements for elements of informed consent related to:

- Secondary research use of data and biospecimens;[28]
- Commercial profit related to biospecimens;
- Return of clinically relevant research results to participants; and
- Whole genome sequencing of biospecimens.[29]

IRB Approval Actions

An IRB must review (and approve) proposed research, including proposed changes to previously approved research, at convened meetings at which a majority of the members of the IRB are present, including at least one member whose primary concerns are in nonscientific areas, except when expedited review is authorized (45 CFR 46.108(b) and 21 CFR 56.108(c)).

According to OHRP, approval with conditions means that "at the time when the IRB reviews and approves a research study (or proposed changes to a previously approved research study), the IRB requires as a condition of approval that the investigator (a) make specified changes to the research protocol or informed consent document(s), (b) confirm specific assumptions or understandings on the part of the IRB regarding how the research will be conducted, or (c) submit additional documents, such that, based on the assumption that the conditions are satisfied, the IRB is able to make all of the determinations required for approval under the HHS regulations at 45 CFR 46.111 and, if applicable, subparts B, C, or D of 45 CFR part 46."

When the IRB grants contingent approval, the IRB should provide the researcher specific modifications required to secure approval. For example, "Participants must be 18 years or older" or "Drop the placebo-controlled arm of the study." Inappropriate use of contingent approval includes statements like, "Explain why participants younger than 18 years of age will be allowed to participate," or "Provide additional justification for the use of placebo."[30]

Continuing Review of Research

HHS regulations at 45 CFR 46.109(e) and FDA regulations at 21 CFR 56.109(f) require that continuing review of research be conducted by the IRB at intervals appropriate to the degree of risk, but not less than once per year. The regulations make no provision for any grace period extending the conduct of the research beyond the expiration date of IRB approval. Additionally, where the convened IRB specifies conditions for approval of a protocol that are to be verified as being satisfied by the IRB chairperson or another IRB member designated by the chairperson, continuing review must occur no later than one year after the date the protocol was reviewed by the convened IRB, not on the anniversary of the date the IRB chairperson or his or her designee verifies that IRB-specified conditions for approval have been satisfied. Under HHS regulations, continuing review is not required for:

- Research previously reviewed under the expedited procedure;
- Research reviewed under limited IRB review;
- Research that has progressed to the point of data analysis and/or access follow-up clinical data from non-research clinical interventions.

IRB Reporting Requirements

HHA and FDA regulations[31] require IRBs to establish and follow written procedures to ensure prompt reporting to the IRB, institutional officials, and the appropriate regulatory agency or agencies of, (i) serious and continuing noncompliance, (ii) suspensions or terminations of IRB approval, and (iii) unanticipated problems involving risks to participants and others. Neither set of regulations defines prompt reporting, serious noncompliance, nor continuing noncompliance, and it is left to local institutional policy to create and implement policies that define those specific terms.

IRB Meeting Minutes

HHS regulations at 45 CFR 46.115(a)(2) and FDA regulations at 21 CFR 56.115(a)(2) require that minutes of IRB meetings be in sufficient detail to show attendance at the meetings; actions taken by the IRB; the vote on these actions including the number of members voting for, against, and abstaining; the basis for requiring changes in or disapproving research; and a written summary of the discussion of controverted issues and their resolution. Thus, per regulations these five items must be documented in IRB meeting minutes.

Moreover, a final guidance document, titled "Minutes of Institutional Review Board (IRB) Meetings—Guidance for Institutions and IRBs," which was prepared jointly by the OHRP and FDA,[32] describes requirements for developing and maintaining IRB minutes and provides recommendations for meeting the regulatory requirements for developing and maintaining IRB minutes. Thus, in addition to the five regulatory requirements noted above, OHRP and FDA recommend that the following information be contained in IRB meeting minutes:

- IRB findings/determinations regarding whether proposed research satisfies all applicable IRB approval criteria;
- IRB findings/determinations as to whether proposed informed consent form(s) meet applicable regulatory requirements;
- IRB decisions regarding waiver of documentation of informed consent;
- IRB decisions regarding waiver or alteration of informed consent;
- IRB findings/determinations for studies involving children;
- IRB findings/determinations relating to emergency research;
- IRB significant risk/non-significant risk determinations, along with the IRB rationale for its determinations;
- IRB findings/determinations for studies involving pregnant women, human fetuses and neonates;
- IRB findings/determinations for studies involving prisoners; and
- Reports of expedited review activities that occurred outside of the convened IRB.

IRB Records

HHS regulations at 45 CFR 46.115(a) and FDA regulations at 21 CFR 56.115(a) provide that an institution, or when appropriate an IRB, shall prepare and maintain adequate documentation of IRB activities, including the following:

- Copies of all research proposals reviewed, scientific evaluations, if any, that accompany the proposals, approved sample consent documents, progress reports submitted by investigators, and reports of injuries to subjects;
- Minutes of IRB meetings, which shall be in sufficient detail to show attendance at the meetings; actions taken by the IRB; the vote on these actions including the number of members voting for, against, and abstaining; the basis for requiring changes in or disapproving research; and a written summary of the discussion of controverted issues and their resolution;
- Records of continuing review activities;
- Copies of all correspondence between the IRB and the investigators;
- A list of IRB members;
- Written procedures for the IRB; and
- Statements of significant new findings provided to subjects.

Other Compliance Considerations Related to the IRB and Human Research Protection Program

IRBs as part of the HRPP are commonly relied upon to perform and oversee compliance functions that are not otherwise directly prescribed by federal regulations. For example, the IRB office might assume primary oversight of investigator training, the HIPAA privacy board, individual investigator conflicts of interest, allegations of noncompliance, harmonization of a clinical research contract with the IRB approved informed consent, and others. This section summarizes some of these core ancillary functions.

HIPAA Privacy Board

The Health Insurance Portability and Accountability Act ("HIPAA") Privacy Rule establishes the conditions under which protected health information ("PHI") may be used or disclosed by covered entities for research purposes. Under the Privacy Rule, covered entities are permitted to use and disclose PHI for research in accordance with an individual's signed authorization, which may be incorporated into a research informed consent form or without individual authorization under limited circumstances.

Commonly, IRBs act as a privacy board for HIPAA-related research issues. The privacy board reviews and approves the proposed access, use, and disclosure of the PHI. As a privacy board, the IRB is responsible for determining whether research subjects are required to sign an authorization for the use and disclosure of their PHI, or if one of the exceptions to the authorization requirements applies. Examples of these exceptions include waivers of authorization and the use of de-identified data or limited data sets.

Harmonization of a Clinical Trial Agreement with IRB Approved Informed Consent

Both FDA and HHS informed consent regulations require IRBs to approve consent forms that, among other things, include information that, (i) describes additional costs that study participants might incur and (ii) describes available compensation for study-related injuries and complications.[33]

The provisions related to subject injury and costs to participants are set forth in the terms and conditions of the clinical trial agreement ("CTA") and study budget. To fully understand potential costs that research participants may incur, a coverage analysis or other procedures that document costs to participants should then be performed.[34] Negotiation of CTAs, budget development, and coverage analysis are procedures performed as part of research administrative pre-award processes. To meet applicable informed consent requirements, procedures should be developed to ensure that the final CTA, budget, and coverage analysis are shared with select representatives from the IRB. IRB staff, pre-award personnel, or others should then reconcile these documents to ensure harmonization of subject injury and cost to participant language with the corresponding sections in the informed consent.

Investigator Training and Education

Although not required by regulation, OHRP recommends that FWA holding institutions establish training and oversight requirements and mechanisms to ensure that investigators maintain continuing knowledge of, and compliance with:

- relevant ethical principles;
- relevant federal regulations;
- written IRB procedures;
- OHRP guidance;
- other applicable guidance;
- state and local laws; and
- institutional policies for the protection of human subjects.[35]

Most institutions that support human research establish training requirements for investigators. Frequently, institutional responsibility for administrative oversight of these training requirements reside in the IRB office and completion of assigned training is a prerequisite that must be completed prior to submission to the IRB.

Managing Noncompliance

IRBs are frequently relied upon to manage allegations of noncompliance. Specifically, in response to an allegation of research noncompliance the IRB office will coordinate the investigation and then present its findings to the IRB committee for review, determination and management. In essence, IRB committees frequently serve as research compliance oversight committees.

Conflicts of Interest

The purpose of the regulations at 42 CFR Part 50 Subpart F, Promoting Objectivity in Research, are to promote objectivity by establishing standards for preventing financial conflicts of interest (COIs) having an impact on the design, conduct, and/or reporting of research funded under Public Health Service grants. These standards are intended to ensure that investigators' work will be free of bias resulting from COIs. Many institutions that support human research apply the requirements of 42 CFR Part 50 Subpart F to all research, regardless of the funding source.

At a minimum, the IRB should receive a copy of COI management plans during its review of research. At some institutions, personnel from the IRB office are required to serve as the COI program administrator, while at other institutions, the IRB committee is required to serve as the research COI committee.

Conclusion

Human subject research is a heavily regulated activity. This chapter merely touches the surface of the many requirements that must be followed to ensure compliance with federal regulations, state law, institutional policies, and accreditation standards. An effective compliance officer must understand these basic requirements. Moreover, the compliance officer should work closely with the HRPP administrator and the IRB committee to stay current with relevant and rapidly evolving hot topics that constantly challenge the compliance environment.

Chapter 6 Endnotes

1. **Scott J. Lipkin, DPM, CIP,** is a Managing Director with Ankura Consulting in Orlando, FL.
2. National Commission for the Protection of Human Subjects of Biomedical and Behavioral Research, The Belmont Report: Ethical Principles and Guidelines for the Protection of Human Subjects of Research. In DHEW Publication No. (OS) 78-0013 and (OS) 78-0014.4, (April 18 1979). www.hhs.gov/ohrp/regulations-and-policy/belmont-report/index.html
3. The Federal Policy for the Protection of Human Subjects, 45 CFR Part 46 subpart A.
4. U.S. Food and Drug Administration, Protection of Human Subjects, 21 CFR Part 50; and Food and Drug Administration, Institutional Review Boards, 21 CFR Part 56.
5. National Research Act, Pub. L. 93-348, 88 Stat. 342 (July 12, 1974).
6. U.S. Dep't of Health and Human Services, Office for Human Research Protections, Federal Policy for the Protection of Human Subjects ("Common Rule"), (last reviewed March 18, 2016), https://www.hhs.gov/ohrp/regulations-and-policy/regulations/common-rule/index.html.
7. U.S. Dep't of Health and Human Services, Office for Human Research Protections, Revised Common Rule, (last reviewed June 19, 2018), https://www.hhs.gov/ohrp/regulations-and-policy/regulations/finalized-revisions-common-rule/index.html.
8. U.S. Food and Drug Administration, Comparison of FDA and HHS Human Subject Protection Regulations (last updated April 3, 2018), https://www.fda.gov/scienceresearch/specialtopics/runningclinicaltrials/educationalmaterials/ucm112910.htm.
9. 21st Century Cures Act, Pub. L. 114-255, 130 STAT. 1033 (December 13, 2016), https://www.congress.gov/114/plaws/publ255/PLAW-114publ255.pdf.
10. 45 CFR Part 46.102(e) and 21 CFR Part 56.102(e).
11. 45 CFR Part 46 102.(l) defines research. Research is at defined in FDA regulations, rather, clinical investigation is defined at 21 CFR Part 56.102(c).
12. 45 CFR Part 46.101(a).
13. 21 CFR Part 50.1(a).
14. For example, a clinical investigation involving an investigational drug under an IND that is funded by the NIH would be subject to both the HHS and FDA regulations.
15. 1978 Cal. Stat., Ch. 360, Protection of Human Subjects in Medical Experimentation Act, http://leginfo.legislature.ca.gov/faces/codes_displayText.xhtml?lawCode=HSC&division=20.&title=&part=&chapter=1.3.&article.
16. See U.S. Dep't of Health and Human Services, Office for Human Research Protections, Federalwide Assurance (FWA) for the Protection of Human Subjects (Updated July 31, 2017), https://www.hhs.gov/ohrp/register-irbs-and-obtain-fwas/fwas/fwa-protection-of-human-subjecct/index.html.
17. U.S. Food and Drug Administration, Institutional Review Boards Frequently Asked Questions—Information Sheet (last updated July 12, 2018), https://www.fda.gov/RegulatoryInformation/Guidances/ucm126420.htm.
18. For example, IRB requirements related to investigational devices, Investigational, drugs, expanded access, emergency use of a test article, and planned emergency research with waiver of informed consent, and others.
19. U.S. Department of Health and Human Services, Office for Human Research Protections, Institutional Review Board (IRB) Written Procedures:Guidance for Institutions and IRBs (May 2018), https://www.fda.gov/downloads/regulatoryinformation/guidances/ucm512761.pdf.
20. 45 CFR Part 46.104.
21. 45 CFR Part 46.104 (d)(2)(iii), (d)(3)(i)(C), (d)(7), and (d)(8).
22. 45 CFR Part 46.111(a)(8)
23. U.S. Department of Health and Human Services Office for Human Research Protections, OHRP Expedited Review Categories (1998), http://www.hhs.gov/ohrp/policy/expedited98.html.
24. Minimal risk is defined at 45 CFR Part 46.102(j).
25. 45 CFR Part 46.109(f)(1)(i).
26. 45 CFR Part 46.111(8).
27. 45 CFR Part 46.116(b)(c) and 21 CFR Part 50.25.
28. 45 CFR Part 46.116(b)(9).
29. 45 CFR Part 46.116(c)(7-9).
30. Association for the Accreditation of Human Research Protection Programs, Inc., Evaluation Instrument for Accreditation, February 2018, page 82.
31. 45 CFR Part 46.108(3)(iii) and 21 CFR Part 56.108(b)(1).
32. U.S. Food and Drug Administration, Minutes of Institutional Review Board (IRB) Meetings - Guidance for Institutions and IRBs, (September 2017), https://www.fda.gov/RegulatoryInformation/Guidances/ucm470046.htm.
33. 21 CFR Part 50.25(a)(6) and 21 CFR Part 50.25(b)(3).
34. U.S. Dep't of Health and Human Services, Centers for Medicare and Medicaid Services, Routine Costs in Clinical Trials, (July 9, 2007), https://www.cms.gov/medicare-coverage-database/details/ncd-details.aspx?NCDId=1&ncdver=2&fromdb=true.
35. U.S. Department of Health and Human Services Office for Human Research Protections, Federalwide Assurance (FWA) for the Protection of Human Subjects, (Updated July 31, 2017), http://www.hhs.gov/ohrp/register-irbs-and-obtain-fwas/fwas/fwa-protection-of-human-subjecct/index.html.

7
FDA-Regulated Clinical Research

By Darshan Kulkarni, Pharm.D, MS, Esq.[1]

Introduction

The U.S. Food and Drug Administration ("FDA") oversees clinical trials involving drugs and medical devices under the Federal Food, Drug, and Cosmetic Act ("FDCA") and implementing regulations. This chapter describes the types of trials regulated by the FDA, the major regulations governing conduct of those trials, responsibilities of sponsors and investigators in performing FDA-regulated trials, what to expect from an FDA inspection of a clinical trial and how to respond.

Legal Framework

Among other things,[2] the FDCA prohibits the shipment of "adulterated" and "misbranded" drugs and devices in interstate commerce.[3] Drugs or devices that are not approved or cleared by the FDA, or that are approved or cleared but offered for a use that is inconsistent with their approved or cleared labeling, are traditionally thought of as adulterated or misbranded. The FDCA facilitates new drug and device development through provisions authorizing the FDA to issue regulations that permit and govern the investigational use of drugs and devices to study their safety and effectiveness before approval or clearance.[4] These regulations include:

- 21 C.F.R. Part 11 (Electronic Records; Electronic Signatures)[5]
- 21 C.F.R. Part 50 (Protection of Human Subjects) and Part 56 (Institutional Review Boards), which correspond substantially with the provisions of the Common Rule[6]
- 21 C.F.R. Part 54 (Financial Disclosures by Clinical Investigators)[7]
- 21 C.F.R. Part 312 (Investigational New Drug Application [IND])
- 21 C.F.R. Part 812 (Investigational Device Exemptions [IDE])

In addition to the FDCA and related laws and regulations, the FDA regularly issues industry guidance to facilitate compliance with legal and regulatory mandates. These guidance documents are not law but represent the agency's current thinking or policy on regulated activities, including clinical research.[8] They do not bind the FDA or the public and do not establish legally enforceable rights or responsibilities. To the contrary, a sponsor or investigator may employ an alternate approach provided its conduct complies with the requirements of all applicable statutes and regulations. Where a sponsor or investigator intends to follow an alternate approach, however, an advance meeting or discussion with the FDA may be prudent.

Importantly, while the laws and regulations referenced above govern the conduct of research involving investigational drugs and devices, they do *not* address the off-label use in clinical practice of approved or cleared drugs or devices. A practitioner who wishes to use an FDA-approved or cleared drug or device off-label should, however, be well informed about the product, base its use on firm scientific rationale and on sound medical evidence, and maintain records of the product's use and effects.[9]

Sponsor and Investigator Responsibilities

A "sponsor" is an individual or organization who initiates but does not actually conduct a clinical investigation.[10] The sponsor is ultimately responsible for the proper conduct of the investigation. An "investigator," by contrast, is the individual who actually performs the investigation.[11] An individual who both initiates and performs an investigation is referred to as a "sponsor-investigator."[12] The FDA prescribes the responsibilities of sponsors and investigators in regulations governing clinical investigations and clarifies its approach in associated guidance posted to the agency's website.[13]

Sponsor Responsibilities

1. Generally

Sponsors are ultimately accountable for assuring that clinical investigations are conducted in accord with approved protocols, or "investigational plans," and with applicable laws and regulations.[14] For example, it is a sponsor's job to:

- Secure FDA approval of an IND, IDE or exemption if required, and comply with the requirements applicable to an IND or IDE
- Select qualified investigators and monitors and provide them with the information they need to conduct and monitor the investigation properly
- Ensure that the investigation is conducted in accordance with the general investigational plan and protocol
- Promptly inform the FDA, the IRB, and investigators of any significant new adverse effects or risks associated with the product
- Appropriately label investigational products
- Initiate, hold, or discontinue clinical trials as required
- Control the distribution and return of investigational products, including shipping only to authorized investigators
- Evaluate and report adverse experiences
- Maintain adequate records
- Submit progress reports and final study results
- Refrain from promotion and commercialization of investigational products, among other things

IND regulations explicitly allow a sponsor to transfer certain obligations to a contract research organization ("CRO"). IDE regulations do not explicitly include such a provision but CROs can be used with appropriate controls. In these cases, the sponsor's responsibilities are delegated under a written agreement and, while a CRO that signs such an agreement must comply with its obligations under the agreement and is subject to the FDA enforcement if it fails, this does not relieve the sponsor of its ultimate accountability.

2. Selecting Investigators

A sponsor must select study investigators who have sufficient training and experience; provide investigators with all the information necessary to properly conduct the study; ensure that the study is monitored properly and on a regular basis; ensure that investigators receive IRB review and approval before starting the study; and ensure that the investigator promptly informs the sponsor and IRB of any significant adverse events relating to the study.

The sponsor is encouraged to conduct a pre-study visit to each site to ensure that each investigator (i) understands the regulatory/specific requirements of the investigation; (ii) understands and accepts the obligations associated with conducting the study; (iii) has access to a suitable number and type of study subjects; and (iv) has adequate facilities to properly conduct the investigation.

A sponsor must secure and maintain a record of a signed agreement for each selected investigator that includes, at a minimum: (i) the investigator's curriculum vitae; (ii) a summary of the investigator's relevant experience; and (iii) a statement of the investigator's commitment to conduct the study in accordance with: all applicable regulations; FDA or IRB imposed conditions; and the investigational plan.

3. Selecting Monitors and Monitoring Investigations

The sponsor is responsible for assuring that the study is monitored properly on a regular basis and that study monitors, like investigators, are qualified to perform their assigned tasks on a study. In recent years, the FDA has begun recommending avoiding a "one size fits all" model of monitoring, where all sites receive similarly routine, on-site visits. It, instead, recommends moving towards a risk-based approach where sponsors and investigators work to risk-stratify facilities based on a variety of factors as may be especially evident by looking at trending conducted by a centralized location. [15] Depending on the nature of the study, the type of product being tested, and the scope of monitoring necessary to oversee its conduct, various professionals ranging from physicians to engineers to nurses may be qualified monitors. Considerations in determining the number of monitors and the level of expertise required include:

- The number of investigators conducting the study
- The number/location(s) of facilities
- The type of product being tested
- The complexity of the study
- The nature of the disease or condition being studied

Sponsors (or their appropriately authorized designees) must monitor clinical investigations periodically to ensure investigator compliance with the requirements of the study and applicable regulations. If an investigator does not comply, the sponsor must implement effective and timely remedial action to correct the non-compliance. Sponsors also must evaluate data regarding safety and effectiveness as it is gathered, make all appropriate reports to the FDA and suspend or terminate the study as required.[16]

Investigator Responsibilities

Investigator responsibilities are described in the IND and IDE regulations; in 21 C.F.R. Parts 50, 54, and 56; in contracts or forms they sign promising to properly conduct studies; and in local institutional policies.[17] Investigators involved in IND studies make the following specific commitments in writing on Form FDA-1572, "Statement of Investigator":

- I agree to conduct the study(ies) in accordance with the relevant, current protocols(s) and will only make changes in a protocol after notifying the sponsor, except when necessary to protect the safety, rights, or welfare of subjects.
- I agree to personally conduct or supervise the described investigation(s).
- I agree to inform any patients, or any persons used as controls, that the drugs are being used for investigational purposes and I will ensure that the requirements relating to obtaining informed consent in 21 C.F.R. Part 50 and institutional review board (IRB) review and approval in 21 C.F.R. Part 56 are met.
- I agree to report to the sponsor adverse experiences that occur in the course of the investigation(s) in accordance with 21 C.F.R. § 312.64.
- I have read and understand the information in the investigator's brochure, including the potential risks and side effects of the drug.
- I agree to ensure that all associates, colleagues, and employees assisting in the conduct of the study(ies) are informed about their obligations in meeting the above commitments.
- I agree to maintain adequate and accurate records in accordance with 21 C.F.R. § 212.62 and to make those records available for inspection in accordance with 21 C.F.R. § 312.68.
- I will ensure that an IRB that complies with the requirements of 21 C.F.R. Part 56 will be responsible for the initial and continuing review and approval of the clinical investigation. I also agree to promptly report to the IRB all changes in the research activity and all unanticipated problems involving risks to human subjects or others. Additionally, I will not make any changes in the research without IRB approval, except where necessary

to eliminate apparent immediate hazards to human subjects.
- I agree to comply with all other requirements regarding the obligations of clinical investigators and all other pertinent requirements in 21 C.F.R. Part 312.

No investigator may participate in an IND investigation until he/she provides the sponsor with a completed, signed "Statement of Investigator". No such formal document exists for IDE investigations but similar provisions are required as part of the "Investigator's Agreement".[18]

Regardless of whether an investigator has made a written commitment to comply with these standards, they reflect existing regulatory mandates in any event and so should be regarded as a minimum standard of conduct in virtually all situations.

INDs and IDEs

Sponsor and investigator responsibilities differ according to the type of "test article" (drug or device) under investigation. Drugs and devices are both generally products intended for use in the diagnosis, cure, mitigation, treatment, or prevention of disease in man or other animals, or intended to affect the structure or function of the body. Drugs act through metabolism or chemical reactions in or on the body.[19] Typical examples include medicines in the form of pills or solutions for ingestion or injection. Some cells, vaccines, and other biological medications derived from living beings are biologics regulated under the Public Health Service Act, but most also meet the definition of a drug, and therefore are subject to regulation by the FDA under the IND provisions if investigational.

Devices do not act through metabolism or chemical reaction; they include everything from pacemakers, stents, dental implants and artificial limbs to hospital beds to medical software applications.[20]

"Combination products" are those composed of any combination of a drug, a biological product, and a device.[21] Regulation of combination products is determined based on their "Primary Mode of Action" or "PMOA".21 The PMOA is the single mode of action that provides the most important therapeutic action of the combination product. Determination of the PMOA will result in a product being assigned to a "lead center" at the FDA that is responsible for determining requirements for the conduct of the investigation and is vested with primary reviewing responsibility for related studies.

Drug Trials

1. When is an IND Required?

An Investigational New Drug Application ("IND") enables a sponsor to ship in interstate commerce a new drug (*i.e.*, one that has not been approved by the FDA or that will be used in a manner inconsistent with its approved labeling) for a clinical investigation. Studies involving investigational new drugs generally require an IND. Those involving lawfully marketed drugs, however, are exempt from IND requirements if *all* of the following criteria are met:

- The investigation is not intended to be reported to the FDA as a well-controlled study in support of a new indication for use or other significant labeling change.
- If the drug is a prescription drug, the investigation is not intended to support a significant advertising change.
- The investigation does not involve a route of administration, dosage level, a patient population or other factor that significantly increases the drug's risks (or decreases the acceptability of the risks).
- The investigation complies with institutional review board (IRB) and informed consent requirements (Parts 50 and 56).

- The investigation is conducted in compliance with the requirements of 21 C.F.R. 312.7, "Promotion and Charging for Investigational Drugs".

The following additional types of investigations also are exempt from IND requirements:

- Investigations of drugs intended solely for in vitro tests or for use in laboratory research animals, if they are shipped in accordance with 21 C.F.R. § 312.160, "Drugs for Investigational Use in Laboratory Research Animals or In-Vitro Tests"
- Investigations involving use of a placebo if they do not otherwise require submission of an IND
- Certain in vivo bioavailability studies [22]

By contrast, clinical investigations exempt from informed consent are not exempt from the requirements of Part 312.

2. What are the Phases of a Clinical Investigation?

Drug development proceeds through a number of different phases, each intended to gather different information about an investigational drug. Sponsor and investigator responsibilities vary somewhat depending on the phase of a given investigation. Figure 1 summarizes these phases:

Figure 1: Phases of a Drug Investigation

PHASE	DESCRIPTION
0	Trials conducted early in product development, prior to Phase I, which involve very limited human exposure and have no therapeutic or diagnostic intent (*e.g.*, screening studies or microdose studies). Also known as "Exploratory IND Studies."
1	Studies typically designed to determine the metabolism and pharmacologic actions of a drug in humans, and the side effects associated with increasing doses; secondary objectives may be to gain early evidence on effectiveness. Focus is on pharmacokinetics and pharmacological effects.
2	Controlled clinical studies conducted to evaluate the effectiveness of a drug for a particular indication or indications in patients with the disease or condition under study and to determine common short-term side effects and risks associated with the drug.
3	Expanded controlled and uncontrolled trials, performed after preliminary evidence suggesting effectiveness has been obtained. Phase 3 trials are intended to gather the additional information about effectiveness and safety that is needed to evaluate the overall benefit-risk relationship of the drug and to provide an adequate basis for physician labeling.
4	Studies performed after the FDA grants marketing approval, also referred to as "post-marketing studies" or "post-market surveillance studies." The FDA may ask or require sponsors to perform certain post-marketing studies to gather additional information about a drug's risks, potential benefits, and optimal use concurrent with marketing approval.

3. IND Applications

Unless a proposed drug study is exempt from IND requirements, a sponsor must file an IND with the FDA and receive FDA approval (or allow thirty days to elapse without FDA notification of a clinical hold) before initiating a study of an investigational new drug. The IND application must include:

- Cover sheet (Form FDA-1571) [23]
- Table of contents
- Introductory statement and general investigational plan
- Investigator's brochure
- Protocols for all planned studies to be conducted under the IND
- Chemistry, manufacturing, and control ("CMC") information
- Pharmacology and toxicology information
- Information about previous human experience with the investigational drug
- Additional information for INDs involving products with drug dependence and abuse potential; radioactive products; or products to be tested in pediatric populations
- A brief statement of any other information that would aid evaluation of the proposed clinical investigations with respect to their safety or design and their potential as controlled clinical trials to support drug marketing

Detailed requirements are described at 21 C.F.R. § 312.23. The FDA also has published guidance describing the limited preclinical support required for exploratory IND studies.[24]

A sponsor may ship an investigational new drug to investigators named in the IND application thirty days after the FDA officially receives the IND provided that no additional information requests or other correspondence have been issued by the FDA. Investigational new drugs may be shipped earlier upon receipt of explicit FDA authorization to ship. Researchers may not administer investigational new drugs to human subjects prior to the effective date of the IND.

At any time after an IND study has been initiated, the FDA may institute a clinical hold and request modification of the IND; terminate the study based on deficiencies in the IND or how the study is being conducted; or inactivate the IND if no subjects have been enrolled in the study for two or more years or if all investigations under the IND remain on clinical hold for one or more years. Sponsors who receive notification of clinical holds should promptly inform all investigators of the holds and assure the investigators notify their respective institutional review boards. Investigations subject to a complete clinical hold may not proceed unless and until the FDA lifts the hold; those subject to partial holds must comply with any imposed restrictions.[25] The FDA alternatively may communicate, either verbally or in writing, identify IND deficiencies or request additional data or information at any time during the application process or the clinical investigation itself. Prompt and complete response to such communications is essential to maintaining a positive working relationship with the FDA and avoiding unnecessary holds.

Once an IND is in effect, a sponsor must amend it as needed to ensure that the clinical investigation is conducted according to protocols included in the application. If a sponsor intends to conduct a study that is not covered by a protocol already contained in the IND, the sponsor must submit an amendment using a Form FDA-1571. The new study may begin after the protocol has been submitted to the FDA for its review and approved by the responsible IRB. Protocol amendments may be initiated only as follows:

- For changes intended to "eliminate apparent immediate hazard to subjects," the changes may be implemented immediately provided that the FDA is promptly notified by an amendment and the reviewing IRB is notified within five (5) working days.
- For other changes to Phase 1 studies that significantly affect subject safety and for changes to Phase 2 or 3 studies that significantly affect subject safety, scope of the

investigation, or its scientific quality, the sponsor must submit the changes to the FDA for review and receive approval from the responsible IRB prior to implementation.
- Changes in investigatorship also must be addressed through protocol amendments, except in the case of treatment protocols performed under 21 C.F.R. § 312.34.

Sponsors are subject to additional reporting requirements in connection with INDs, as follows:

- IND safety reports must be made to the FDA and all participating investigators for any serious and unexpected adverse experiences associated with use of the drug, as well as findings from tests in laboratory animals that suggest a significant risk for human subjects, including reports of mutagenicity, teratogenicity, or carcinogenicity. Safety report requirements are described at 21 C.F.R. § 312.32(c).
- Annual reports must be made within sixty days of the anniversary of the IND's effective date, describing the progress of the investigation and additional information specified in the regulations. Requirements for annual reports are identified at 21 C.F.R. § 312.33.
- Other essential information relevant to an IND, such as new toxicology, chemistry, or other technical information; or notice of suspension or termination of an investigation, must be reported in an "information amendment" as described at 21 C.F.R. § 312.31.

4. Early and Expanded Access

The FDA has developed special mechanisms to facilitate access to promising therapeutic agents where no satisfactory alternative treatments exist and standard IND requirements may result in unnecessary and counterproductive delays. These mechanisms are designed to ensure that human subject protection and the scientific integrity of the product development process are not compromised.

- **Single Patient INDs for Emergency Use.** Emergency use (also known as compassionate use) is the use of an investigational drug with a human subject in a life-threatening (or severely debilitating) situation in which no standard acceptable treatment is available and in which there is not sufficient time to obtain IRB approval. This exemption from prior IRB review and approval is limited to a single use. FDA regulations require that any subsequent use of the investigational product at the institution have prospective IRB review and approval. The FDA acknowledges, however, that it would be inappropriate to deny emergency treatment to a second individual if the only obstacle is that the IRB has not had sufficient time to convene a meeting to review the issue.

IRBs may, but are not required to, establish procedures requiring notification prior to an emergency use. Notification does not substitute for approval, but rather is used solely to initiate tracking to ensure the investigator files a report within five days. Expedited approval is not permissible for emergency use; full board approval is required unless the requirements for an exemption as described above are met and it is not possible to convene a quorum within the time available.[26]

Regardless of local IRB policies, the emergency use of an investigational drug requires an additional IND or amendment.[27] If the intended subject does not meet the criteria of an existing study protocol, or if an approved protocol does not exist, the usual procedure is to contact the manufacturer and determine if the drug can be made available for the emergency use under the company's IND. However, the need for an investigational drug may arise in an emergency situation that does not allow time for submission of an IND or required amendment. In such a case, the FDA may authorize shipment of the test article in advance of the IND submission.[28]

- **Treatment INDs.** A treatment IND may be granted only after sufficient data have been collected to show that the drug in question "may be effective" and does not pose unreasonable risks. In addition, the following criteria must be met: (i) the drug must be intended to treat a serious or immediately life-threatening disease; (ii) there is no satisfactory alternative treatment available; (iii) the drug is already under investigation, or trials have been completed; and (iv) the trial sponsor is actively pursuing marketing approval.

  An immediately life-threatening disease means a stage of a disease in which there is a reasonable likelihood that death will occur within a matter of months or in which premature death is likely without early treatment. For example, advanced cases of AIDS, herpes simplex encephalitis, and subarachnoid hemorrhage are all considered to be immediately life-threatening diseases. Treatment INDs are made available to patients before general marketing begins, typically during Phase 3 studies. Treatment INDs also allow the FDA to obtain additional data on the safety and effectiveness of the drugs in question.

- **Parallel Track Studies.** The FDA has adopted a "Parallel Track" policy,[29] which facilitates access to promising new drugs for AIDS/HIV related diseases under a separate protocol that "parallels" the controlled clinical trials that are essential to establish the safety and effectiveness. It provides an administrative system that expands the availability of drugs for treating AIDS/HIV. These studies require prior IRB review and approval and informed consent. The FDA is responsible for assuring that the availability of a drug under the parallel track program does not interfere with the drug sponsor's ability to carry out well-controlled studies on the drug and does not encourage patients with other approved treatment alternatives to resort to untested investigational drugs.

- **Open Label Protocols or Open Protocol INDs.** These are usually uncontrolled Phase 3 studies, carried out to obtain additional safety data. They typically are used when the controlled trial has ended and treatment is continued so that subjects and controls may continue to receive the benefits of the investigational drug until marketing approval is obtained. These studies require prior IRB review and approval, and informed consent.

- **Real World Evidence.** The FDA has begun paying closer attention to opportunities to generate valid scientific evidence, using electronic health records, registries, and administrative and claims data, which was originally collected for non-regulatory purposes, to support regulatory decision making.[30] This, together with other real world evidence as combined with patient preference data and other information, can be used for a variety of purposes in the context of biologics and devices including the support for the validity of a biomarker and support for a petition to reclassify certain medical devices or in the context of post approval studies.

Device Trials

The FDA has established a series of regulations designed to prevent unsafe or ineffective devices from being marketed or promoted in interstate commerce. These are referred to collectively as "device controls" and include requirements for registration of device manufacturing and other facilities, listing of devices manufactured or distributed by those facilities, compliance with "good manufacturing practice" standards, the FDA marketing approval or clearance requirements, reporting requirements, and more. An investigational device exemption, or IDE, permits the shipment of a device otherwise subject to these device controls for use in a clinical trial to assess its safety and effectiveness. Note, however, that many investigational devices are still subject to design controls under the FDA's Quality System Regulation ("QSR"). The FDA exempts from its IDE requirements investigations of the following categories of devices:

- Many devices in commercial distribution before May 28, 1976, when used or investigated in accordance with the labeled indications in effect at that time
- Certain devices determined by the FDA to be substantially equivalent to other devices that are used or investigated under the indications for use reviewed by the FDA as part of the substantial equivalence determination
- Diagnostic devices that meet certain requirements specified by the FDA [31]
- Devices undergoing consumer preference testing, testing of modifications, or testing of a combination of two or more devices in commercial distribution if the testing is not for the purpose of determining safety or effectiveness and does not put subjects at risk
- Devices intended solely for veterinary or animal research use
- Custom devices unless they are being used to determine safety or effectiveness for commercial distribution

1. Significant Risk and Non-Significant Risk Determinations

A significant risk (SR) device is an investigational device that (i) is intended as an implant and presents potential for serious risk to the health, safety or welfare of subjects; (ii) is intended to be used to support or sustain human life and presents a potential for serious risk to the health, safety or welfare of subjects; (iii) is for a use of substantial importance in diagnosing, curing, mitigating or treating disease or otherwise preventing impairment of human health and presents a potential for serious risk to the health, safety or welfare of subjects; or (iv) otherwise presents a potential for serious risk to the health, safety or welfare of subjects.[32] A non significant risk (NSR) device is one that does not meet the criteria listed above, is not a banned device and is not the subject of a notification from the FDA that an IDE application is required.[33]

2. IDE Applications

A sponsor must submit an IDE application to the FDA if:

- The sponsor intends to use an SR device in a clinical investigation
- The sponsor intends to conduct an investigation that involves an exception from informed consent under 21 C.F.R. § 50.24
- The FDA notifies the sponsor that an application is required for an investigation

A clinical investigation involving an SR device may not be initiated until the FDA has approved the IDE application. The FDA Center for Devices and Radiological Health, which oversees medical device investigations, has not developed a form similar to the 1571 used for studies of investigational new drugs. FDA regulations do, however, specify the required content of an IDE application:

- Name and address of the sponsor
- Detailed information about prior investigations and a summary of their outcomes
- Detailed information about the investigational plan
- Information about the methods, facilities, and controls used for the manufacture, processing, packing, storage, and installation of the device in sufficient detail to appropriately evaluate quality control
- An example of the agreements to be entered into by all investigators to comply with investigator obligations under Part 812, and a list of the names and addresses of all investigators who have signed the agreement (similar to the content provided on a Form-1572 in investigational drug studies)
- A certification that all investigators who will participate in the investigation have signed the agreement, that the list of investigators includes all the investigators participating in the investigation, and that no investigators will be added to the investigation until they have signed the agreement.
- A list of the name, address, and chairperson of each IRB that has been or will be asked to review the investigation and a certification

of the action concerning the investigation taken by each such IRB.
- The name and address of any institution at which a part of the investigation may be conducted that has not been identified in accordance with 21 C.F.R. § 812.20(b)(6).
- If the device is to be sold, the amount to be charged and an explanation of why the price does not constitute commercialization of the device
- Environmental assessment information
- Copies of all labeling for the device
- Copies of all forms and informational materials to be provided to subjects to obtain informed consent
- Any other relevant information the FDA requests for review of the application.

Once the FDA has received a completed application, the agency may approve the application, approve it with modifications, disapprove it, or request additional information. An SR investigation may begin after the FDA and the relevant IRB have approved the application, or thirty days after the FDA receives the application, as long as IRB approval has been secured and the FDA has not notified the sponsor to delay initiation. An NSR study may begin after the IRB approves the protocol and consent documents.[34]

As with drug studies, the FDA generally requires advance approval of changes to investigational plans that are likely to have a significant effect on scientific soundness of trial design and/or validity of data resulting from the trial such as a change in indication, or a change in type or nature of the study control.[35] Approval must be granted by the FDA and the IRB in SR studies and by the IRB only in NSR studies. There are exceptions, however, including for emergency use, certain developmental changes to the device, and other minor changes to the clinical protocol. Notice of these types of changes must be provided to the FDA within five (5) working days.

FDA and IRB approval also is required for each site that will participate in a device investigation. The FDA will consider IDE applications that do not contain a certification of IRB approval for each site, but the sponsor must submit that certification in an IDE supplement when that approval is secured and to open any new study sites to enrollment.

A sponsor may report minor changes in the following areas as part of its annual progress report: study purpose, risk analysis, monitoring procedures, labeling, informed consent materials and IRB information. If, however, the changes affect the validity of the data, risk-benefit analysis, scientific soundness of the investigational plan, or the rights, safety, or welfare of subjects involved in the study, they must be approved in advance.

3. Documentation and Reporting Requirements

The IDE regulations require sponsors and investigators to prepare and submit specified reports in a complete, accurate, and timely manner. These include, but are not limited to, reports of:

- Study progress generally
- Significant risk device determinations
- Failure to secure informed consent for any reason [36]
- Certain adverse events and unanticipated problems affecting risks to subjects and others
- Deviations from the investigational plan for any reason
- Withdrawal of IRB or FDA approval
- Final report

A complete listing of all the required reports may be found at 21 C.F.R. § 812.150.

4. Early and Expanded Access

The FDA has described four ways providers may access investigational devices prior to FDA approval and outside the scope of an approved clinical trial. These are: (i) emergency use for life-threatening or serious diseases or conditions; (ii) compassionate use for patients who do not meet the criteria for inclusion in a trial but may benefit from use of the device; (iii) treatment use, to expand the number of subjects who may be permitted to participate in a trial that shows promise; and (iv) continued access to investigational devices for subjects participating in a trial after the trial is complete but prior to FDA approval.[37]

- **Emergency Use.** To qualify for emergency use, the prospective patient must be suffering a life-threatening or serious disease or condition that requires immediate treatment; there must be no available, generally acceptable alternatives for treating the patient; and there must be no time to use existing procedures to obtain FDA approval. It is the treating physician's responsibility to determine whether these criteria have been met, to assess a patient's potential for benefits from the unapproved use, and to have substantial reason to believe that benefits will exist. Where emergencies are reasonably foreseeable, sponsors or physicians should obtain FDA approval through standard IDE procedures or through the compassionate, treatment or continued use procedures described below. The FDA considers an emergency reasonably foreseeable if the device could be used in an emergency.[38]

In the event an unapproved investigational device is used in an emergency under this exception, the device developer must notify the FDA immediately after shipment. In addition, the physician employing the device should make every effort to protect subjects including, as applicable: (i) obtaining an independent assessment by an uninvolved physician; (ii) obtaining informed consent from the patient or legally authorized representative; (iii) notifying the appropriate IRB as soon as practicable; and (iv) obtaining authorization from the IDE holder, if an approved IDE for the device exists.

After the emergency, the physician must: (i) report to the IRB within five days and otherwise comply with IRB requirements; (ii) evaluate the likelihood of a similar need occurring again and, if future use is likely, immediately initiate efforts to obtain IRB approval and an approved IDE for subsequent use; and (iii) if an IDE for the use already exists, notify the sponsor of the emergency use, or if an IDE does not exist, notify the FDA of the emergency use, and provide the FDA with a written summary of the conditions constituting the emergency, subject protection measures, and results. Subsequent emergency use may not occur unless the physician or another person obtains approval of an IDE for the device and its use. If one has been filed and disapproved by the FDA, the device may not be used even in an emergency.

- **Compassionate Use.** The FDA allows patients who do not meet the requirements for participation in a clinical investigation but for whom the treating physician believes the device may provide a benefit in treating or diagnosing their disease or condition to access that device during the clinical trial. The patient's condition must be serious and there must be no available, generally acceptable alternatives for treatment. This provision is typically approved for single patients, but may be approved to treat a small group.

Prior FDA approval is needed before compassionate use occurs. In order to obtain FDA approval, the sponsor should submit an IDE supplement requesting approval for a protocol deviation. The physician should not treat the patient (or patients) identified in the supplement until the FDA and the appropriate IRB both approve the use of the device under the proposed circumstances.[39]

- **Treatment Use.** Approved IDEs specify the maximum number of clinical sites and the maximum number of human subjects that may be enrolled in a study. During the course of a clinical trial, if the data suggest that the device is effective, then the trial may be expanded to include additional patients with life-threatening or serious diseases. To qualify for a treatment use IDE, the disease or condition must be life threatening or serious, and patients must have no comparable or satisfactory alternatives to the investigational device. If the disease is life-threatening (*i.e.,* there is a reasonable likelihood that death will occur within a matter of months or premature death is likely without early treatment), a device may be eligible for a treatment use IDE prior to completion of all clinical trials; if the disease is serious, a device ordinarily may be made available for treatment use only after all clinical trials have been completed.

Thus, in summary, the FDA will consider the use of an investigational device under a treatment use IDE if all of the following criteria are met:[40] (i) the device is intended to treat or diagnose a serious or immediately life-threatening disease or condition;

(ii) there is no comparable or satisfactory alternative device or other therapy to treat or diagnose that stage of the disease or condition in the intended patient population; (iii) the device is under investigation in a controlled clinical trial for the same use under an approved IDE, or the clinical trials have been completed; and (iv) the sponsor of the investigation is actively pursuing marketing approval/clearance of the investigational device with due diligence.

Treatment use may begin 30 days after the FDA receives the treatment IDE submission, unless the FDA notifies the sponsor otherwise.

- **Continued Access.** The FDA may allow continued enrollment of subjects after a controlled clinical trial under an IDE has been completed to allow access to the investigational device, while a marketing application is being prepared by the sponsor or reviewed by the FDA, and to facilitate the collection of additional safety and effectiveness data to support the marketing application or to address new questions regarding the investigational device. This is referred to as an "extended investigation." The FDA will approve an extended investigation only if it identifies a public health need or preliminary evidence is submitted that the device will be effective and no significant safety concerns have been identified for the proposed indication.[41]

The difference between a treatment use IDE and use of an investigational device under the continued access policy is that a treatment use IDE can be submitted earlier in the IDE process (*i.e.,* as soon as promising evidence of safety and effectiveness has been collected but while the clinical study is ongoing) but is intended only for patients with serious or immediately life-threatening diseases or conditions, whereas continued access generally is available only after completion of a clinical trial but for a broader range of patients.

- **Additional Exceptions.** The FDA from time to time approves additional exceptions to standard approval processes. For instance, guidance issued in June 2005 under the Project Bioshield Act of 2004 permits the FDA to allow the use of unapproved medical products or approved medical products for unapproved purposes during a declared emergency involving a heightened risk of attack on the public or U.S. military forces.

Additional Requirements

1. Labeling and Marketing

The FDA also regulates how investigational drugs and devices are labeled[42] and the circumstances under which a sponsor may promote or charge for their use[43]. The immediate package of an investigational new drug intended for human use must include the following statement: "Caution: New Drug—Limited by Federal (or United States) law to investigational use." The label of an investigational drug may not contain any statement that is false or misleading, and may not represent that the drug is safe or effective for the purposes for which it is being investigated. A similar ban applies to promotion, test marketing, or commercial distribution of the investigational drug by sponsors and individuals not independent of, or under the control of, a sponsor[44], and investigators. Sponsors may not charge for investigational drugs in clinical trials proceeding under an IND without the FDA's prior written approval. Even then, sponsors are limited to the amount necessary to recover costs of manufacture, research, development, and handling. In addition, a sponsor may not unduly prolong an investigation after finding that the results of the investigation appear to establish sufficient data to support a marketing application.

An investigational device or its immediate package must include a label with the following information: (i) name and place of business of the manufacturer, packer, or distributor; (ii) quality of contents, if appropriate; (iii) quantity of contents, if appropriate; and (iv) the following statement: "CAUTION—Investigational device. Limited by Federal (or United States) law to investigational use." In the case of a device study, at a minimum, the label or other labeling also must describe all relevant contraindications, hazards, adverse effects, interfering substances or devices, warnings, and precautions.

As with drugs, sponsors of investigational devices may not promote or profit from their products. The label of an investigational device may not bear any statement that is false or misleading, and may not represent that the device is safe or effective for the purposes for which it is being investigated. A similar ban applies to promotion, test marketing, or commercial distribution of the device by sponsors and investigators. Sponsors may not charge for investigational devices in clinical trials proceeding under an IDE other than the amount necessary to recover costs of manufacture, research, development, and handling and may not unduly prolong an investigation.

While marketing or promoting investigational drugs or devices is prohibited, the FDA recognizes the practical need to recruit clinical investigators and study subjects through dissemination of information on investigational products. An FDA guidance entitled "Guidance for Industry and FDA Staff: Preparing Notices of Availability of Investigational Medical Devices and for Recruiting Study Subjects" (March 19, 1999)[45] defines the recommendations and restrictions regarding such information dissemination for devices. See also the "Recruiting Study Subjects—Information Sheet" which applies to both drugs and devices.[46]

2. Waiver of IND or IDE Requirements

A sponsor may request the FDA to waive any of the requirements found at 21 C.F.R. Part 312.[47] A waiver request may be submitted either in an IND or in an IND information amendment. In an emergency, a request may be made by telephone or other rapid communication means. The request must contain at least one of the following:

- An explanation why the sponsor's compliance with the requirement is unnecessary or cannot be achieved
- A description of an alternative submission or course of action that satisfies the purpose of the requirement; or
- Other information justifying a waiver.

The FDA may grant the waiver if it finds that the sponsor's noncompliance would not pose a significant and unreasonable risk to human subjects and that one of the following is met: (i) the sponsor's compliance with the requirement is unnecessary for the agency to evaluate the application, or compliance cannot be achieved; (ii) the sponsor's proposed alternative satisfies the requirement; or (iii) the applicant's submission otherwise justifies a waiver.

As with drugs, sponsors may request the FDA to waive any requirement of 21 C.F.R. Part 812.[48] A waiver request, with supporting documentation, may be submitted separately or as part of an IDE application. The FDA may grant a waiver of any requirement it deems not required by the act, nor necessary to protect the rights, safety or welfare of the study subjects. It is important to understand, however, that each requirement applies unless and until the FDA expressly waives it.

In May 2018, President Trump signed the "Trickett Wendler, Frank Mongiello, Jordan McLinn, and Matthew Bellina Right to Try Act of 2017."[49] More commonly known as the "Right to Try Act," the Act aims to help terminally ill patients who have exhausted approved treatment options and are unable to participate in a relevant clinical trial. The Act potentially provides access to drugs that have completed a Phase 1 clinical trial but has not been approved or licensed by the FDA. The Act also limits the liability of the sponsor, the manufacturer, the prescriber, or the dispenser who provides or declines to provide the eligible investigational drug to the eligible patient. Additionally, the act also limits the use of clinical outcomes associated with the use of an eligible investigational product to delay or adversely affect the review or approval of the drug.

FDA Inspections

The FDA regularly monitors sponsors, clinical investigators, institutional review boards, and non-clinical laboratories to assure compliance with FDA regulations and, ultimately, the quality of the data that is relied upon to determine whether new drugs or devices should come to market. Inspections fall into two primary categories: "routine" and "directed" (or for-cause) inspections. Routine inspections are just what they sound like: The FDA randomly selects regulated organizations for inspection through its bioresearch monitoring program to review adherence to the investigational plan, the FDA regulations, and institutional policies. Directed or for-cause inspections, on the other hand, are initiated when some specific problem has been identified within one or all aspects of a clinical trial, such as integrity of source data or compliance of sponsors or investigators with regulation mandates. The problem may be observed during review of sponsor submissions regarding ongoing clinical investigations, or following evaluation of clinical data submitted with marketing applications. Verbal and written complaints from patients, physicians, or competitors may also result in a directed inspection. The FDA may also target sites for inspection when they are studying products of special interest, for example, because they implicate significant public health concerns.

What to Expect at the Inspection

The FDA typically initiates routine and even some for-cause inspections by contacting the regulated party (*e.g.*, sponsor, investigator or institutional official for an IRB) and setting an appointment. Because the FDA is a law enforcement agency, its inspectors generally present their credentials and a notice of inspection (Form FDA-482) upon their arrival at the site to be inspected and conduct an entrance interview. After the interview they review applicable records and, during the course of the inspection, which may extend only a day or two or a few weeks or even longer, they may conduct additional interviews. During this time, they may review:

- Who performed various aspects of the protocol, and their qualifications
- Degree and appropriateness of delegation of authority, and documentation of delegation
- Documentation of research procedures and other information in research records and source documents (case report forms, medical records, and so forth)
- Accountability for investigational products (how they were tracked from receipt through distribution)
- Investigator/monitor/sponsor/IRB communications
- Monitor evaluation of the progress of an investigation
- Adherence to approved protocols, regulatory mandates, and local policies and procedures

At the conclusion of the inspection, the FDA will conduct an exit conference during which the inspector(s) will discuss findings with the appropriate personnel.[50] If the findings require no corrective action, they will issue no written report to the inspected site and may recommend to the appropriate District office and/or the appropriate FDA center that no further action be taken. If the findings are more significant, the inspector(s) may issue written

"Inspectional Observations" on a Form FDA-483. Depending on the severity of the findings, the inspector(s) may recommend voluntary action—meaning that objectionable conditions were found, but they can be addressed voluntarily. In more serious cases, the inspector will recommend that official action is indicated, *i.e.*, objectionable conditions were found that merit further regulatory response from the agency.

The inspected organization or individual is given time to respond formally to the observations listed on the 483. If the FDA finds the response adequate, generally no further action is taken. If not, or where the observations were very serious, the FDA may issue a "Warning Letter" which describes deficiencies identified during the inspection or through related activities, including those deficiencies not addressed to its satisfaction in the original response (if any).[51] Other FDA enforcement tools include product seizures, court-ordered injunctions, civil penalties, investigator disqualification or debarment. The FDA, in conjunction with the U.S. Department of Justice, may also legally prosecute individuals and/or companies via Supreme Court decisions like the Park Doctrine[52] and/or in accordance with the Yates memo.[53]. For example, where a physician investigator's enrollment of ineligible subjects on a trial through falsification of lab values resulted in one patient's death, the physician investigator was prosecuted and received a prison sentence.[54]

Promoting Compliance

Occasional reports of criminal conduct notwithstanding, most researchers and research institutions engaged in clinical investigations proceed with all of the best intentions. Following are steps that should be taken to promote compliance and avoid poor outcomes following inspections:

- Assure that investigators, research staff, monitors, and institutional review boards understand their obligations under FDA regulations and institutional policy. In many cases, training and certification on applicable requirements is available for physician-investigators, research staff, and IRB professionals and should be pursued wherever feasible. At a minimum, assure sufficient expertise at an institutional level so that those at the site with questions regarding their obligations have a good resource for assistance.
- Conduct regular and targeted training on current Good Clinical Practices ("cGCP"),[55] as well as applicable FDA regulations and guidances.
- Assure adequate staffing to conduct clinical trials including selection of qualified investigators and monitors.
- Promote clear allocation of responsibilities among sponsors, investigators, monitors, and others involved in the work.
- Maintain clear written records of all relevant communications, source documents, research documents, investigations, and procedures. Review the documentation for accuracy throughout the course of the study, not just at the end. Each subject's research record should include a complete case history, which includes a signed copy of the informed consent document, relevant source documents and case report forms, documentation of study visits and follow up, and documentation of adverse events and protocol deviations. General study records should include correspondence among sponsors, investigators, and IRBs; records of all on-site visits by study monitors and records of drug or device receipt, storage, distribution, and final disposition.
- Assure proper oversight of and financial disclosure by all involved investigators.
- When inspectors initiate a visit, be prepared. Have all files ready and available before they arrive. Invite legal counsel to attend at least the entrance and exit interviews so that they can help prepare any necessary response.

Treat the inspectors at all times with the respect they expect and deserve.

It is, however, interesting that on January 25, 2018, the Associate Attorney General Rachel Brand issued a memorandum to the Heads of the Civil Litigating Components of the U.S. Attorneys stating that, "Guidance documents cannot create binding requirements that do not already exist by statute or by regulation. Accordingly, effective immediately for [Affirmative civil enforcement] cases, the [Department of Justice] may not use its enforcement authority to effectively convert agency guidance into binding rules." This change in prosecution priorities and methods signals the potential for noteworthy future changes.[56]

Current Good Manufacturing Practices

FDCA also requires that the methods used in, and facilities and controls used for, the manufacture, processing, packing and storage of a new drug or device and, in the case of a device, its installation, conform to current good manufacturing practice to assure they are safe and effective and otherwise comply with the requirements of the law.[57] Drugs and devices are considered "adulterated" when they fail to comply with these requirements. FDA regulations describe minimum cGMP requirements.[58]

- **Drugs**. A drug is considered to be adulterated if the methods used in, or the facilities or controls used for, its manufacture, processing, packing, or holding do not conform to or are not operated or administered in conformity with current good manufacturing practices to assure that such drug meets the requirements of the Act as to safety and has the identity and strength, and meets the quality and purity characteristics, which it purports or is represented to possess. Most Phase I investigational drugs are exempt from complying with the regulatory cGMP requirements (21 C.F.R. Parts 210 and 211). The FDA will still oversee the manufacture of these drugs under its general statutory cGMP authority and review of investigational new drug applications (INDs). The FDA has issued guidance to assist manufacturers in complying with cGMP requirements for Phase I studies.[59] When drug development reaches the stage where drugs are being produced for Phase II and III clinical trials, however, then full compliance is necessary.[60]

- **Devices**. A device is considered to be adulterated if the methods used in, or the facilities or controls used for, its manufacture, packing, storage, or installation are not in conformity with applicable good manufacturing practice requirements. Device cGMPs are part of the "Quality System Regulations." IDE devices are exempt from Quality System requirements except for the design control requirements found at 21 C.F.R. § 820.30 when applicable to the type of device in question. Design controls require that a manufacturer establish and maintain procedures to control the design of a device in order to ensure that specific design requirements are met. Since most of the device design occurs prior to and during the IDE stage, it is necessary that manufacturers who intend to commercially produce the device follow design control procedures when applicable. An IDE application must contain a description of the methods, facilities and controls used to manufacture and/or install the product in sufficient detail such that a person familiar with quality systems can make a knowledgeable judgment about the level of quality control used to manufacture the investigational device. Once the device is approved/cleared by the FDA, all manufacturing activities must conform to all applicable cGMP requirements.

Acknowledgement

The author wishes to thank Neil F. O'Flaherty, Esq. and Nancy W. Mathewson, Esq. for their contributions to previous versions of this chapter.

Chapter 7 Endnotes

1. **Darshan Kulkarni, Pharm.D, MS, Esq.** is the Vice President of Regulatory Strategy and Policy at Synchrogenix in Philadelphia, PA. He is responsible in guiding the policy development and engagement strategies of the company using various methodologies including, but not limited to, artificial intelligence, blockchain, and big data. He has multiple patent filings to his name and owns various forms of intellectual property rights including copyrights and trademarks.
2. A comprehensive list of the laws that FDA enforces is available online at http://www.fda.gov/opacom/laws/.
3. "Interstate commerce" means commerce between any State or Territory and any place outside thereof, and commerce within the District of Columbia or within any other Territory not organized with a legislative body. FDA has no jurisdiction over activities that occur solely within a single state's jurisdiction. However, most medical care and biomedical research touch interstate commerce, and many states have adopted "mini" food and drug laws imposing restrictions similar to FDCA's. Thus, investigators, research institutions, and responsible compliance officials are encouraged to consult with expert legal counsel before making any assumption that a particular activity is not regulated by FDA or corresponding state agencies.
4. See 21 U.S.C. § 355(i) (permitting promulgation of regulations to exempt drugs from otherwise applicable drug controls solely for investigational use to study their safety and effectiveness); 21 U.S.C. § 360j(g) (exempting from certain device controls investigational use of devices to study their safety and effectiveness).
5. Part 11 principally addresses security standards applicable to individuals and organizations who utilize electronic systems to create, use, store, or sign documents required by other FDA regulations. These security standards are discussed in Chapter 12.
6. The federal policy for protection of human research subjects, or Common Rule, is codified at 45 C.F.R. Part 46 and discussed in some depth in Chapter 1. FDA has published a comparison of its regulations against the Common Rule, which is available online at http://www.fda.gov/oc/gcp/comparison.html.
7. Financial disclosure and conflict of interest issues are discussed in depth in Chapter 2.
8. See http://www.fda.gov/opacom/morechoices/industry/guidedc.htm.
9. See "'Off-Label' and Investigational Use of Marketed Drugs, Biologics, and Medical Devices," available online at http://www.fda.gov/oc/ohrt/irbs/offlabel.html. Practitioners who are unsure about whether an IND or IDE may be required in a given situation may contact the individuals listed at this site for informal guidance. A formal determination typically can be secured only by submitting an IND or IDE application.
10. See 21 C.F.R. §§ 312.3, 812.3(n).
11. See 21 C.F.R. §§ 312.3, 812.3(i).
12. See, e.g., 21 C.F.R. §§ 50.3(f), 312.3(b), 812.3(o).
13. See, e.g., Guidance for Industry Investigator Responsibilities – Protecting the Rights, Safety, and Welfare of Study Subjects, available at https://www.fda.gov/downloads/Drugs/GuidanceComplianceRegulatoryInformation/Guidances/UCM187772.pdf; Guidance for Industry Oversight of Clinical Investigations – A Risk-Based Approach to Monitoring, available at https://www.fda.gov/downloads/Drugs/GuidanceComplianceRegulatoryInformation/Guidances/UCM269919.pdf. Additional guidance is found at http://www.fda.gov/oc/gcp/default.htm and the CDER, CDRH, and CBER web pages.
14. See 21 C.F.R. §§ 312.50, 812.40.
15. FDA guidance for risk based monitoring entitled, "Oversight of Clinical Investigations – A Risk-Based Approach to Monitoring," is available at https://www.fda.gov/downloads/Drugs/Guidances/UCM269919.pdf.
16. FDA's guidelines for the establishment and operation of data monitoring committees – also known as data safety monitoring boards – are posted online at https://www.fda.gov/RegulatoryInformation/Guidances/ucm127069.htm; see also the National Institutes of Health's policy, available online at http://grants.nih.gov/grants/guide/notice-files/not98-084.html.
17. In October 2009, FDA published an easy-to-read guidance document, available online at https://www.fda.gov/downloads/Drugs/GuidanceComplianceRegulatoryInformation/Guidances/UCM187772.pdf and titled, Guidance for Industry Investigator Responsibilities – Protecting the Rights, Safety, and Welfare of Study Subjects, describing some of the central responsibilities of a clinical investigator.
18. See 21 C.F.R. § 812.43.
19. A complete definition is found at 21 U.S.C. § 201(g)(1). Foods and dietary supplements, even so-called "nutriceuticals," generally are not regulated as drugs, as long as no disease claims are made in the labeling or marketing materials. Id; see also "Structure/Function Claims: Small Entity Compliance Guide" online at https://www.fda.gov/Food/GuidanceRegulation/GuidanceDocumentsRegulatoryInformation/ucm103340.htm; "Is it a Cosmetic, a Drug, or Both? Or Is it Soap?"online at https://www.fda.gov/cosmetics/guidanceregulation/lawsregulations/ucm074201.htm.
20. See 21 U.S.C. § 321(h).
21. A complete definition is provided at 21 C.F.R. § 3.2(e).
22. A discussion of bioavailability studies and their regulation is beyond the scope of this chapter.
23. FDA electronic forms are available online at http://www.fda.gov/opacom/morechoices/fdaforms/.
24. See "Guidance for Industry, Investigators and Reviewers: Exploratory IND Studies," available online at https://www.fda.gov/downloads/drugs/guidancecomplianceregulatoryinformation/guidances/ucm078933.pdf.
25. FDA has published industry guidance on responding to clinical holds, available online at https://www.fda.gov/downloads/Drugs/GuidanceComplianceRegulatoryInformation/Guidances/UCM080581.pdf; see also related FDA Standard Operating Procedures, available online at https://www.fda.gov/downloads/RegulatoryInformation/Guidances/UCM126997.pdf; and Office of Medical Policy, Clinical Hold /Refusal-to-File Committee, at https://www.fda.gov/BiologicsBloodVaccines/DevelopmentApprovalProcess/InvestigationalNewDrugINDorDeviceExemptionIDEProcess/ucm094301.htm.
26. See http://www.fda.gov/oc/ohrt/irbs/drugsbiologics.html#emergency.
27. Instructions for completing a single patient IND for emergency (or compassionate use) are available online at https://www.fda.gov/Drugs/DevelopmentApprovalProcess/HowDrugsareDevelopedandApproved/ApprovalApplications/InvestigationalNewDrugINDApplication/ucm343022.htm. Contact information for submission of an emergency use IND is available at http://www.fda.gov/oc/ohrt/irbs/drugsbiologicsNEW.html.
28. Requests for such authorization may be made at any time by contacting FDA as provided at: http://www.fda.gov/oc/ohrt/irbs/drugsbiologicsNEW.html.
29. 57 Fed. Reg. 13250 (May 21, 1990).
30. Guidance for Industry and Food and Drug Administration Staff, Use of Real-World Evidence to Support Regulatory

Decision-Making for Medical Devices, https://www.fda.gov/downloads/medicaldevices/deviceregulationandguidance/guidancedocuments/ucm513027.pdf.
31. See 21 C.F.R. § 809.10(c).
32. See 21 C.F.R. § 812.3(m).
33. Guidance for determining whether a device is SR or NSR is available online at http://www.fda.gov/oc/ohrt/irbs/devrisk.pdf.
34. A separate IDE application is required for studies involving an exception from the informed consent process under 21 C.F.R. §§ 50.24, 812.20(a)(4)(i).
35. See https://www.fda.gov/MedicalDevices/DeviceRegulationandGuidance/HowtoMarketYourDevice/InvestigationalDeviceExemptionIDE/ucm046706.htm#idemod.
36. It is important to note that state or local requirements relating to informed consent and interpretations thereof may differ. A recent Pennsylvania Supreme Court case has supported the argument that informed consent may not be a delegable duty and must be performed by the physician. Shinal v Toms MD, 162 A. 3d 429 - Pa: Supreme Court, 2017.
37. Additional guidance on early and expanded access to investigational devices is available from FDA online at https://www.fda.gov/NewsEvents/PublicHealthFocus/ExpandedAccessCompassionateUse/ucm429687.htm.
38. See the IRB Information Sheet available at http://www.fda.gov/oc/ohrt/irbs/devices.html#emergency, "Emergency Use of Unapproved Medical Devices," for additional information.
39. Additional requirements apply and are discussed at https://www.fda.gov/NewsEvents/PublicHealthFocus/ExpandedAccessCompassionateUse/ucm613609.htm.
40. Specific requirements for a treatment IDE application are available at: https://www.fda.gov/NewsEvents/PublicHealthFocus/ExpandedAccessCompassionateUse/default.htm.
41. See https://www.fda.gov/NewsEvents/PublicHealthFocus/ExpandedAccessCompassionateUse/ucm431769.htm for a description of the requirements for a continued access IDE application; see also https://www.fda.gov/MedicalDevices/DeviceRegulationandGuidance/HowtoMarketYourDevice/InvestigationalDeviceExemptionIDE/ucm051345.htm#treatment.
42. 21 C.F.R. §§ 312.6, 812.5.
43. 21 C.F.R. §§ 312.7, 812.7.
44. The FDA currently believes that sponsors are responsible for the communications on the internet and internet-based platforms by its employees or any agents acting on behalf of the firm. Organizations, such as clinical research organizations, may therefore want to be careful about the inappropriate sharing of information. https://www.fda.gov/downloads/Drugs/GuidanceComplianceRegulatoryInformation/Guidances/UCM401079.pdf.
45. See https://www.fda.gov/downloads/MedicalDevices/DeviceRegulationandGuidance/GuidanceDocuments/UCM073585.pdf.
46. See https://www.fda.gov/RegulatoryInformation/Guidances/ucm126428.htm.
47. See 21 C.F.R. § 312.10.
48. 21 C.F.R. § 812.10.
49. Trickett Wendler, Frank Mongiello, Jordan McLinn, and Matthew Bellina Right to Try Act of 2017 https://www.congress.gov/bill/115th-congress/senate-bill/204.
50. A list of the types of findings that may be made during an inspection of a clinical investigation is available online at https://www.fda.gov/Drugs/GuidanceComplianceRegulatoryInformation/EnforcementActivitiesbyFDA/ucm073059.htm.
51. Warning Letters and Notices of Initiation of Disqualification Proceedings and Opportunity to Explain ("NIDPOE") Letters are posted on FDA's website: http://www.fda.gov/foi/electrr.htm.
52. U.S. FDA Regulatory Procedures Manual, Chapter 6 https://www.fda.gov/downloads/iceci/compliancemanuals/regulatoryproceduresmanual/ucm074317.pdf.
53. Individual Accountability for Corporate Wrongdoing, https://www.justice.gov/archives/dag/file/769036/download.
54. See, e.g., "FDA Law Enforcers Protect Consumers' Health: Inside the Office of Criminal Investigations," FDA Consumer Health Information, August 4, 2008.
55. Supporting resources abound. One is originally published by the International Conference on Harmonisation and recently updated by the FDA. U.S. Dep't of Health and Human Services, Food and Drug Administration, Center for Drug Evaluation and Research (CDER) Center for Biologics Evaluation and Research (CBER), "E6(R2) Good Clinical Practice: Integrated Addendum to ICH E6(R1) Guidance for Industry," (March 2018). It is available at https://www.fda.gov/downloads/Drugs/Guidances/UCM464506.pdf.
56. Limiting Use of Agency Guidance Documents In Affirmative Civil Enforcement Cases, https://www.justice.gov/file/1028756/download.
57. 21 U.S.C. §§ 351(a)(2)(B), 351(h), 360(j)(f).
58. 21 C.F.R. Parts 210 and 211 (drugs); and Part 820 (devices); see also the drug cGMP summary websheet at https://www.fda.gov/Drugs/DevelopmentApprovalProcess/Manufacturing/ucm090016.htm and Q&A, at https://www.fda.gov/Drugs/DevelopmentApprovalProcess/Manufacturing/ucm124740.htm. The agency also has posted substantial guidance on this subject. See "A Risk-Based Approach to Pharmaceutical Current Good Manufacturing Practices (cGMP) for the 21st Century," available online at https://www.fda.gov/downloads/drugs/developmentapprovalprocess/manufacturing/questionsandanswersoncurrentgoodmanufacturingpracticescgmpfordrugs/ucm176374.pdf. See "GMP Information / Quality Systems Information," at https://www.fda.gov/MedicalDevices/DeviceRegulationandGuidance/PostmarketRequirements/QualitySystemsRegulations/default.htm or "Medical Device Quality Systems Manual: A Small Entity Compliance Guide" which may be found at https://ntrl.ntis.gov/NTRL/dashboard/searchResults/titleDetail/PB97148001.xhtml for guidance regarding devices.
59. "Guidance for Industry, CGMP for Phase 1 Investigational Drugs", July 2008. See https://www.fda.gov/downloads/drugs/guidances/ucm070273.pdf.
60. See the March 1991 FDA guidance entitled "Guideline on the Preparation of Investigational New Drug Products (Human and Animal)", available online at https://www.fda.gov/downloads/Drugs/GuidanceComplianceRegulatoryInformation/Guidances/ucm070315.pdf.

8

Research Privacy and Security: Myths, Facts, and Practical Approaches

By Marti Arvin, JD, CCEP-F,CHC-F,CHPC,CHRC, Kathleen Price, RN, MBA, CIP, and David Vulcano, LCSW, MBA, CIP, RAC[1]

Introduction

An individual's right to privacy has been a well-established principle in the American healthcare system for a long time. A healthcare provider or researcher has an obligation to protect the confidentiality of a patient's or subject's identifiable private information against unauthorized use or disclosure. These principles have deep historical roots. Indeed, a physician's duty to treat as confidential any information gained when caring for a patient dates back to around the time of the Greek philosophers,[2] and is well-ensconced in Anglo-American law and jurisprudence.[3] It is also one of the general principles articulated in the Declaration of Helsinki: "It is the duty of the physician in medical research to protect the life, health, *privacy*, and dignity of the human subject."[4]

This chapter includes descriptions of federal and state privacy, confidentiality, and security laws and regulations that govern clinical research in the United States, as well as practical recommendations for compliance consistent with the efficient conduct of that research.

Federal Privacy Rules

The Health Insurance Portability and Accountability Act of 1996 (HIPAA) and its implementing regulations[5] are perhaps the best-known federal privacy rules today. The Common Rule,[6] corresponding FDA regulations,[7] and other federal laws and regulations also protect the privacy and confidentiality of records created, used, and disclosed in human research. These federal mandates are discussed below.

Health Insurance Portability and Accountability Act of 1996 (HIPAA)

Congress enacted HIPAA in 1996 to assure individuals the ability to move from one job to another without risking their health insurance coverage and to strengthen federal fraud and abuse laws. The law included "administrative simplification" provisions designed to encourage standardization of health insurance claims submission and processing and to promote overall efficiency in the healthcare system.[8] Recognizing that standardization would facilitate electronic storage and transmission of health information, and concerned that a move to use of electronic records would increase risks to health privacy, Congress included privacy protection provisions and a mandate that, absent further legislative action, the Secretary of Health and Human Services would develop and implement regulations to protect individually identifiable health information.[9] Those regulations were released as a "final rule" in December 2000[10] and the HIPAA Privacy Rule became effective in April 2003.

The HIPAA Omnibus (Final) Rule

In 2013 the Department of Health and Human Services (HHS) released the "Omnibus Rule," which resulted in modifications to the HIPAA Privacy, Security, Breach Notification, and Enforcement Rules.[11] HHS published the Omnibus Rule, also known as the Final Rule, in January and it went into effect on March 26, 2013. Covered entities and business associates were required to be in compliance with most of the directives in the rule since September 23, 2013.

The Omnibus Rule implements most of the privacy and security provisions of the Health Information Technology for Economic and Clinical Health (HITECH) Act. The rule provides for increased focus on patient rights and providing health information to patients. Restrictions on some uses and disclosures of protected health information (*e.g.*, sale of PHI, marketing, fundraising limitations, and allowance for patient out-of-pocket payment without notification of payers) are included. The rule extends the provisions of the Security Rule to business associates and subcontractors.

Changes in the Enforcement Rule altered HIPAA enforcement from a program with very little punitive power to a more substantive penalty-based system. The penalties range from $100–$50,000 per violation, with a $1.5 million cap per calendar year for all violations of an identical provision, and criminal penalties of up to 10 years' imprisonment. Where there is a possibility of a violation occurring due to willful neglect, HHS can impose civil monetary penalties in the higher ranges of $10,000–$50,000 per violation per provisions.

Uses and disclosures of PHI for research purposes are included in 45 CFR 164.512, Standard (i) of the regulations, "Uses and disclosures for which an authorization or opportunity to agree or object is not required." This section describes the waiver process, IRB and privacy board requirements, and reviews preparatory to research and review and approval procedures.

The Omnibus Rule removed significant barriers to clinical research and provided more flexibility for future research endeavors. Authorizations for the use or disclosure of PHI for a research study may be combined with any other type of written permission for the same or for another research study. Previously, a participant in a clinical trial could only authorize the use of PHI for one clinical trial per authorization. The Privacy Rule prohibited combining an authorization that conditioned treatment, payment, enrollment in a health plan, or eligibility for benefits (*i.e.*, a conditioned authorization) with an authorization for another purpose for which treatment, payment, enrollment, or eligibility might not be conditioned (*i.e.*, an unconditioned authorization). Thus, prior to the Omnibus Rule, a covered entity could not, for example, combine an authorization to use and disclose PHI for research in connection with a clinical trial (which is a conditioned authorization) with an authorization to create a central research repository or tissue bank for future research (which might be an unconditioned authorization). Authorizations for unspecified future research were prohibited.

The Omnibus Rule harmonizes authorization requirements with federal human subject protection rules, and permits the use of compound authorizations, combining conditioned and unconditioned authorizations, and permitting the use or disclosure of PHI for future, unspecified research. Thus, a single document that includes consent and authorization for a clinical trial and a future study, as long as the authorization includes a general description of the types of research that might be conducted, can now be used. The authorization must clearly differentiate between conditioned and unconditioned authorizations for research and provide the individual with the option to opt in to the unconditioned research activities. The change to compound authorizations will simplify the administration of clinical trials and facilitate outcomes research involving tissue and data banking information.

The use of compound authorizations requires covered entities to revise authorization processes and forms, including the process for future revocations by subjects.

Authorization for use or disclosure of psychotherapy notes continue to have the restriction that the form may only be combined with another authorization for use or disclosure of psychotherapy notes, and may not be combined with other authorizations.

Prior to enactment of the Omnibus Rule, authorization for research had to be study-specific. The change provides that a valid authorization can be used for future research studies and will benefit secondary research efforts. Future research need not be related to a current study, as long as the authorization adequately describes potential future research in a way that it would be reasonable for the subject to expect that PHI could be used or disclosed for the research.

In the Omnibus Rule, HHS also confirmed that researchers may be business associates if they perform a service for covered entities, *e.g.*, de-identifying PHI or creating a limited data set, even if the de-identified PHI or limited data set is created for use by the researcher—provided there is separation between the business associate activity of creating the data set and the activity of performing the research. As stated in the Rule:

> However, a researcher may be a business associate if the researcher performs a function, activity, or service for a covered entity that does fall within the definition of business associate, such as the health care operations function of creating a de-identified or limited data set for the covered entity. See paragraph (6)(v) of the definition of "health care operations." Where the researcher is also the intended recipient of the de-identified data or limited data set, the researcher must return or destroy the identifiers at the time the business associate relationship to create the data set terminates and the researcher now wishes to use the deidentified data or limited data set (subject to a data use agreement) for a research purpose.[12]

Although HIPAA does not directly govern research, its privacy and security rules do regulate healthcare providers, health plans, and clearinghouses (collectively "covered entities"[13] that often control data researchers need to conduct clinical studies). Moreover, HIPAA violations may result in significant penalties ranging from small assessments per violation up to 10 years' imprisonment and multi-million dollar fines in the most egregious cases,[14] not to mention negative publicity and loss of public trust. As a result, some covered entities have adopted very conservative—and sometimes unnecessarily restrictive—approaches to data sharing that hinder good clinical research.[15] A strong grasp of the legal and regulatory requirements that govern privacy, confidentiality, security, and data sharing can help researchers, IRBs, and privacy officers avoid this problem.

1. Basic Privacy Rights

Under the Privacy Rule, as it is known, a covered entity may not use or disclose an individual's PHI unless the use or disclosure is authorized in writing by the individual (or his or her personal representative[16]), or a specified regulatory exception applies.[17] These exceptions are described in detail in subsection below. To be valid, an authorization to use or disclose PHI for research must include the following elements and statements:[18]

- A description of the study (*e.g.*, the title and purpose)
- A description of any PHI to be used or disclosed for the study
- The names or groups of persons involved in the research (*e.g.*, "researchers and their staff")
- A statement that the subject's PHI may not be protected under HIPAA once it is disclosed outside the covered entity
- A statement either that: (i) authorization is voluntary, but failure to agree to the requested use or disclosure will bar the prospective subject from participating in the study (for any research conducted by a covered entity that involves treatment); or (ii) participation is voluntary and the covered entity may not

condition testing or treatment on whether the prospective subject signs the authorization (for research that does not involve research-related treatment)
- Information about withdrawal
- Information regarding future revocation, when a compound authorization is used
- Expiration date or event (a date may be given, or an event such as "the end of the study,"); researchers may extend authorizations indefinitely by explicitly stating that there is no expiration date
- Signature of subject or subject's personal representative
- Date of signature

The Privacy Rule identifies essential privacy rights and requires covered entities to develop and implement policies and procedures designed to protect those rights. For a complete listing and information regarding these rights, refer to the 45 C.F.R. §164, Subpart E, "Privacy of Individually Identifiable Health Information." Key privacy rights described in Subpart E include rights to the following.

Notification of a Covered Entity's Privacy Practices[19]

The Privacy Rule requires covered entities to provide written notice of their privacy practices to individual patients or health plan members, to post those notices on their public websites, and to promptly publish information about material changes. A covered entity may provide the notice to an individual by Email, if the individual agrees to electronic notice and such agreement has not been withdrawn. The notices must inform individuals of the circumstances under which their PHI may be used without their permission including, if applicable, for research or public health activities.

The Omnibus Rule requires that covered entities revise the notice of privacy practices to include the following:

a. Prohibition against health plans using or disclosing genetic information for underwriting purposes;
b. Prohibition on the sale of PHI without the express written authorization of the individual, and other uses and disclosures that expressly require the individual's authorization (marketing and disclosure of psychotherapy notes);
c. Duty of a covered entity to notify affected individuals of a breach involving their PHI;
d. Individual's right to opt out of receiving fundraising communications for entities that have stated their intent to fundraise in the notice of privacy practices; and
e. Individual's right to restrict disclosures of PHI to a health plan where the individual pays out of pocket in full for the service.

Inspect and Copy Healthcare Records[20]

The Privacy Rule defines a "designated record set" (DRS) to include medical and billing records, as well as other records used to make decisions about individuals, and requires covered entities to maintain DRS records for at least six years and make those records available to the individuals to whom they pertain.[21] Because the definition of a DRS is broad, it extends to clinical research records created, received, or maintained by a covered entity, even if solely for research purposes and even if they involve only "research subjects" and not "patients."

Access of Individuals to Protected Health Information

Individuals have a right to request copies of their own PHI in any form they choose, including electronic copies, provided the PHI is "readily producible" in that format. Covered entities must provide copies of PHI to other parties as designated by the individual, based upon a written and signed request that clearly identifies the designated recipient and where to send the copy of PHI. Of note, however, HIPAA allows the covered entity to withhold the release of certain research related information for a period of time if the patient agreed to it up front as part of their signed authorization. This would be important in studies that require blinding of the participants for scientific purposes. All requests for access must be addressed (granted or denied) within 30 days. Covered entities may also be permitted a one-time 30-day extension by providing notice to the individual of the reasons for the delay.

Covered entities must permit individuals to request their records and must accommodate reasonable requests by individuals to receive communications of PHI by alternative means or at alternate locations. Covered entities may send individuals unencrypted Emails including electronic protected health information (ePHI), if the individual requests it, provided that the covered entity has advised the individual of the risk and the individual accepts that the message will be delivered via unencrypted email.

Amendment of Protected Health Information[22]

An individual has the right to have a covered entity amend PHI or a record about the individual in a DRS for as long as the PHI is maintained in the DRS. The covered entity may deny the request for amendment, if it determines that the PHI or record was not created by the covered entity, is not part of the DRS, would not be available for inspection, or is accurate and complete. The covered entity must act on the individual's request for an amendment no later than 60 days after receipt of the request. The covered entity may extend the time for action by no more than 30 days provided that the individual is provided with a written statement about the reasons for the delay and the date by which the covered entity will complete its action on the request. The covered entity must maintain information about any objections.

Receive an Accounting of Certain Unauthorized Disclosures[23]

The Privacy Rule requires covered entities to maintain records of certain disclosures done without written authorization, including disclosures for public health purposes and for research conducted pursuant to a waiver of authorization by an Institutional Review Board (IRB) or Privacy Board, reviews preparatory to research and research on decedent information. The covered entity must provide information about those disclosures to patients upon request.

This list must be tied to each disclosure of the identifiable record and must contain, among other things, the name(s) and address of the accessing researchers and the date and the purpose of the access (*i.e.*, the title of the research activity). If, however, the researcher accesses more than 50 identifiable records for that research activity, the covered entity may, in lieu of tagging each identifiable record disclosed, keep a master list of such projects. This abbreviated list requires information additional to that of the above, such as the name and phone number of the sponsor. When utilizing the abbreviated listing for documenting more than 50 records accessed, that list would be given to all patients whose records might have been accessed in addition to the list of the known accesses. Specifically, when a patient asks the covered entity for their accounting of disclosures, the covered entity would provide the list of the activities of known access of that patients record as well as the master list of which their record might have been accessed when not documenting it individually.

2. Authorization Exceptions

The Privacy Rule permits use or disclosure of PHI without an individual's written authorization for "treatment," "payment," and "healthcare operations" (TPO). These terms do not include most research activities.[24] HIPAA also permits use or disclosure to law enforcement and public health authorities, subject to specified limitations.[25]

HIPAA includes five additional exceptions to the written authorization requirement relevant to research activities, which are described below.

Waiver of Authorization[26]

The Privacy Rule empowers an institutional review board (IRB) whose membership meets the membership criteria under the Common Rule, or a properly constituted privacy board, to grant a waiver or alteration of written authorization if the proposed use or disclosure will pose minimal risk to participants' privacy and other specified criteria are met. A comparison of Common Rule and HIPAA waivers and detailed discussion of the role of a privacy board under HIPAA is discussed later in this chapter. Of note, although there is overlap in the criteria for this waiver of authorization and the waiver of obtaining informed consent to be in the research, these are separate and distinct decisions the IRB must make and document separately.

Review Preparatory to Research[27]
A covered entity may allow researchers, whether or not affiliated with the covered entity, to review PHI without written authorization from affected individuals if the researchers certify that: (1) the use or disclosure is sought solely to review PHI as necessary to prepare a research protocol or for similar purposes preparatory to research; (2) no PHI will be removed from the covered entity by the researcher in the course of the review; and (3) the PHI for which use or access is sought is necessary for the research purposes.

Through its FAQ process, the Office of Civil Rights clarified that this exception could be used to permit individuals to identify potential research subjects. OCR specified that for recruitment purposes, the exception could only be used by individuals considered to be members of the covered entity's workforce.[28] Using or disclosing PHI for recruitment by a non-workforce member must meet one of the other exceptions to be permitted by the Privacy Rule.

Research on decedents' Information[29]
A covered entity may use or disclose PHI of a decedent to the researcher, if the researcher provides: (1) a representation that the use or disclosure sought is solely for research on the PHI of decedents; (2) documentation, at the covered entity's request, of the death of the specified individuals; and (3) a representation that the PHI for which use or disclosure is sought is necessary for the research purposes.

De-identified Data Sets
Section 164.514(a) of the HIPAA Privacy Rule provides the standard for de-identification of protected health information. Under this standard, health information is not individually identifiable if it does not identify an individual and if the covered entity has no reasonable basis to believe it can be used to identify an individual. A covered entity may use or disclose de-identified health information for any purpose without restriction (although other laws may apply). The Privacy Rule designates two ways by which a covered entity can determine that health information is de-identified. The first is the "Safe Harbor" approach, which permits a covered entity to consider data to be de-identified if it removes 18 types of identifiers (*e.g.*, names and other direct identifiers, such as medical record numbers or social security numbers, all elements of dates other than year, age if over 89, all geography smaller than a state, and all but the first three digits of zip codes unless the first three digits represent a population with less than 20,000 inhabitants (to which it must be replaced with 000, and some other identifiers). The covered entity must also have no actual knowledge that the remaining information could be used to identify an individual, either alone or in combination with other information. An alternative is the statistical approach, which permits covered entities to disclose health information in any form provided that a qualified statistical or scientific expert concludes, through the use of accepted analytic techniques, that the risk the information could be used alone, or in combination with other reasonably available information, to identify the subject is very small.

The Privacy Rule permits covered entities to develop procedures under which a statistician or similarly qualified person may determine that the risk of re-identification of the information in a given data set is very small.[30]

Section 13424(c) of the HITECH Act requires the secretary of HHS to issue guidance on how best to implement the requirements for the de-identification of health information contained in the Privacy Rule.

In the Omnibus Rule, HHS notes that "we decline to completely exempt limited data sets from these provisions as, unlike de-identified data, they are still protected health information. However, disclosures of limited data sets for purposes permitted under the Rule would be exempt from the authorization requirements to the extent the only remuneration received in exchange for the data is a reasonable, cost-based fee to prepare and transmit the data or a fee otherwise expressly permitted by other law."[31]

The Privacy Rule, modified by the Omnibus Rule, includes a new Section 164.532(f). This section indicates "that a covered entity may continue to use or disclose a limited data set in accordance with an existing data use agreement that meets the requirements of Section 164.514(e), including for research purposes, until "the data use agreement is renewed or modified or until one year from the compliance date of this final rule [September 23, 2013], whichever is earlier, even if such disclosure would otherwise constitute a sale of protected health information upon the effective date of this rule."[32]

Limited Data Sets[33]

Soon after the final Privacy Rule was released in 2000, many researchers found that the restrictions imposed by its de-identification standards were impractical and would force researchers to seek waivers for research that otherwise was exempt from IRB review.[34]

In amendments to the regulation released in August 2002, the HHS created an alternative mechanism to use or disclose data for research, dubbed a "limited data set." Unlike a de-identified data set, a limited data set may include geographic information other than street address, all elements of dates and ages, and certain other unique identifying characteristics or codes.

For information to be shared in a limited data set, the recipient must agree to sign a Data Use Agreement (DUA). The use of a DUA assures the covered entity that the recipient will, among other things, protect the limited data set and not make any effort to re-identify individuals using the data set or contact individuals if re-identified. A researcher may be a business associate if the researcher performs a function, activity, or service for a covered entity that does fall within the definition of business associate, such as the healthcare operations function of creating a de-identified or limited data set for the covered entity. Where the researcher is also the intended recipient of the de-identified data or limited data set, the researcher must return or destroy the identifiers at the time the business associate relationship to create the data set terminates and the researcher may then wish to use the de-identified data or limited data set (subject to a DUA) for research purpose.

In the Omnibus Rule, the HHS encourages covered entities and business associates to take advantage of the safe harbor provision of the breach notification rule by encrypting limited data sets and other protected health information pursuant to the Guidance Specifying the Technologies and Methodologies that Render Protected Health Information Unusable, Unreadable, or Indecipherable to Unauthorized Individuals (74 FR 42740, 42742). "If protected health information is encrypted pursuant to this guidance, then no breach notification is required following an impermissible use or disclosure of the information."[35]

3. Additional Protections and Mandates

To protect against inappropriate use or disclosure of PHI, the Privacy Rule imposes numerous detailed administrative requirements on covered entities, many of which affect research. These include a "minimum necessary" standard applicable to many research-related uses and disclosures of PHI, as well as a requirement that covered entities contracting with third parties to perform treatment, payment, or healthcare operations activities (note, this list intentionally does not include research) on their behalf must enter into "business associate agreements" with those third parties.

Minimum Necessary Standard

HIPAA requires covered entities to make reasonable efforts to limit the PHI used, disclosed, or requested for any purpose other than direct treatment to the "minimum necessary" to accomplish the intended purpose of the use, disclosure, or request.[36] Although the principle addressed by the standard is laudable, its application is sometimes overly restrictive and may hamper appropriate research activities. It is, therefore, important for covered entities and researchers alike to understand the circumstances where the minimum necessary standard does *not* apply. These include:

- Disclosures to or requests by a healthcare provider for treatment (which may include research-related treatment)
- Uses or disclosures made pursuant to a written authorization
- Uses or disclosures required by law, including uses or disclosures made to public health authorities such as the Public Health Service's Office for Human Research Protections (OHRP) or the Food and Drug Administration (FDA); and uses or disclosures made to FDA-regulated entities that in turn are required to make safety, efficacy, or quality reports to FDA related to drugs, devices, or biologics that they manufacture.

Business Associate Agreements

The HIPAA statute's administrative simplification and privacy standards apply only to covered entities. To address concerns that the legislation left unregulated scores of individuals and organizations—ranging from software vendors to disease management companies to accreditation agencies—with broad access to PHI, the HHS imposed on covered entities an obligation to enter into specific written agreements (called "business associate agreements" or BAAs) with these third parties that, in effect, extended the Privacy Rule (and, later the Security Rule) to a much broader segment of the healthcare industry.

The Omnibus Rule clarified the role of researchers and business associates. The rule includes a new definition of a business associate as an entity that "creates, receives, maintains or transmits PHI"[37] for a function or activity regulated by HIPAA, on behalf of a covered entity.

An external researcher is not a business associate of a covered entity by virtue of its research activities, even if the covered entity has hired the researcher to perform the research thus other HIPAA compliant methods must be utilized other than Business Associate Agreements for a covered entity to disclose identifiable PHI to a researcher.[38] Similarly, an external or independent IRB is not a business associate of a covered entity by virtue of its performing research review, approval, and continuing oversight functions. However, a researcher may be a business associate if the researcher performs a function, activity, or service for a covered entity that does fall within the definition of business associate, such as the healthcare operations function of creating a de-identified or limited data set for the covered entity.

Common Rule and FDA Privacy and Confidentiality Provisions

The Common Rule defines "private information" to include "information about behavior that occurs in a context in which an individual can reasonably expect that no observation or recording is taking place, and information which has been provided for specific purposes by an individual and which the individual can reasonably expect will not be made public (for example, a medical record)."[39] One can argue that, since implementation of the Privacy Rule, private information includes (though may not be limited to) any information that constitutes PHI under HIPAA.

Ethical guidelines that influenced the adoption and content of the Common Rule and corresponding FDA regulations stress the importance of participant privacy and the need to protect the confidentiality of research data. The regulations include standards requiring researchers to inform participants of their privacy rights and requiring IRBs to assure research plans include adequate provisions to protect the *privacy* of subjects and maintain the *confidentiality* of data.[40] The distinction between these two terms is not conceptually obvious to many, but understanding it can help IRBs and researchers to assure that both sets of interests are well protected. In general, *privacy* "refers to persons; and to their interest in controlling the access of others to themselves." *Confidentiality*, by contrast, "refers to data; and to the agreements that are made about ways in which information is restricted to certain people."[41]

1. Participant Privacy and Informed Consent

Research participant privacy interests are addressed primarily through the informed consent process. The Common Rule and corresponding FDA regulations require the consent to include information about the study and the subject's participation in the study, as well as a "statement describing the extent, if any, to which confidentiality of records identifying the subject will be maintained." FDA regulations also require explicit discussion of the possibility that FDA may inspect research records.[42] Collectively, these requirements assure that prospective subjects can make an informed choice about whether they are willing to accept some intrusion as a condition of participating in a study.

It is difficult to protect subjects before they are contacted. Accordingly, researchers must understand that prospective subjects and their families are at risk of harm particularly during the identification and recruitment phases of a study, before they are provided an opportunity to agree or decline to participate. For example, subjects may not be aware of their condition before they are contacted; or the process of contacting them may result in disclosures to family or household members who are unaware of their condition.[43] A researcher can minimize these risks in a number of ways, including approaching a prospective participant through his or her physician and using any predetermined methods and/or limitations of such contact.

2. Confidentiality Protections

It is often the case in data research that there is enough –built-in "privacy/confidentiality by design" protections that the research activity is exempt from further oversight of an IRB. This exempt classification is reserved for when the researchers do not use any identifiers for the research, in essence making the research de-identified. In research that does not include interaction or intervention with the subjects and only involves use of their de-identified data that was or (under the revised Common Rule) would have been gathered absent the research, such an –IRB-exempt determination can be made by the institution.

For non-exempt research, confidentiality concerns are reviewed and addressed primarily through the IRB's evaluation of the non-exempt research protocol and, in particular, its provisions for securing research data against inappropriate use and disclosure. These might include any combination of physical safeguards (*e.g.*, maintaining data in locked file cabinets in secure buildings or offices); electronic safeguards (*e.g.*, encrypting data and storage devices); and policy safeguards (*e.g.*, limiting data access to those with a documented need-to-know, training those with access to comply with approved security procedures, coding data and maintaining links in separate paper files or separate computers or servers, and destroying links at the earliest possible opportunity).

Researchers may also take advantage of available legal safeguards. For example, the National Institutes of Health (NIH), issues certificates of confidentiality(COCs) to protect research data against involuntary disclosure. COCs are available for both federally and non-federally supported research, and exempt a researcher from compliance with subpoenas, court orders, and even demands from law enforcement authorities, although they do not exempt researchers from mandatory public health disclosures such as communicable disease or abuse/neglect reports to state authorities.[44] The 21st Century Cures Act (passed in December 2016) made COC coverage automatic for affected federally funded research (thus eliminating the need to actually apply for one), while also supporting that non-federally funded research could still obtain one through application.

3. Secondary Use

The secondary use of one's personal data is hotly debated in contemporary times. While most of the press focuses on items such as social media and retail/service giants using one's data for purposes not disclosed or permissioned, the importance is not lost on the secondary use of research data. Under today's standards, unless otherwise committed to with the participant, information provided for one purpose can be de-identified and used for secondary purposes as de-identified data is not regulated by HIPAA or the Common Rule. This introduces many ethical questions on the appropriateness of secondary use of one's data in a manner that is not inconsistent with the original consent. While regulatory compliance can be met (through de-identification), such use may be inconsistent with the original intent (whether implied or written). One of the most famous examples of this was the secondary use of data and biospecimens from the Havasupai Tribe, where Arizona State University researchers were accused of using the data in manners inconsistent with the original informed consent.

This issue is becoming more complicated as just as there are efforts to secure privacy and confidentiality of one's data, there is growing interest in making research data more transparent. Many institutions that conduct large amounts of NIH-funded studies have been familiar with data transparency requirements for many years (*i.e.*, data bought using taxpayer dollars belongs to the taxpayers, assuming privacy and confidentiality of the individuals to which the data is about is maintained)[45]. Similarly, many nonprofit foundations (such as the Wellcome Foundation or the Bill & Melinda Gates Foundation) that fund research also require that the de-identified data generated from their funding be made available to future researchers. In addition to sponsors of research making these demands for data sharing, a growing number of influential external entities are also making similar demands. Clinical (de-identified) data transparency is now required under Policy 0070 for approval filings with the European Medicines Agency and Canada is drafting a similar policy. Although FDA has yet to initiate such a requirement for filings in the United States, research data is often gathered and used for international filings thus a site in the United States could have their de-identified data made available to the public when filed in these other countries. In July 2018, the International Committee of Medical Journal Editors (ICMJE), whose members are editors of more than 4,000 medical journals, passed their requirement that requests to publish clinical trials in their member journals must be accompanied with a (de-identified) data sharing plan, and the requirement expands to require a data sharing plan posting on the trial's public registration beginning January 2019. Technically the submitted data sharing plan can be that the researchers will not share the data, however, it is expected that the journals will react negatively to the requirement in their consideration to publish or not publish the results of clinical trials in their journals.

In the revised Common Rule, a new element of consent requires that researchers disclose up front if they will or will not intend to use the data gathered for secondary research. Specifically, the new regulation requires the following in the consent form:

> "One of the following statements about any research that involves the collection of identifiable private information or identifiable biospecimens:
>
> (i) A statement that identifiers might be removed from the identifiable private information or identifiable biospecimens and that, after such removal, the information or biospecimens could be used for future research studies or distributed to another investigator for future research studies without additional informed consent from the subject or the legally authorized representative, if this might be a possibility; or

(ii) A statement that the subject's information or biospecimens collected as part of the research, even if identifiers are removed, will not be used or distributed for future research studies."[46]

Given just the above demands for data transparency much less the growing ones from other stakeholders, it would be extremely impractical for a researcher to commit to option (ii) above. If a researcher wants to make such a commitment, the researchers should assure they have complete control over the data (including data that any subcontractors or vendors may have) and its destruction.

Research Regulations vs. HIPAA

Although the Common Rule and corresponding FDA regulations do not regulate covered entities that are not engaged in human research,[47] and HIPAA does not regulate the conduct of human research, but only the use and disclosure of data created, received, or maintained by covered entities, the regulations do overlap. Many researchers and research institutions are responsible for compliance with both.[48]

Overlap

Of note, there are some important nuances regarding the difference between HIPAA privacy protection and Common Rule/FDA privacy protection. HIPAA protects protected health information of patients where not all subjects of research, even in a healthcare setting, are patients. It is not uncommon for subjects to be the treating physicians, other clinical or non-clinical staff, the general public, or even the patient's visitors. This is where the Common Rule protections play the primary role. There also may be other regulations protecting the privacy of those who are not patients (*e.g.*, The Family Educational Rights and Privacy Act (FERPA) for a student's U.S. academic records, The General Data Protection Regulation for European Union citizens etc.). This and other key differences between HIPAA and the Common Rule as they deal with privacy on a medical setting are described in the table below.

COMMON RULE / FDA	HIPAA
Protects all research subjects' privacy (identity of patients, providers, employees, visitors, etc.)	Protects PHI Only
Less prescriptive on what is "de-identified"	Very prescriptive on what is "de-identified"
Waiver criteria for research consent only, not waiver of HIPAA Authorization to disclose identifiable PHI	Waiver criteria for HIPAA authorization to disclose identifiable PHI only, not the consent to participate in the research
Applies to living individuals (expires at death)	Expires 50 years after death

1. Authorization and Consent

The Common Rule, FDA regulations, and HIPAA all protect individual privacy by requiring, in most instances, written permission prior to enrolling a person in a research study or using or disclosing his or her PHI for the study.[49] These different regulatory standards share some essential features.

Each of the regulations typically requires written documentation of an individual's or legally authorized representative's voluntary agreement to participate in a study or use or disclose identifiable private information for the study. Each requires documentation of information critical for the individual to make an informed choice, including purpose, risks, and right to withdraw. Yet there are important differences. The Common Rule and FDA human subject regulations are designed to protect the rights and welfare of living individual research participants—of people; HIPAA is intended to protect information—even when associated with deceased individuals for up to 50 years after their death. These differences are reflected in part in the differing requirements for consent under the Common Rule and corresponding FDA regulations, on one hand, and authorization under the Privacy Rule, on the other.

Absent local institutional policies to the contrary, researchers generally have discretion to decide whether or not to integrate the requirements of the research regulations with those imposed by HIPAA in a single document. The HHS Office for Civil Rights, which is responsible for enforcing HIPAA's privacy and security standards, has made clear that HIPAA does not require IRBs to review and approve stand-alone authorizations.[50] Nor do OHRP or FDA require IRBs to do so, unless IRB policies require review of *all* materials provided to prospective research participants during the recruitment or enrollment process.[51] Indeed, FDA has issued guidance "intended to encourage IRBs to permit the enrollment of subjects in clinical investigations without prior IRB review and/ or approval of stand-alone HIPAA authorizations, since such review and/or approval is not required by the HIPAA Privacy Rule." ThePrivacy Rule generally prohibits combining an authorization with any other document. However, the regulation exempts from this prohibition combining the consent to participate in a research study with authorization for the use or disclosure of PHI in connection with that study.[52]

In determining whether to utilize compound or stand-alone authorizations for all studies or particular types of studies, IRBs and researchers should consider the implications of their decisions. These may include, among other challenges:

The likelihood of subject confusion resulting from two potentially inconsistent documents. For example, consent documents may reference a potential risk to privacy but generally promise that researchers will protect subject privacy and data confidentiality. Authorization forms, however, are required to state that once disclosed outside a covered entity, PHI is no longer regulated by HIPAA—an implication that privacy may not be protected when data is shared for research.

Documentation challenges. Research records generally must be maintained for a minimum of three years, although requirements vary depending on the nature of the study and funding source. PHI, including authorization or waiver to use or disclose PHI for research, must be maintained at least six years.

Administrative burden. In hybrid covered entities, such as large research universities, imposition of a requirement that consents and authorizations be integrated can result in non-covered components using overly complex forms and, in some cases, inadvertently implying that they are subject to HIPAA.

2. Research and Quality Improvement

Both the Common Rule and HIPAA define research as a: "systematic investigation... designed to develop or contribute to generalizable knowledge."[53] The Common Rule equally regulates activities undertaken solely for research purposes and those undertaken primarily for other reasons (*e.g.*, quality improvement and program evaluation) if there is also a research component, no matter how insignificant. HIPAA, by contrast, treats the following activities as "healthcare operations" rather than research:

- Conducting quality assessment and improvement activities, including outcomes evaluation and development of clinical guidelines, if the obtaining of generalizable knowledge is not the primary purpose of studies resulting from the activities
- Population-based activities relating to improving health or reducing healthcare costs
- [Clinical] protocol development, case management and care coordination.

Thus, while the Common Rule requires individual consent (or IRB-approved waiver of consent) to conduct quality improvement activities that contain activities meeting the definition of research with human subjects, HIPAA does *not* require a covered entity to secure individual authorization (or IRB-or Privacy Board approved waiver) for use or disclosure of PHI for those same activities, as long as the covered entity describes the activities in its Notice of Privacy Practices.

3. The Role of the Privacy Board and Authorization Waivers

Like HIPAA, the Common Rule recognizes circumstances where securing informed consent is unreasonable and unnecessary for the ethical conduct of a research project. Though similar, the Privacy Rule and Common Rule requirements are not identical because of the different concerns addressed by each. The regulatory standards are summarized as follows in the table below:

WAIVER OF HIPAA AUTHORIZATION	COMMON RULE WAIVER OF INFORMED CONSENT
The use or disclosure involves no more than minimal risk to the privacy of individuals because there's an adequate plan to protect identifiers from improper use and disclosure; to destroy identifiers consistent with the conduct of the research; and to not reuse or re-disclose the data except as required by law, for oversight of the study, or for other permitted research	Research poses no more than minimal risk to prospective participants. "Minimal risk" means the probability and magnitude of harm or discomforts anticipated in the research are not greater in and of themselves than those ordinarily encountered in daily life or during the performance of routine physical or psychological examinations or tests of healthy individuals.
N/A	The waiver or alteration will not adversely affect participants' rights and welfare
The research could not practicably be conducted without the waiver or alteration; nor without access and use of the PHI	The research could not practicably be carried out without the waiver or alteration. In the revised Common Rule, to obtain a waiver for the use of identifying data and/or biospecimens, the researcher must justify why the identifiers are needed as opposed to using de-identified information. Also of note, the definition of the term "practicably" has been debated with some credence in the 09/08/2015 Federal Register clarifying that the criteria means it is impractical to conduct the research (as it has been defined in the protocol by its specific aims and objectives) if consent was required, not it is impractical (*i.e.*, in time or cost) to obtain consent. For example. A research project involving deceit of the research intent would be impractical but a research project that would lose money or take a lot of time if consent was obtained would not meet the criteria.

WAIVER OF HIPAA AUTHORIZATION	COMMON RULE WAIVER OF INFORMED CONSENT
N/A	Whenever appropriate, the subjects will be provided with additional pertinent information after participation
Documentation of the waiver reflecting that it was properly awarded must be maintained by the covered entity for at least 6 years.	Documentation of the waiver must be maintained by the IRB for at least 3 years after the closure of the study under U.S. regulation. The overall institution may have longer regulatory and/or contractual requirements.

The Privacy Rule empowers IRBs to grant HIPAA authorization waivers.[54] The regulation's drafters also recognized, however, that while not all covered entities have an established IRB, many contribute data for research activities. Accordingly, the regulation permits covered entities or others to designate a "Privacy Board" to grant such waivers.[55]

A Privacy Board must include (1) members with varying backgrounds and appropriate professional competency as necessary to review the effect of the research protocol on the individual's privacy rights and related interests; (2) at least one member who is not affiliated with the covered entity, not affiliated with any entity conducting or sponsoring the research, and not related to any person who is affiliated with any of such entities; and (3) does not have any member participating in a review of any project in which the member has a conflict of interest.

The Privacy Rule does not confer any additional obligations or entitlements on privacy boards, although covered entities sometimes assign them broader authority. For example, privacy boards may be responsible for identifying, and perhaps addressing, broader privacy and confidentiality concerns related to proposed studies, or they may be empowered to grant requests for use of PHI preparatory to research or use of PHI for research on decedents' information.

When institutions engage in multisite research activities, the revised Common Rule requires each engaged institution to certify IRB approval (including approval of written informed consent forms or of consent waivers) from a single IRB, typically under an IRB Authorization Agreement.[56]

With that said, OHRP guidance on what it means to be engaged in research indicates that institutions that are only releasing information or biospecimens (even if identifiable) are generally not meeting the criteria of "engaged in research" thus only standard privacy rules germane to the release of the information would apply.[57]

The Privacy Rule, by contrast, does not require multiple approvals but instead allows a covered entity to rely on a properly documented waiver granted by any IRB or Privacy Board constituted in compliance with the requirements of the Privacy Rule. The rule requires documentation of waiver approval to include identification and date of action, waiver criteria, PHI needed, and review and approval procedures. Waiver criteria must include a statement that the Privacy Board or IRB has determined that alteration of the waiver, in whole or in part, satisfies the following criteria:

a. Use or disclosure of PHI involves no more than a minimal risk to the privacy of individuals, based on, at least the presence of the following elements: (1) an adequate plan to protect the identifiers from improper use and disclosure; (2) an adequate plan to destroy the identifiers at the earliest opportunity consistent with conduct of the research, unless there is a health or research justification for retaining the identifiers or such retention is required by law; and (3) adequate written assurances that PHI will not be reused or disclosed to any other person or entity,

except as required by law, for authorized oversight of the research study, or for other research for which use or disclosure of PHI would be permitted;
b. The research could not practicably be conducted without the waiver or alteration; and
c. The research could not practicably be conducted without access to and use of the PHI.

Research Repositories

Researchers increasingly rely on research repositories to facilitate clinical research. Recruitment registries are thought to improve efficiency in recruitment efforts. Large specimen and data banks can facilitate analyses not possible in individual interventional studies. Moreover, once specimens or data are deposited in a repository, subsequent research may be unregulated under the Common Rule altogether,[58] or exempt from continuing IRB oversight.[59]

The Common Rule and corresponding FDA regulations require informed consent documents to include an "explanation of the purposes of the research."[60] This requirement has been interpreted to permit researchers to collect specimens and data for future research whose specific purposes may be unknown. The National Cancer Institute, for example, has developed a widely utilized informed consent template for collection of excess tissue.[61] The form offers three non-exclusive choices to those who agree to participate:

- Tissue may be kept for use in research to learn about, prevent, or treat cancer.
- Tissue may be kept for use in research to learn about, prevent, or treat other health problems.
- Specimen bank may contact the participant in the future to invite the participant to take part in more research.

Similar to the Common Rule, the Privacy Rule requires covered entities to describe with specificity the purposes of any proposed current *or future* use or disclosure of PHI, including for research. A statement that PHI will be transferred to a specimen or databank is considered sufficiently specific to meet this HIPAA standard,[62] but before accessing, using, or disclosing PHI maintained in such a repository for an individual project, the investigator(s) must secure written authorization or an IRB and/or Privacy Board-approved waiver. Researchers interested in developing registries to address perceived impediments to recruitment created by the Privacy Rule should be aware of the following considerations before making a final decision:

- **Registries are not necessary to identify and recruit eligible subjects.** A certification for review preparatory to research may be used if no PHI will be removed from the covered entity's site; and if removal is necessary, a partial waiver of authorization can also do the trick. Of note, however, contacting subjects for recruitment purposes under preparatory to research is only allowed for members of the covered entity's workforce, meaning that while an external entity can use the preparatory to research provision to view records for protocol preparation and/or study feasibility, if they are not part of the HIPAA-covered entity's workforce they must stop short of actually contacting participants. This may be worked around with a business associate agreement contracting with the external entity to contact patients and set appointments.
- **Creation of a registry may result in additional risk to participants.** Researchers who may be experts in their scientific fields are not necessarily experts in data security and do not always enjoy sufficient technical support to assure data security consistent with HIPAA or other industry standards. Well-publicized breaches at major research institutions have exposed major weaknesses in security systems in an academic environment.[63] These include failure to encrypt data stored on portable devices (*e.g.*, laptops), storage of coded data in separate files but on the same computer or server as the codes necessary to identify involved individuals, sharing of access passwords among users (*e.g.*, with secretaries), and more. When registries are created solely for recruiting purposes, re-

search participant privacy can be placed at unnecessary risk. Researchers are required under the Common Rule, corresponding FDA regulations, and underlying ethical principles to minimize such risks.

- **Registries may be problematic from an ethical or scientific perspective.** The total pool of potential subjects may be demographically different from a registry pool. Indeed, researchers have observed "consent bias" when patients are asked whether they want to participate in actual projects—bias that can impact the generalizability and validity of results.[64]
- **Use of a registry may result in confusion among participants.** It is easy to create an (often incorrect) expectation among prospective subjects that, by refusing to participate in a registry, they can protect themselves from future contact about research participation. In these cases, recruiting materials and consent and authorization forms should make clear to subjects that a decision not to participate will not necessarily protect them from being contacted for possible participation in individual studies utilizing the registry or unrelated studies conducted locally by the same institution.

A recent development in repositories brought on by the revised Common Rule deals with a newly created kind of consent called "Broad Consent" which is approved under a new kind of IRB review called "Limited IRB Review". This Broad Consent has different criteria than the usual research consent as it pertains to the secondary use of their healthcare data. Broad Consent, also called "front door consent" prior to the new rule giving it an official regulatory name, is generally intended to occur when a person enters into a health system and is asked (presumably with other admission or check-in paperwork) whether or not they want to have their identifiable information and/or biospecimens available for future unspecified research. While many applaud the idea of giving patients this level of autonomy in theory, health systems are generally not adopting the broad consent option due to the logistical challenges, operational costs, and technical infeasibility to guarantee the sequestration of the data for those who refuse to give Broad Consent. For one, the new regulation is clear that an IRB cannot override a Broad Consent decline with a waiver of authorization, essentially meaning that "no" means "no". Secondly, while technically under a Broad Consent "no," the identifiers can be removed and information used anyway, this is likely not the understanding that patient would have and they would possibly see that as a violation of their "no". Therefore, while Broad Consent is a new regulatory option, the usual practice of just informing participants that their data may be used in research in accordance with current research and privacy regulations will remain the norm for the foreseeable future.

Other Federal Privacy Protections

HIPAA is the best-known federal privacy law, but other federal standards also address individual privacy and impact research. These include:

- The Public Health Service Act and implementing regulations, which protect mental health and substance abuse treatment records and related research records.[65]
- The Family Educational Rights and Privacy Act ("FERPA") and Protection of Pupil Rights Amendment ("PPRA"), which protect educational records including, in some cases, student health records.[66]
- The Privacy Act, which contains protections similar to HIPAA with respect to identifiable private information collected by federal agencies.[67] These include individual access rights, imposition of "minimum necessary" requirements on agency collection and retention activities, limitations on agency disclosure, and more. Although the Privacy Act does not typically affect researchers or research institutions directly, they may be required to comply with its requirements when serving as contractors to federal agencies.
- Substance Abuse and Mental Health Services Administration (SAMHSA) has regulations at 42 C.F.R. Part 2 pertaining to confiden-

tiality of substance abuse disorder patient records that provide protections and restrictions above and beyond HIPAA for data that (i) contains information relating to a patient, whether recorded (electronically or on paper) or not, that is created, received, or acquired by a Part 2 covered program; (ii) contains Patient Identifying Information (as defined in 42 C.F.R. § 2.11); and (iii) contains information about being or having been diagnosed with a substance use disorder (or to a condition which is identified as having been caused by that substance use disorder), having or having had a substance use disorder, or being or having been referred for treatment of a substance use disorder either directly, by reference to publicly available information, or through verification of such identification by another person.

Privacy advocates have advanced additional proposals to further protect health information privacy, including laws restricting access to and use of genetic testing and results information or to limit use of social security numbers. The Genetic Information Nondiscrimination Act (GINA) became law in 2008. The Omnibus Rule, effective in 2013, provides for implementation of GINA. HHS includes "genetic information" as a type of health information subject to HIPAA rules, including the imposition of restrictions that prohibit health plans from using genetic information for underwriting purposes.

Efforts at the national level to better protect social security numbers have been equally ineffective, though a number of local initiatives have succeeded.[68]

State Privacy and Mandatory Disclosure Laws

Researchers must also be aware of any applicable state law requirements.

Special Protections

Many states have adopted additional protections for sensitive information, even if de-identified, such as alcohol and substance abuse, behavioral health, reproductive health, sexually transmitted diseases, genetic testing, cancer, and HIV/AIDS. Examples of such protections include requiring specific language in authorization forms, further limiting the circumstances under which sensitive data may be used or disclosed without a patient's authorization, and severely restricting the use of social security numbers.[69] Often the application of these laws is not limited to the context in which the information is obtained in the healthcare setting. This means, whether the information is obtained through a clinical interaction or a research project, the protections may still apply.

Who May Authorize Use or Disclosure of Health Information

In addition to the laws that govern sensitive information, state laws also govern *who* is empowered to determine whether a person's health information can be used in research (where authorization is required). For example, minors (usually, but not always, individuals under age 18)[70] may have the right to control certain health information. HIPAA provides that a minor who is empowered under state law to consent to certain healthcare services (e.g., prenatal care or substance abuse) without a parent's or guardian's permission is also empowered to exercise control of resulting health information.[71] If the minor is involved in research using such information, these laws will determine who has the legal authority to sign research documents, including authorization forms.[72] This may create complexities in the research project if certain information requires the minor's authorization while other information requires the legal representative's authorization.

Electronic Records and Signatures

In addition to the challenges of complying with HIPAA, the Common Rule, and a patchwork of sometimes inconsistent state privacy laws, researchers and research institutions have obligations under HIPAA and other federal and state laws to adopt policies, procedures, and systems to secure electronic health and research information.

Food and Drug Administration (FDA): 21 C.F.R. Part 11

The Federal Food, Drug, and Cosmetic Act,[73] governs the use of new and approved drugs, devices, and biologics in human research. Investigators engaged in FDA-regulated research are required under various "predicate rules" (*e.g.*, regulations in 21 C.F.R. parts 50, 54, 56, 312, and 812) to create, maintain, and transmit to sponsors and FDA numerous records and reports. When utilizing electronic systems to comply with these requirements, investigators must also comply with the security provisions of 21 C.F.R. Part 11.[74] These "Part 11" regulations were issued in 1997 to permit the use of electronic records and signatures, as well as handwritten signatures executed in electronic records. Although the regulations seem to broadly address the use of electronic systems to generate research records, FDA has stated that it will exercise "enforcement discretion" when electronic records are maintained in paper form.[75]

Part 11 defines an "electronic record" as "any combination of text, graphic, data, audio, pictorial, or other information representation in digital form, that is created, modified, maintained, archived, retrieved, or distributed by a computer system."[76] The rule establishes data security and integrity standards that are not uncommon across the healthcare industry. Thus, in looking at Part 11 requirements, many organizations can review their overall security measures. Those that are covered entities under HIPAA will have covered many Part 11 requirements in the compliance program implemented for the HIPAA Security Rule.

Part 11 applies to records in "electronic form that are created, modified, maintained, archived, retrieved, or transmitted, under any records requirement set forth in agency regulations."[77] FDA will permit use of electronic records *in lieu of* paper records if the provisions of Part 11 are met for those records that are submitted to the agency and those that must be maintained locally under the agency regulations. The regulations outline the required controls for both "closed" and "open" systems.

1. Closed Records Systems

A closed system is one that is controlled by the persons who are responsible for the information that is in the system.[78] A closed system must have a method to maintain the "authenticity, integrity and when appropriate, the confidentiality" of the records.[79] A closed system must also have a method for validation of the system that will ensure the accuracy and reliability of the records.[80] In addition, there must be a way for the system to identify invalid or altered records.[81]

If an entity is maintaining electronic records in a closed system it must be able to produce both human readable and electronic form copies of the records.[82] The copies must be suitable for review, inspection, and copying by FDA.[83] Access to the closed system must be limited to authorized users.[84] Organizations should establish a standard process for user authentication and authorization that includes basic security measures. This control is intended to ensure that records are properly signed and that changes to records are made only by individuals who have been assigned that authority.[85]

Another required provision for a closed system is a secure audit trail with a time stamp. The audit trail must include the capability to track the date and time of entries and actions that create, modify, or delete electronic records.[86] Any changes in the system may not obscure previous entries.[87] This means that all versions of documents must be maintained in the electronic system for the time required by the relevant predicate rules (typically for at least two years following application for approval or termination of the study, whichever is later).

An organization using a closed system must establish a process to assure that individuals who use the system have proper education, training, and experience.[88] Individuals who use the system must be held accountable for actions performed under their electronic signatures, and the organization must develop and adopt appropriate policies and procedures to reflect this requirement.[89]

Finally, a closed system must have a method to exercise control over system documentation.[90]

2. Open Records System

Like a closed system, an open system must have the controls described above. In addition, an open system must impose special measures like encryption and appropriate digital signature standards to ensure the authenticity, integrity, and confidentiality of the records.[91]

3. Electronic Signatures

Electronic signatures must comply with specific criteria established by the regulations. Each signature must carry with it a clear indication of the printed name of the signer, and a date and time.[92] The meaning associated with the signature must be identified in the system.[93] The system must link the electronic signature to the applicable electronic record so that the signature cannot be removed, copied, or transferred to other records.[94]

Electronic signatures must be unique to the individual signer.[95] Once an electronic signature is assigned, it may not be used by or reassigned to another person.[96] Before an electronic signature can be assigned, the organization must verify the individual's identity.[97] Before an individual can use an electronic signature, the person must verify that the electronic signature is intended to be legally binding equivalent of the handwritten signature.[98] This verification must be in a paper form, signed with a traditional handwritten signature, and submitted to the FDA Office of Regional Operations.[99]

If an electronic signature is not based on biometrics, then it must have at least two distinct identification methods, such as an identification code and password.[100] If the electronic signature uses biometrics, then a system must be in place to ensure that only the genuine owners have the ability to use the signature.[101] There also must be a process to ensure that the signer cannot repudiate the authenticity of an electronically signed record.[102]

In sum, the requirements of Part 11 can be especially challenging for large organizations that maintain records in multiple systems. Every system used must meet the above criteria. Research organizations and even individual researchers may be asked by sponsors to certify that their systems comply with all Part 11 requirements. It is important that organizations and researchers understand the implications of such a certification. If the electronic information will be stored in multiple systems, someone with knowledge of each of those systems must work closely with the organization's contract negotiators or the researchers regarding the certification. Without this type of communication, an organization or researcher might inadvertently certify to compliance with Part 11 for systems that are incapable of meeting the regulatory requirements.

Other Laws Governing Electronic Signatures and Records

Part 11 applies only to electronic signatures and records used in FDA-regulated research. Other laws governing electronic commerce can have an impact on research even though the laws were not specifically drafted with research in mind. Two that are of particular interest are the federal Electronic Signatures in Global and National Commerce (eSIGN)[103] and the Uniform Electronic Transactions Act (UETA).[104]

1. Electronic Signatures in Global and National Commerce (eSIGN) Act

eSIGN is a federal statute that governs the use of electronic documents and signatures in commercial transactions. It defines an electronic signature as "an electronic sound, symbol, or process, attached to or logically associated with a contract or other record and executed or adopted by a person with the intent to sign the record."[105] The law essentially provides that a document may not be denied legal effect, validity, or enforceability simply because it is in electronic form or electronically signed.[106] Under eSIGN, if a consumer transaction is required to be in writing, the consumer must affirmatively consent to receiving information in electronic form if the parties wish to conduct the transaction electronically.[107]

This act may apply to some research transactions. The applicability will depend on whether the state has adopted the UETA and elected to preempt certain eSIGN provisions.

2. Uniform Electronic Transactions Act (UETA)

UETA was developed by the National Conference of Commissioners on Uniform State Laws in 1999 and was recommended to the states for adoption. All but a few states have adopted UETA and the remaining ones have enacted laws recognizing electronic signatures. UETA recognizes electronic records and signatures (defined consistently with eSIGN) as valid and binding to the same degree as their paper equivalents, so long as both parties agree to the electronic transaction. The legislation establishes security, authentication, authorization, and non-repudiation standards for creation, use, and storage of electronic records and signatures. While this law does not specifically apply to research, it may be applicable to data maintained electronically and the use of electronic signatures.

Breach Notification Rules

The Breach Notification Rule, finalized with the passage of the Omnibus Rule in 2013, requires that a covered entity notify the individual and the secretary of HHS Office for Civil Rights (OCR) of any breach of "unsecured" protected health information that has occurred or which they reasonably believe has occurred. The notification must be without undue delay but not more than 60 days from when the breach was discovered. If the breach involves more than 500 individuals OCR must be notified immediately (at the same time as the individuals). If there are more than 500 individuals within a state or jurisdiction then local news media must also be notified. For breaches involving fewer than 500 individuals, covered entities must notify OCR within 60 days of the end of the calendar year in which the breach occurred or at the same time as the individual. An incident is not considered a breach if the data involved is considered secure, which means it has been rendered unusable, unreadable, and indecipherable. Encryption will make data secure as identified by guidance provided by the OCR.

Business associates of covered entities must notify the covered entity without undue delay but not more than 60 days from when a breach occurs on their watch. Subcontractors of business associates must notify business associates who, in turn, notify the covered entity. The covered entity has the responsibility of notifying the individuals affected by the breach.

Information Security and Human Research

Information security is an essential component of an effective system to protect the confidentiality of research data.

HIPAA Security Rule

While the Privacy Rule directly affects the conduct of clinical research by controlling how researchers gain access to much of the information needed to perform clinical studies, the Security Rule[108] covers electronic protected health information (ePHI) that a covered entity or business associate creates, receives, maintains, or transmits. HITECH included provisions to make business associates responsible for compliance with the HIPAA Security Rule and Breach Notification Rule. With the enactment of the Omnibus Rule in 2013, business associates and their subcontractors became directly liable for compliance with all the requirements of the Security Rule, a limited number of the requirements of the Privacy Rule, the requirements of the Breach Notification Rule, and are subject to the Enforcement Rule.

The Security Rule includes administrative, physical, and technical safeguards to protect ePHI.

Administrative safeguards refer to "administrative actions, and policies and procedures, to manage the selection, development, implementation, and maintenance of security measuresto protect electronic protected health information and to manage the conduct of thecovered entity's workforce in relation to the protection of that information.[109] The standards include provisions that a covered entity or business associate must implement. Some of the standards include: conduct a risk assessment, manage the workforce's access to information, designate a security official, conduct security awareness training for the workforce, establish access and audit controls, provide for contingency planning and disaster recovery.[110]

Physical safeguards include "physical measures, policies, and procedures to protect a covered entity's electronic information systems and related buildings and equipment, from natural and environmental hazards, and unauthorized intrusion."[111] It is important to the integrity of the research that only individuals with a need to access the data are permitted to do so. In this increasingly mobile world, it is also important that researchers understand the critical need to secure data when is it is being transmitted on mobile devices such as USB drives, laptops, CDs, smart phones, and other types of portable devices. Devices must be encrypted and users trained in how to safely use them to protect any ePHI or other confidential information. It is far too easy to download significant amounts of sensitive data to these types of devices, resulting in possible data leakage or potential security incidents. In addition to loss of data, a security breach can cause embarrassment to the organization and affect reputation, result in the loss of trust by research participants, require meeting the notification requirements of the Breach Rule, and can lead to significant fines and enactment of corrective action plans.

Technical safeguards represent the "technology and the policy and procedures for its use that protect electronic protected health information and control access to it."[112] Covered entities and business associates are required to use technology to help safeguard electronic protected health information. The regulations require all users to have a unique user name and authentication methods to protect the security of the data. Covered entities and business associates must implement capabilities to audit systems and to control access.

Covered entities engaged in research should have implemented these standards and implementation specifications, as the Security Rule has been in effect since 2005. If the research is not being conducted by a covered entity, the organization may still be asked to comply with the Security Rule's requirements. Regardless, the Security Rule provides a good outline of basic security measures any organization should be using to protect sensitive information and arguably establishes an "industry standard" even for those organizations that are not directly regulated by HIPAA.

Federal Information Security Management Act ("FISMA")

The Federal Information Security Management Act (FISMA) was enacted in 2002 as part of the E-Government Act.[113] The legislation was introduced to, among other purposes, "provide a comprehensive framework for ensuring the effectiveness of information security controls over information resources that support Federal operations and assets."[114] FISMA does not directly regulate non-federal researchers, but the law requires federal agencies to adopt stringent security standards. Because implementation occurs at the agency level, standards vary by agency.

On January 9, 2008, the National Institutes of Health released a "Notice Regarding the Applicability of the Federal Information Security and Management Act to NIH Grantees." FISMA applies to grantees only when they collect, store, process, transmit, or use information on behalf of HHS or any of its component organizations. In all other cases, FISMA is not applicable to recipients of grants, including cooperative agreements with grantees. The grantee retains the original data and intellectual property, and is responsible for the security of this data, subject to all applicable laws protecting security, privacy, and research. If and when information collected by a grantee is provided to HHS, responsibility for the protection of the HHS copy of the information is transferred to HHS and it becomes the agency's responsibility to protect that information and any derivative copies as required by FISMA."[115]

In contrast to NIH's hands-off approach, the Veterans Administration (VA) has implemented policies to assure that veterans' health information never leaves VA control and, accordingly, remains protected under FISMA standards at all times. These rules have had a significant impact on a number of research and public health initiatives.[116]

Some VA implementation initiatives have involved requests directed to individual researchers, rather than institutional officials, to make certifications on behalf of their organizations that they are not always in a position to make. Researchers faced with requests for such certifications should be sure to coordinate any response with their information security officials and others with sufficient knowledge to respond accurately to VA.

State Breach Notification Laws

All fifty states now have data breach notification laws. A state's data breach notification requirements may differ from what's required under HIPAA, and data breach notification required under HIPAA may not trump state laws. Notice requirements vary by state (*e.g.*, California requires notice to the state agency within fifteen business days of the breach by an entity regulated by the California Department of Health; Connecticut requires that the Insurance Commissioner be notified if the entity is licensed by the state Department of Banking and Insurance). In the event of a data breach involving PHI, a covered entity may not only have to notify the OCR and other parties as required by the HIPAA Breach Notification Rule, but notification may also be required under state laws.

Because many of these laws may be applicable to research activity depending on the nature of the organization and/or the information being gathered, it is important for researchers and research organizations to be familiar with the requirements in their states. Even if the entity doing the research is not a covered entity under HIPAA, state breach notification laws may be applicable. For those researchers who conduct their projects out-of-state, or who recruit out-of-state residents, multiple state laws may apply.

Mandatory Reporting

Many states require healthcare providers and others to report certain information to public health or law enforcement authorities. HIPAA permits such reports without authorization from the patient. These requirements do not generally differentiate information learned in a clinical setting from information generated as part of research activities. Examples of typical state mandatory disclosure laws include child/vulnerable adult abuse or neglect, violent crimes, serious communicable disease and cancer.

Conclusion

Researchers and research organizations must familiarize themselves with the many laws and regulations that protect the privacy and security of health and other information that may be generated, stored, or transmitted in connection with research studies. Failure to do so can result not only in legal or regulatory exposure and reputational harm, but also in loss of public trust and resulting unwillingness of individuals to volunteer to participate in future studies. On a brighter note, however, knowledge can yield power. Researchers who are well-versed in the actual requirements of the various federal and state mandates, including the HIPAA Omnibus Rule that streamlines authorization requirements under HIPAA and enables future research studies, can educate institutional officials and administrators, assisting in compliance with regulations while eliminating unnecessary roadblocks and barriers to effective and timely research.

Chapter 8 Endnotes

1. **Marti Arvin, JD, CCEP-F,CHC-F,CHPC,CHRC**, is Vice President, Audit Strategy, for CynergisTek in Austin, TX; **Kathleen Price, RN, MBA, CIP**, is Director, Office of Human Subjects' Protection at St. Jude Children's Research Hospital in Memphis, TN; **David Vulcano, LCSW, MBA, CIP, RAC**, is Vice President, Research Compliance and Integrity for HCA Healthcare in Nashville, TN.
2. U.S. National Institutes of Health, National Library of Medicine, History of Medicine Division, "The Hippocratic Oath," Translated by Michael North, National Library of Medicine (2002), last modified February 7, 2012, https://www.nlm.nih.gov/hmd/greek/greek_oath.html.
3. Neil M. Richards & Daniel J. Solove, "Privacy's Other Path: Recovering the Law of Confidentiality," *The Georgetown Law Journal* 96 (2007): 123.
4. "World Medical Association Declaration of Helsinki: Ethical Principles for Medical Research Involving Human Subjects," *Bulletin of the World Health Organization* 79, no. 4 (2001): 373.
5. P. L. 104-191 (Aug. 21, 1996); 45 C.F.R. pts. 160 and 164.
6. The "Common Rule" is a policy adopted by more than a dozen separate federal agencies governing the conduct of federally funded human research. The version adopted by the U.S. Public Health Service is found at 45 C.F.R. pt. 46. Detailed information about the history of the regulation, agency guidance, and agency enforcement activities is available at http://www.hhs.gov/ohrp.
7. 21 C.F.R. pts. 50 and 56.
8. P. L. 104-191, Title II, subtitle F, pt. C (Aug. 21,1996).
9. P.L. 104-191 § 264 (Aug. 21, 1996).
10. 65 Fed. Reg. 82462 (Dec. 28, 2000). The regulations were revised somewhat about 18 months later, prior to their effective date. 67 Fed. Reg. 53181 (Aug. 14, 2002). The complete current HIPAA privacy, security, and related administrative rules are available online at https://www.hhs.gov/sites/default/files/ocr/privacy/hipaa/administrative/combined/hipaa-simplification-201303.pdf.
11. 78 Fed. Reg., 17, 5565-5702 (codified at 45 CFR 160 and 45 CFR 164) (January 25, 2013), "Modifications to the HIPAA Privacy, Security, Enforcement, and Breach Notification Rules under the Health Information Technology for Economic and Clinical Health Act and the Genetic Information Nondiscrimination Act; Other Modifications to the HIPPA Rules," https://www.federalregister.gov/documents/2013/01/25/2013-01073/modifications-to-the-hipaa-privacy-security-enforcement-and-breach-notification-rules-under-the.
12. Id.
13. These terms are defined at 45 C.F.R. § 160.103. HIPAA also recognizes "hybrid" covered entities—single legal entities that include two or more distinguishable, but not legally separate, units or components, where some but not all of the components would be "covered entities" as defined under HIPAA. Typical examples of hybrid entities include insurance companies that offer both life and health policies or Universities whose faculty practices or health facilities offer clinical services. Some healthcare organizations that conduct research initially declared themselves hybrid covered entities and drew the line between their covered and non-covered components not along organizational boundaries but instead based on what activities were being performed at any given time. The Department of Health and Human Services subsequently clarified that a hybrid covered entity may not define its components along functional lines. *See* U.S. Dep't of Health and Human Services, "HIPAA Frequent Questions: When Does a Covered Entity Have Discretion to Determine Whether a Research Component of the Entity is Part of Their Covered Functions, and Therefore, Subject to the HIPAA Privacy Rule?," last modified July 26, 2013, https://www.hhs.gov/hipaa/for-professionals/faq/315/when-does-a-covered-entity-have-discretion-to-determine-covered-functions/index.html. *See also* "When is a Researcher a Covered Health Care Provider Under HIPAA?," HHS, last modified October 10, 2017, https://www.hhs.gov/hipaa/for-professionals/faq/314/when-is-a-researcher-considered-a-covered-health-care-provider-under-hipaa/index.html.
14. P.L. 104-191, § 1177 (Aug. 21, 1996); 42 U.S.C. § 1320d-6.
15. Rachel Nosowsky and Thomas J. Giordano, "The Health Insurance Portability and Accountability Act of 1996 (HIPAA) Privacy Rule: Implications for Clinical Research," *Annual Review of Medicine* 57, (Feb. 2006): 575-90.
16. A personal representative may, depending on state law, be a legal guardian, attorney-in-fact, patient advocate, or next-of-kin. An unemancipated minor's personal representative generally is his or her parent or legal guardian. In cases where the minor may, under state law, consent to healthcare services without an adult's permission (for example, for prenatal care, treatment of STDs, or mental health or substance abuse treatment), the parent or legal guardian is not considered the minor's personal representative. (45 C.F.R. § 164.502(g)). HIPAA also permits covered entities to withhold PHI from a parent or legal guardian in domestic violence cases. (*Id.*).
17. 45 C.F.R. § 164.502(a). An "individual" is the living or deceased individual who is the subject of any given protected health information ("PHI"). PHI, in turn, is defined to include information that (i) is created or received by a health care provider, health plan, employer, or clearinghouse; (ii) relates to an individual's past, present, or future condition, provision of healthcare to the individual, or related payment; and (iii) identifies the individual or reasonably could be used to identify the individual. *Id.* at § 160.103.
18. Detailed guidance on drafting research authorizations is available on the NIH website at: https://privacyruleandresearch.nih.gov/authorization.asp.
19. 45 C.F.R. § 164.520.
20. 45 C.F.R. § 164.524.
21. 45 C.F.R. § 164.520(a); *id.* at 164.530(j).
22. 45 C.F.R. § 164.526.
23. 45 C.F.R. § 164.528. The accounting requirement can be onerous, and requires patient-specific disclosure tracking, unless 50 or more subjects are involved in the study. *Id.* at 164.528(b)(4).
24. 45 C.F.R. § 164.501. See subsection C(2) below for a discussion of activities that include a research component but are primarily intended for quality assessment and improvement purposes.
25. 45 C.F.R. §§ 164.510 and 164.512.
26. 45 C.F.R. § 164.512(i)(1)(i).
27. 45 C.F.R. § 164.512(i)(1)(ii).
28. U.S. Dep't of Health and Human Services, "Can the preparatory research provision of the HIPAA Privacy Rule at 45 CFR 164.512(i)(1)(ii) be used to recruit individuals into a research study?," last modified March 14, 2006, https://www.hhs.gov/hipaa/for-professionals/faq/317/can-the-prepatory-research-provision-be-used-to-recruit-individuals-to-a-research-study/index.html.
29. 45 C.F.R. § 164.512(i)(1)(iii).
30. 45 C.F.R. § 164.514(b)(1).
31. 78 Fed. Reg. 17, 5609, Modifications to the HIPAA Privacy, Security, Enforcement, and Breach Notification Rules

Under the Health Information Technology for Economic and Clinical Health Act and the Genetic Information Nondiscrimination Act; Other Modifications to the HIPAA Rules; Final Rule, (Jan. 25, 2013).
32. Ibid.
33. 45 C.F.R. § 164.514(e).
34. See, *e.g.*, 67 Fed. Reg. 53181, 53234-38 (Aug. 14, 2002).
35. 45 C.F.R. Parts 160 and 164.
36. 45 C.F.R. § 164.502(b).
37. 45 C.F.R. Parts 160 and 164.
38. U.S. Dep't of Health and Human Services, "Is a business associate contract required for a covered entity to disclose protected health information to a researcher?," accessed November 15, 2018, https://www.hhs.gov/hipaa/for-professionals/faq/239/is-a-business-associate-contract-required-for-a-covered-entity-to-information-to-a-researcher/index.html.
39. 45 C.F.R. § 46.102(f).
40. 45 C.F.R. § 46.111(a)(7); 21 C.F.R. §21.44.
41. National Science Foundation, "Frequently Asked Questions and Vignettes: What's the difference between privacy and confidentiality?", accessed November 15, 2018, http://www.nsf.gov/bfa/dias/policy/hsfaqs.jsp#difference. *See also*, Robin Levin Penslar, *Protecting Human Research Subjects: Institutional Review Board Guidebook*, Ch. 4, Pt. E (1993), https://www.hhs.gov/ohrp/education-and-outreach/archived-materials/index.html.
42. 45 C.F.R. § 46.116(a)(5); 21 C.F.R. § 50.25(a)(5).
43. Robin Levin Penslar, *Protecting Human Research Subjects: Institutional Review Board Guidebook*, Ch. 4, Pt. E (1993), https://www.hhs.gov/ohrp/education-and-outreach/archived-materials/index.html.
44. Detailed information on certificates of confidentiality and the application and approval process are available on the NIH website at http://grants.nih.gov/grants/policy/coc/; *see also* Joan E. Sieber, *Summary of Human Subjects Protection Issues Related to Large Sample Surveys*, at pp. 21-22, U.S. Dep't of Justice, Bureau of Justice Stats. (Jun. 2001), available at http://www.ojp.gov/bjs/pub/pdf/shspirls.pdf.
45. See U.S. Dep't of Health and Human Services, National Institutes of Health, Final NIH Statement On Sharing Research Data (February 26, 2003), https://grants.nih.gov/grants/guide/notice-files/NOT-OD-03-032.html. See also, Director of the Office of Science and Technology Policy, Memorandum For The Heads Of Executive Departments And Agencies (the "Holdren Memorandum") (February 22, 2013), https://obamawhitehouse.archives.gov/sites/default/files/microsites/ostp/scientific-integrity-memo-12172010.pdf.
46. 46 C.F.R. § 46.116(b)(9).
47. U.S. Dep't of Health and Human Services, Office for Human Research Protections, "Coded Private Information or Specimens Use in Research, Guidance" (2008) last modified October 5, 2018,https://www.hhs.gov/ohrp/regulations-and-policy/guidance/research-involving-coded-private-information/index.html; Dep't of Health and Human Services, Office for Human Research Protections, "Engagement of Institutions in Human Subjects Research" (2008) last modified March 7, 2016, https://www.hhs.gov/ohrp/regulations-and-policy/guidance/guidance-on-engagement-of-institutions/index.html.
48. For a detailed analysis of the interaction among these regulations, *see* Erin D. Williams, *Federal Protection for Human Subjects: An Analysis of the Common Rule and Its Interactions with FDA Regulations and the HIPAA Privacy Rule*, Congressional Research Service Report for Congress Order Code RL32909 (Jun. 2, 2005), last modified June 13, 2018, http://www.fas.org/sgp/crs/misc/RL32909.pdf; *see also* Dep't of Health and Human Services,OCR HIPAA Privacy,"Research," (December 3, 2002), last modified June 13, 2018, https://www.hhs.gov/hipaa/for-professionals/special-topics/research/index.html.
49. 45 C.F.R. § 46.116-46.117 (Common Rule); 21 C.F.R. pt. 50, subpt. B (FDA regulations); 45 C.F.R. § 164.502(a)(1)(iv) (HIPAA).
50. U.S. Food and Drug Administration, "Guidance for Industry: IRB Review of Stand-Alone HIPAA Authorizations Under FDA Regulations." (October 21, 2003), https://www.fda.gov/downloads/RegulatoryInformation/Guidances/UCM126952.pdf.
51. 68 Fed. Reg. 63110 (Nov. 7, 2003); "Institutional Review Boards and the HIPAA Privacy Rule,"revised July7, 2003, https://privacyruleandresearch.nih.gov/irbandprivacyrule.asp.
52. 45 C.F.R. § 164.508(c)(3); see also U.S. Dep't of health and Human Services, Health Information Privacy "HIPAA Frequent Questions: Do the HIPAA Rule's Requirements for Authorization and the Common Rule's Requirements for Informed Consent Differ?," (December 20, 2002), last modified July 26, 2006, https://www.hhs.gov/hipaa/for-professionals/faq/313/does-the-hipaa-requirement-for-authorization-differ-from-the-common-rule/index.html.
53. 45 C.F.R. § 46.102(d); 45 C.F.R. § 164.501.
54. 45 C.F.R. § 164.512(i)(1)(i)(A).
55. 45 C.F.R. § 164.512(i)(1)(i)(B).
56. 45 C.F.R. § 46.114; *see also* U.S. Dep't of Health and Human Services, Office for Human Research Protections, "Assurance Process Frequently Asked Questions(FAQs): Who is covered by a Federalwide Assurance (FWA)?," last reviewed February 19, 2016, https://www.hhs.gov/ohrp/register-irbs-and-obtain-fwas/fwas/assurance-process-faq/index.html.
57. U.S. Dep't of Health and Human Services, Office for Human Research Protections, "Engagement of Institutions in Human Subjects Research" (2008), https://www.hhs.gov/ohrp/regulations-and-policy/guidance/guidance-on-engagement-of-institutions/index.html.
58. *See, e.g.*, U.S. Dep't of Health and Human Services, Office for Human Research Protections, *Guidance on Research Involving Coded Private Information or Biological Specimens* (Aug. 10, 2004), available at http://www.hhs.gov/ohrp/humansubjects/guidance/cdebiol.htm; *see also*, U.S. Dep't of Health and Human Services, Office for Human Research Protections, *DRAFTOHRP Guidance of Engagement of Institutions in Human Subjects Research* (Dec. 8, 2006), available at http://www.hhs.gov/ohrp/requests/com120806.html.
59. 45 C.F.R. § 46.101(b)(4).
60. 45 C.F.R. § 46.116(a)(1); 21 C.F.R. § 50.25(a)(1).
61. Nat'l Cancer Inst. Cancer Diagnosis Program, *Legal and Ethical Issues: Informed Consent*, http://www.cancerdiagnosis.nci.nih.gov/specimens/legal.htm#3b; *see also* National Action Plan on Breast Cancer, National Biological Resource Banks Working Group, *Sunset Report* (Jul. 1998), http://www.4woman.gov/napbc/catalog.wci/napbc/sunset2.htm; *see also*, Nat'l Action Plan on Breast Cancer, *Consent Form for Use of Tissue for Research* (May 1997), http://www.4woman.gov/napbc/catalog.wci/napbc/consent.htm; *see also*, Nat'l Action Plan on Breast Cancer, *How is Tissue Used for Research* (May 1997), http://www.4woman.gov/napbc/catalog.wci/napbc/q&a.htm.
62. U.S. Dep't of Health and Human Services, National Institute of Health, "Research Repositories, Databases, and the HIPAA Privacy Rule," https://privacyruleandresearch.nih.gov/research_repositories.asp (explaining that collecting and

63. See, Anick Desjanun, "Hacker Teams Breach Powerful Research Networks," *USA Today,* April 14, 2004; see also, Tim Gray, "Another University Suffers Security Breach," *eSecurity Planet,* March 30, 2005, https://www.esecurity-planet.com/trends/article.php/3493721/Another-University-Suffers-Security-Breach.htm; *see also,* "Data Breaches," *Privacy Rights Clearinghouse,* http://www.privacyrights.org/ar/ChronDataBreaches.htm#CP.
64. L. Joseph Melton, III, "The Threat to Medical-Records Research," *New England Journal of Medicine* 337 (Nov. 13, 1997):1466-1470; see also, Steven H. Woolf, et al., "Selection Bias from Requiring Patients to Give Consent to Examine Data for Health Services Research," *Archives of Family Medicine* 9 (Nov. 2000):1111-1118.
65. 42 C.F.R. pts. 2 and 2a.
66. For information about these acts, see the U.S. Dep't of Education website, "Family Educational Rights and Privacy Act (FERPA)," (last modified March 1, 2018), https://www2.ed.gov/policy/gen/guid/fpco/ferpa/index.html?src=rn; also see "Protection of Public Rights Amendment (PPRA)," (last modified February 17, 2005), https://www2.ed.gov/policy//gen/guid/fpco/ppra/index.html.
67. 5 U.S.C. § 552a; "The Privacy Act of 1974," Electronic Privacy Information Center, https://epic.org/privacy/1974act/.
68. "Social Security Numbers," Electronic Privacy Information Center, , https://epic.org/privacy/ssn/.
69. U.S. Government Accountability Office, *Social Security Numbers: Use is Widespread and Protections Vary,* GAO-04-768T (Washington, DC, 2004), http://www.gao.gov./new.items/d04768t.pdf; *see also,* "Social Security Numbers," Electronic Privacy Information Center, https://www.epic.org/privacy.ssn.
70. The National Conference of State Legislatures maintains a list of state "Age of Majority" laws, available at http://www.ncsl.org/research/human-services/termination-of-child-support-age-of-majority.aspx.
71. 45 C.F.R. § 164.502(g)(3).
72. "Security Breach Notification Laws," National Conference of State Legislators, http://www.ncsl.org/research/telecommu-nications-and-information-technology/security-breach-notification-laws.aspx.
73. 21 U.S.C. ch. 9.
74. 21 C.F.R. pt. 1.1.
75. U.S. Food and Drug Administration, "Guidance for Industry: Part 11, Electronic Records; Electronic Signatures—Scope and Application," (August 2003), last modified July 12, 2018, https://www.fda.gov/RegulatoryInformation/Guidances/ucm125067.htm.
76. 21 C.F.R. § 11.3(6).
77. 21 C.F.R. § 11.1(b).
78. 21 C.F.R. § 11.3(a)(4).
79. 21 C.F.R. § 11.10.
80. 21 C.F.R. § 11.10(a).
81. 21 C.F.R. § 11.10(a).
82. 21 C.F.R. § 11(b).
83. 21 C.F.R. § 11(b).
84. 21 C.F.R. § 11.10(d).
85. 21 C.F.R. 11.10(g).
86. 21 C.F.R. 11.10(e).
87. 21 C.F.R. § 11.10(g).
88. 21 C.F.R. § 11.10(j).
89. 21 C.F.R. § 11.10(j).
90. 21 C.F.R. 11.10(k).
91. 21 C.F.R. § 11.30.
92. 21 C.F.R. § 11.50(a)(1)-(2).
93. 21 C.F.R. § 11.50(a)(3).
94. 21 C.F.R. § 11.70.
95. 21 C.F.R. § 11.100(a).
96. 21 C.F.R. § 11.70.
97. 21 C.F.R. § 11.100(b).
98. 21 C.F.R. § 11.100(c).
99. 21 C.F.R. § 11.100(c)(1).
100. 21 C.F.R. § 11.200(a)(1).
101. 21 C.F.R. § 11.200(b).
102. 21 C.F.R. § 11.10.
103. Pub. Law 106-229 (Jun. 30, 2000).
104. "Electronic Transactions Act," Uniform Law Commission, http://www.uniformlaws.org/Act.aspx?title=Electronic%20Transactions%20Act.
105. 15 U.S.C. § 7006(5).
106. 15 U.S.C. § 7001 (a).
107. 15 U.S.C. § 7001 (c); *see also,* U.S. Federal Trade Commission, "Report to Congress On The Electronic Signatures In Global And National Commerce Act: The Consumer Consent Provision in Section 101(c)(1)(C)(ii)," https://www.ftc.gov/reports/report-congress-electronic-signatures-global-national-commerce-act-consumer-consent.
108. 45 C.F.R. pt. 164, subpt. C.
109. 45 C.F.R. §164.304.
110. 45 C.F.R. §164.308.
111. 45 C.F.R. §164.304.
112. *Id.*
113. P.L. 107-347 (Dec. 17, 2002). *See also* U.S. Dep't of Commerce, National Institute of Standards and Technology, Computer Security Resource Center, "Federal Information Security Management Act (FISMA) Implementation Project Overview," last modified November 16, 2018, https://csrc.nist.gov/projects/risk-management.
114. P.L. 107-347, § 3541(1).
115. U.S. Dep't of Health and Human Services, National Institutes of Health, "Notice Regarding the Applicability of the Federal Information Security Management Act to NIH Grantees," (January 9, 2008), http://grants.nih.gov/grants/guide/notice-files/NOT-OD-08-032.html.
116. U.S. Department of Veterans Affairs, Veterans Health Administration, VHA Handbook 1200.12, "Use of Data and Data Repositories in VHA Research" (March 9, 2009).

9
Research Records Management

By Carole A. Klove, RN, JD, with assistance from Heather Kopeck, CHRC[1]

Introduction

Records management presents an ongoing challenge for all healthcare entities; however, it is especially complex and challenging for clinical research due to the existence of two separate sets of records—the legal medical record and the research record. Each record set has a set of regulatory requirements that govern the management of documents included in the record. Navigating those myriad requirements requires a systematic approach.

General Overview

The records generated in conjunction with clinical research must serve several purposes, so it is understandable that their management is governed by multiple external organizations with specific standards and/or rules and regulations. The research study record includes documentation prepared by the principle investigator and contains study notes, informed consent forms, Health Insurance Portability and Accountability Act (HIPAA) authorization forms, offsite lab results, as well as other outside records. A legal medical record must also be maintained for each patient as per federal regulatory and state licensing requirements and should contain clinical data (both inpatient and outpatient), as well as consent forms and the specific entity admission terms and conditions.

The primary guidance for creating a compliance-based records retention system is based upon the Food and Drug Administration's (FDA) good clinical practices (GCPs),[2] which provides resources within the FDA for the review of issues surrounding clinical research trials. In addition, the following list (which is not exhaustive) includes standards, laws, and other types of regulations that must be considered when establishing a sound records retention system:

- HIPAA privacy and security regulations;
- General Data Protection Regulation (EU GDPR);[3]
- Joint Commission accreditation requirements;
- Association for the Accreditation of Human Research Participation Programs (AAHRPP) accreditation requirements;
- Federal rules in the Code of Federal Regulations (CFR);
- U.S. Food & Drug Administration (FDA) guidelines; and
- Individual state laws and regulations governing medical record confidentiality and privacy.

While development of the research record is essential from a regulatory and GCP perspective, ensuring that the subject/participant is aware of the record and its contents is very important and a right of the participant. That right is included in the subject's bill of rights and includes the following elements:

- HIPAA authorization
- Definition of the patient safety considerations for including and excluding information in the chart
- Documentation expected to be found in the medical record

- Records excluded from the medical record and found only in the research record
- Review of the study, possible risks and benefits, alternatives, participation and care, personal and financial concerns, ability to withdraw, and confidentiality

The following chapter outlines the basic structure for the establishment of a compliance-based research records retention system.

What is the Role of the Investigator in Record Management?

The primary role of the investigator is to ensure the safety of the patient; however, the investigator provides administrative, as well as scientific, leadership to the research team. An essential role of the investigator in research includes instituting appropriate processes to maintain research records that comprehensively document the progress of the study. Record keeping requirements should be formalized and incorporated into the institution's policies and procedures. In addition, the Institutional Review Board (IRB) approval letter for the specific study should include the specifications of what must be included in the research record, such as the informed consent form, HIPAA authorization, etc. In addition, if the IRB approval letter does not specifically state that certain records relating to the patient should be excluded from the patient's medical record, then all records should be maintained and included in the medical record.

The investigator must maintain documentation of, and comply with:

- Procedures as described in the protocol,
- Decisions of the IRB,
- GCP guidelines,
- Institutional policies and procedures, and
- Other standard operating procedures and/or other applicable regulations, including registration of the study as applicable in ClinicalTrials.gov.[4]

To document the safety of the participant in the study, the investigator must document any deviations from the protocol and/or the approval process. Should there be deviations from the protocol without prior IRB approval, the investigator must document that the deviations support the elimination of immediate danger to the subject and the reason there was not enough time to obtain the appropriate approvals. Documentation occurring after approval of the study must follow the requirements imposed by federal regulations and the institution permitting the study. The written consent form should be revised whenever important new information becomes available that may be relevant to the subject's consent.[5] If the new information might impact a study participant's willingness to participate, the information must be communicated to the participants and the IRB. These changes, along with new consent forms should be documented in the research record.

Investigational new drug (IND) and investigational device exemption (IDE) protocols require additional reporting to FDA for problems that are serious, unexpected, and possibly related to the experimental treatment. Records should be maintained for the notification by the investigator to the sponsor of the serious adverse event. Adverse events are those that result in death, life threatening experience, hospitalization or prolonging of hospitalization, significant disability, or a birth defect. Investigators must file a serious adverse event report with the sponsor and the IRB, which will initiate a report to the FDA. IND sponsors must notify FDA and the National Institute of Allergy and Infectious Diseases (NIAID) within 24 hours of such events. In some circumstances the investigator must also file an adverse event report.

FDA-regulated studies require the investigator to maintain records that document disposition of an investigational drug. Section 21 of the

Code of Federal Regulations (CFR) 312.62 states that the record should include dates, quantity used, and use by human subjects. If the investigation is terminated, suspended, discontinued, or completed, the investigator shall return the unused supplies of the drug to the sponsor, or they must be destroyed. Federal regulations require investigators maintain these records for a period of two years following the date a marketing application is approved for investigation of an indicated use of the drug; or, if no application is to be filed or if the application is not approved for such indication, until two years after the investigation is discontinued and FDA is notified.[6]

Components of the Research Study Record

There is always a question of who decides what needs to be included in the research and medical records. For most research institutions, the possible decision makers may include, but may not be limited to:

1. IRB. The IRB bases its ability to determine the content of the research study record versus the medical record on the Criteria for IRB approval of research as detailed in the CFRs: "When appropriate, there are adequate provisions to protect the privacy of subjects and to maintaining the confidentiality of the data"[7]

2. Health System Governing Body. For health systems that have been or want to be accredited by outside organizations such as the Joint Commission, certain accreditation standards specify the content of the medical record.

What records are typically needed?

Every human subject protocol needs a research record, a medical record, and a billing record (intended for the grant or payer) that documents each encounter and/or visit. FDA-regulated studies require investigators to maintain "case histories."[8] An investigator is required to prepare and maintain adequate and accurate case histories that record all observations and other data pertinent to the investigation on each individual administered the investigational drug or employed as a control in the investigation. Case histories comprise the case report forms and supporting data including, but not limited to, signed and dated consent forms and medical records, *e.g.*, progress notes of the physician, the individual's hospital chart(s), and nurses' notes. The case history for each individual shall document that the informed consent was obtained prior to participation in the study. For an IND, the regulations require that the case history be maintained for a period of two years following the approval date of a marketing application for the drug's indicated use that is being investigated.

The essential elements of a research study record include, at a minimum, the following documents:

- Comprehensive agreement between the sponsor and investigator that clearly outlines the roles and responsibilities of both the sponsor and investigator during the life of the research study. This should include such elements as formal reporting requirements, publication agreements, etc.
- Investigator brochure developed and provided to the investigator by the sponsor prior to the initiation of the study. The brochure should be the most recent version (all obsolete versions should be removed) and should include relevant and current scientific information about each of the investigational drugs or devices that have been provided to the investigator.
- Signed protocol and amendments, if any, and a sample case report form (CRF).
- Information given to the trial subject to provide a potential subject with sufficient data to make an informed decision regarding his or her participation in the study. The main categories of information include:

- Informed consent: This form documents that consent was obtained in accordance with regulations, GCP, and the specific protocol. The informed consent form should be dated prior to the initial participation date for each participant in a clinical trial. Non-English-speaking patients must receive information and give consent in a language they can understand, and the written translations should be maintained.
- Recruitment information and advertisements: Inclusion of the recruitment and advertising information in the legal record documents that study participants were given the appropriate written information supporting their ability to give fully informed consent. It also demonstrates that the recruitment measures were designed appropriately and were not coercive. Recruitment information and advertisements should include advertisements for participant recruitment, educational materials specific to the protocol, and any other recruitment information provided to potential participants.
- Any other information provided to the subject to assist in the decision making process.

■ Financial aspects of the trial, including the approved budget, should be included in the record to provide a framework for understanding the scope and complexity of the study and potential impact of decision-making as related to budgetary concerns.
■ Insurance coverage analysis and potential study-related injuries are important elements for study participants to understand and agree to prior to the initiation of the study. Written documentation in the record should include a description of routine costs that will be billed to a participant's insurance and the research-related costs covered by the study. This information must include a clearly defined intention of when the participant's insurance will be billed (and whether the participant will be responsible for payment of co-payments and deductible(s)), and finally, who will be responsible for the healthcare costs related to injuries suffered as a result of the study. A signed agreement by participants to these terms must also be included.
■ Dated documentation of IRB approval should be obtained prior to the beginning of a trial. Typically, the IRB will review the study's written informed consent form and any other written information that will be provided to subjects, including:
- Protocol and amendments, as applicable
- CRF (if applicable)
- Recruitment documentation
- Informed consent forms including HIPAA documentation

In addition to the above, the following list of required documentation elements should also be included:

■ Compensation to the subject (if any)
■ Curriculum vitaes/résumés of the investigator and any sub-investigators
■ Normal ranges for any clinical laboratory studies or other diagnostic tests used in the protocol
■ Documentation to support the testing facilities and/or the procedures or tests that have been done
■ Documentation outlining the handling instructions of clinical trial-related material(s) and shipping instructions
■ Decoding procedures for blinded studies
■ Pre-trial and trial monitoring reports
■ Other documentation related to the study, such as:
- Documents sent to other committees (*e.g.*, a radiation use committee)
- Communications for IRB clarification memos, as required by the IRB
- Documents related to the type of study or trial (*e.g.*, observational study, HIV studies)

Medical Records for Research Studies

Why should certain research documents exist in the medical record? The advantages for combining the information include patient safety, facilitation of billing compliance, accurate accounting for the cost allocations associated with research activities at your institution, and HIPAA regulatory considerations. HIPAA regulates the use and disclosure of patient data created, received, or maintained by covered entities. The privacy rule requires a covered entity to obtain written patient authorization to use or disclose an individual's protected health information (PHI). HIPAA regulations include five exemptions to its written authorization requirements relevant to research activities:

- Waiver of patient authorization by the IRB
- Review of PHI preparatory to research
- Research on decedents
- De-identified data sets
- Limited data sets, which require a researcher to sign a data use agreement

As discussed in the "Research Privacy and Security: Myths, Facts and Practical Approaches," chapter 8 of this book, the FDA has issued guidance "intended to encourage IRBs to permit the enrollment of subjects in clinical investigations without prior IRB review and/or approval of stand alone HIPAA authorizations, since such review and/or approval is not required by the HIPAA Privacy Rule."[9] Research records generally must be maintained for three years; however, PHI (including the authorization or waiver to use or disclose PHI for research) must be maintained for at least six years. In addition, it is important to consider the placement of clinical laboratory and radiology procedure documentation in the record. The primary rationale for that inclusion is the relevance of the diagnostic data to the total patient care delivered by providers outside of the research team. However, this data inclusion will document the provision of quality patient care and improve communications to help "tell the story" about the patient.

Special Considerations for Certain Types of Studies

Certain types of studies require special consideration when reviewing the composition of the research record. An example of such a record is an epidemiologic study that may include questionnaires and sensitive information; those that link data from many sources such as insurance, employment, medical records, etc.; those that involve privacy and confidentiality concerns that support obtaining IRB approval; those that require review for ethical considerations by an epidemiologist or the Office for Human Research Protections; and those that need assurance that information will be protected and disclosure will not compromise a subject's right of privacy.

What other studies would give rise to confidentiality of the information? Sensitive studies can include those that evaluate the use of alcohol, drugs, or other illicit products; or those involving mental health, genetic testing, and other sensitive issues that typically include certificates of confidentiality. Blinded drug studies that require patient aliases as a basis of participation are also included.

Research Misconduct in Record Management

Research misconduct is defined in part as "fabrication, falsification, or plagiarism" in performing, reviewing, or reporting research results.[10] The definition includes activities such as making up data, reporting erroneous data, manipulating study results, and/or taking another person's idea, process, or results and reporting them as one's own. Lack of PI oversight could potentially result in research misconduct from erroneous data or reporting. The HHS Office of Research Integrity (ORI) oversees and directs Public Health Service (PHS) research integrity activities on behalf of the HHS secretary, with the exception of the regulatory research integrity activities conducted by the FDA.[11] ORI carries out its responsibilities by:

- Developing policies, procedures, and regulations related to the detection, investigation, and prevention of research misconduct and the responsible conduct of research;
- Reviewing and monitoring research misconduct investigations conducted by applicant and awardee institutions, intramural re-

search programs, and the Office of Inspector General (OIG) in the HHS;
- Recommending research misconduct findings and administrative actions to the Assistant Secretary for Health at HHS for decision, subject to appeal;
- Assisting the Office of the General Counsel (OGC) to present cases before the HHS Departmental Appeals Board;
- Providing technical assistance to institutions that respond to allegations of research misconduct;
- Implementing activities and programs to teach the responsible conduct of research, promote research integrity, prevent research misconduct, and improve the handling of allegations of research misconduct;
- Conducting policy analyses, evaluations, and research to build the knowledge base in research misconduct, research integrity, and prevention; and to improve HHS research integrity policies and procedures;
- Administering programs for maintaining institutional assurances, responding to allegations of retaliation against whistleblowers, approving intramural and extramural policies and procedures, and responding to Freedom of Information Act and Privacy Act requests.

One noted study, which reviewed closed ORI cases of research misconduct, documented how the failure of a mentor, or the person the institution identified as being in an advisory role, was a major contributing factor to research misconduct among trainees. The authors noted that "when the mentor did not review the source documentation, there was a tendency for the mentor to have lax supervisor standards for conducting research—particularly standards for recording and reporting data."[12] More detail on research misconduct can be found in Chapter 3, "Scientific and Research Misconduct," in this book.

General Rules for the Record

When establishing research records, consider the following when determining the content and retention of the record:

- Inclusion of the following documentation in both the research and medical records:
    - Informed consent
    - HIPAA authorization
    - Test results that are relevant to the care of the patient, even if the tests were part of the research protocol and paid for by the grant
- Confidentiality of the patient
- Patient safety concerns—sensitive matters that should be in the medical record, including:
    - Clearly defined information in the patient locator or other prominent portion of the record that the patient is enrolled in a clinical trial; the investigator's contact information to notify in the event of an emergency or question pertaining to care
    - Processes to ensure confidentiality and safety for patients enrolled in General Clinical Research Center (GCRC) research studies
- Exclusion of certain tests or procedures from the record due to the nature of the study and/or nature of the test:
    - Exclusion might be appropriate for:
        - Test results from a central lab designed for the study, as defined by the sponsor
        - Test results from facilities not authorized to provide clinical services, (*e.g.*, a research lab which is not licensed or credentialed)
    - It is important to know the licensure of the laboratories, especially those associated with General Clinical Research Centers (GCRC) and now Clinical and Translational Science Awards (CTSA) and/or laboratories which are purely research in nature and may have quality

control measures that differ from other types of research laboratories.

Common record management issues include, but may not be limited to the following:

- Failure to report changes to the protocol
- Misuse or lack of informed consent
- Untimely submission of the protocol to the IRB

Conclusion

Research records management is a very complex process that requires standardized approaches to its structure. Today, research sites have the choice of using electronic regulatory systems that enhance the management of regulatory files for studies. Electronic medical records and Clinical Trial Management Systems (CTMS) can also streamline documentation and record keeping efforts, while also assisting in information sharing with stakeholders. This improves collaboration and communication efforts and also makes it easier for researchers to manage the scientific data of a study. Training on all systems within a research participant's record can be complex. The need for stricter privacy and security measures to prevent unintended breaches stretches a study's limited resources. Realize and appreciate the challenges and responsibilities of record management in the research process. They are necessary elements of a research study's operations.

Chapter 9 Endnotes

1. **Carole Klove, RN, JD**, is General Counsel / Chief Nursing Office for Elemeno Health in San Francisco, CA; **Heather Kopeck, CHRC**, is Director of Development Policy and Advancement Relations at University of California Office of the President.
2. U.S. Food and Drug Administration, Clinical Trials and Human Subject Protection (Last Updated December 20, 2018), https://www.fda.gov/ScienceResearch/SpecialTopics/RunningClinicalTrials/.
3. European Commission, 2018 reform of EU data protection rules, https://ec.europa.eu/commission/priorities/justice-and-fundamental-rights/data-protection/2018-reform-eu-data-protection-rules_en.
4. U.S. Dep't of Health and Human Services, National Institutes of Health, U.S. National Library of Medicine, ClinicalTrials.gov, "FDAAA 801 and the Final Rule," (last reviewed November 2018), https://clinicaltrials.gov/ct2/manage-recs/fdaaa.
5. See U.S. Dep't of Health and Human Services, "Guidance for Industry E6 Good Clinical Practices: Consolidated Guidance," (March 2018), https://www.fda.gov/downloads/Drugs/Guidances/UCM464506.pdf.
6. 21 C.F.R. § 312.62 (c).
7. 45 C.F.R. § 46.111(a) (7).
8. 21 C.F.R. 312.62 (b) and (c).
9. U.S. Food and Drug Administration, Office of the Commissioner, "Guidance for Industry: IRB Review of Stand-Alone HIPAA Authorizations Under FDA Regulations," (October 21, 2003), https://www.fda.gov/downloads/RegulatoryInformation/Guidances/UCM126952.pdf.
10. 42 CFR Part 93.
11. U.S. Department of Health and Human Services, Office of Research Integrity (website), https://ori.hhs.gov.
12. David E. Wright, Sandra Titus, Jered B. Cornelison, "Mentoring and Research Misconduct: An analysis of Research Mentoring in Closed Office of Research Integrity Cases," *Science and Engineering Ethics*, 14 (September 2008): 323-336.

10
Data and Safety Monitoring

By Susan Partridge, BSN, MBA, CCRC and L. Steven Brown, MS, CPH[1]

Introduction

Data and safety monitoring of a clinical trial consists of oversight of an ongoing study. This oversight ensures that study participants are protected from unforeseen and potentially avoidable risks, and that the trial produces valid data. The premise for data and safety monitoring is that despite one's best efforts in designing a trial, one can never fully anticipate what happens as a study progresses. During the course of a trial, study populations may respond differently than expected, accrual of subjects may be skewed for unforeseen reasons, unexpected operational or compliance problems could impact outcomes, unanticipated adverse events or new drug toxicities may emerge, and minor adverse events may prove to be more important than one thought. As a result, data and safety monitoring has evolved to become one way that the clinical research enterprise can ensure the quality and safety of the trials they conduct.

This type of monitoring is different from sponsor-directed monitoring; the latter is also conducted in real time, but the purpose of sponsor-directed monitoring is to verify study site performance and compliance with the protocol, sponsor requirements, and good clinical practices. Data and safety monitoring is also distinct from the requirement for study review and approval by an institutional review board (IRB).

Data and safety monitoring takes into consideration what could possibly happen during a trial, not just what is expected to happen. Prior to the start of a study, a plan outlines how accumulating data will be reviewed to focus on the following:

1. study participant safety and protection from risks;
2. trial validity and integrity;
3. ensuring that the study continues to be ethical, scientifically valid, worthwhile, and feasible for the entire study period; and,
4. ensuring that the trial is stopped as soon as reliable conclusions can be drawn from the data.

Another important element of effective data and safety monitoring is the ability to objectively assess the data and make recommendations to continue the trial as designed, modify the trial or terminate the trial. Study sponsors and investigators may have recognized or unrecognized interests in the conduct and results of a trial. Ensuring that data and safety monitoring is performed by individuals who are not only knowledgeable but independent of the vested parties is critical to unbiased decision making.

Data and Safety Monitoring: A Background

Data and safety monitoring and the introduction of data monitoring committees (DMCs) can be traced to the 1960s. It started with the Framingham Heart Study, which began in 1948. Starting in the mid-1950s, the study began releasing its findings about the role of cigarettes, high blood pressure, and elevated cholesterol in the risk of heart disease. Those results led to the development and National Heart Institute (NHI)[2] funding of the Coronary Drug Project, a nine-year trial from 1966-1975. The project was designed to evaluate the long-term efficacy and safety of five lipid-influencing drugs and their impact on the incidence of myocardial infarction (heart attack). To meet statistical requirements, the study methods called for enrollment and long-term follow-up of more than 8,300 subjects, resulting in an operationally challenging study involving 53 study sites. Because trials of this size, complexity, and cost were not typical at the time, there were many questions by study investigators and sponsors about how best to oversee and ensure the participants' safety and the validity of the trial while it was ongoing.

The NIH commissioned an external advisory group to develop a plan for the conduct of these types of trials. Under the leadership of Dr. Herbert Greenberg, the Heart Special Project Committee produced the report in May 1967, titled *Organization, Review, and Administration of Cooperative Studies (Greenberg Report): a Report from the Heart Special Project Committee to the National Advisory Heart Council*. The committee recognized that interim monitoring of study data was essential for ensuring study participants' safety, and that individuals closely involved in the design, sponsorship, or conduct of the trial may not be fully objective in reviewing that data. The report called for establishing an expert panel of advisors who could review the accumulating data in an unbiased manner and make recommendations. *The Greenberg Report* recommended that this group of advisors (which we now call a Data and Safety Monitoring Board or Committee) should be "... a Policy Board or Advisory Committee of senior scientists, experts in the field of study but not data-contributing participants in it, is almost essential for a large complex cooperative project."[3]

The *Greenberg Report* also anticipated that not all studies should be permitted to continue to completion:

> A mechanism must be developed for early termination if unusual circumstances dictate that a cooperative study should not be continued. Such action might be contemplated if the accumulated data answer the original question sooner than anticipated, if it is apparent that the study will not or cannot achieve its stated aims, or if scientific advances since initiation render continuation superfluous. This is obviously a difficult decision that must be based on careful analysis of past progress and future expectation. If the National Heart Institute must initiate such action, it must do so only with the advice and on the recommendation of consultants.[4]

The *Greenberg Report* and Coronary Drug Project contributed significantly to the way in which clinical research is practiced today. In addition to establishing the concept of formal independent data and safety monitoring, the Coronary Drug Project is also notable for establishing a model for the design, organization, standardization, quality control, and monitoring of multicenter trials.

In summary, the *Greenberg Report* defined the forerunner of the current DMC: a body of experts independent of the study that conducts ongoing reviews of the study's data in order to ensure the scientific and operational integrity of the clinical trial. The following ideas, generated by the *Greenberg Report*, became official National Institute Health (NIH) policy by 1979:

1. Every clinical trial should have provision for data and safety monitoring.
2. The mechanism(s) for data and safety monitoring should be presented to and approved by the Institutional Review Board as an integral part of its review of the project proposal. A variety of types of monitoring may be anticipated depending on the nature, size, and complexity of the clinical trial. In many cases, the principal investigator would be expected to perform the monitoring function.
3. Large or multicenter trials and trials in which the protocol requires blinding of the

investigators, should have a data and safety monitoring unit. The unit should consist of clinical experts in the disease under investigation, biostatisticians, and scientists from other pertinent disciplines. Physicians engaged in the care of study patients or directly responsible for evaluating clinical status are excluded.[5]

The NIH standard is closely echoed in the 1998 NIH Policy for Data and Safety Monitoring. It is also reflected in the definitions we see today in the FDA guidance of 2006: "A clinical trial DMC is a group of individuals with pertinent expertise that reviews on a regular basis accumulating data from one or more ongoing clinical trials. The DMC advises the sponsor regarding the continuing safety of trial subjects and those yet to be recruited to the trial, as well as the continuing validity and scientific merit of the trial."[6]

Likewise, the International Conference on Harmonisation of Technical Requirements for Registration of Pharmaceuticals for Human Use (ICH) guidance of 2005 defines a data monitoring committee as: "A group of independent experts external to a study assessing the progress, safety data and, if needed, critical efficacy endpoints of a clinical study. In order to do so a DMC may review unblinded study information (on a patient level or treatment group level) during the conduct of the study. Based on its review, the DMC provides the sponsor with recommendations regarding study modification, continuation or termination."[7]

What Kind of Monitoring is Needed?

In today's environment, it is expected that a clinical trial will have a Data and Safety Monitoring Plan (DSMP) unless there are compelling reasons why there should not be one, such as studies where the interventions carry no or minimal risks or where there is evidence that monitoring would not help protect study participants. In general, clinical trials that require monitoring are those where: 1) the treatments or interventions carry a risk, 2) clinical events are an outcome measure, and/or 3) the trial could generate definitive findings prior to the official end of the trial. Data and safety monitoring in this context is focused on clinical trials, rather than observational studies or those that do not test an intervention.

Although most clinical trials require safety monitoring, not all trials require oversight by a formal committee that is independent from the trial organizers and investigators. The degree of monitoring, as well as the structure and plan for monitoring, are customized to each study based on the risk and complexity associated with that study. Considerations such as the phase of the investigation (Phase 1, 2, or 3 for investigational drugs or biologics), the known side effects of the investigational agent or similar agents, the complexity of the study design, the nature of the disease process, the vulnerability of the study population, and the anticipated outcomes are important factors when determining the type of monitoring plan needed.

For some types of minimal risk studies, effective monitoring may be accomplished by the principal investigator (PI) or an independent safety monitor (ISM), whereas other higher risk, high impact, and complex trials may require a formal data and safety monitoring board (DSMB). To determine which type of monitor is needed, consider the following:

1. **Monitoring by an individual investigator:** This type of monitoring may be appropriate for small studies conducted at a single study site with relatively low-risk interventions. Close, continuous monitoring by the PI with reporting to the IRB and sponsor may be adequate.
2. **Monitoring by an individual or group other than the investigator:** For clinical trials where additional expertise or objec-

tivity is needed to oversee safety or clinical outcomes, an ISM may be appropriate. The ISM is external to the investigator, the trial design, and the conduct of the study. In some cases, the ISM may be associated with the sponsor, depending on potential conflict of interest trial concerns.

3. **Monitoring by a committee or board:** For studies that involve large numbers of study participants, multiple study sites, complex study designs, blinded study groups, interventions that are higher risk, or sophisticated data review or statistical analyses, a DMC may be required. A DMC (also referred to as a DSMB or data and safety monitoring committee (DSMC)) is a group of independent experts—with no tie to the trial investigators, the pharmaceutical sponsor, or the funding agency—that periodically review the progress and data from an ongoing clinical trial, assess the trial's safety and continuing scientific integrity, and make recommendations as to whether the trial should continue as planned, or be modified or stopped.

DSMBs are generally required by NIH for phase III clinical trials and may be recommended for certain other studies (phase I and II) if the research involves high risk interventions, significant outcomes or vulnerable populations. The following chart developed by NIH provides a general guide for determining when a DSMB is required.

Many institutions and IRBs have specific criteria and requirements for data and safety monitoring. Some study sponsors, particularly federal granting agencies, also have specific requirements for monitoring as outlined in the *NIH Policy for Data and Safety Monitoring*[8] and the NIH National Cancer Institute (NCI) guidance, *Essential Elements of a Data and Safety Monitoring Plan for Clinical Trials Funded by the National Cancer Institute.*[9]

The degree and elements for monitoring are determined prior to the start of a clinical trial and are summarized in a DSMP. Typically, this plan is part of the initial IRB submission process.

The Data and Safety Monitoring Plan (DSMP)

A DSMP describes who, what, where, when, and why of how the trial data will be monitored, assessed, and reported. Examples of data monitoring include ongoing assessment of recruitment, patient eligibility, follow up, completion and drop-out rates, accessing unbalanced randomization, study resource management, critical patient characteristics or demographics, and endpoints. Examples of safety monitoring include tracking, tabulation, and interpretation of adverse events and plans for communication of safety data to the IRB, sponsor, FDA, and others.

The elements of a data and safety monitoring plan include the following:

1. Delineation of oversight responsibilities (*e.g.*, Who will monitor the trial? What is the person's expertise? What is the person's relationship to the research?)
2. Specific data and events that need to be monitored to follow study protocol compliance
3. The frequency of monitoring (*e.g.*, after a specified number of subjects have received a dose of an investigational drug or after a specified level of enrollment has been achieved)
4. A plan for reporting data and events to the monitoring entity, which should include data audits and data management strategies
5. A description of the planned analyses and interpretation of the data
6. A description of specific study events that would trigger halting or modifying a trial (*e.g.*, stopping rules or lack of data quality)
7. The type and frequency of communications to various groups, including investigators, the sponsor, the IRB, and applicable regulatory agencies

8. The appropriate resources available in the study, which include study personnel, equipment, and study supplies

The DSMP should consider the oversight role of the study sponsor and how the independent monitoring group will communicate information to the sponsor. The plan should also consider the activities and responsibilities of other oversight committees, such as those seen with cooperative group trials.

The DSMP elements listed here are conceptually the same regardless of whether monitoring will be accomplished by the PI, ISM, or DMC. In the following section, greater attention is given to DMCs to better characterize their structure, function, and operating processes.

Data Monitoring Committees

Membership

The DMC should be composed of individuals with sufficient expertise and experience to evaluate data from the clinical trial. The DMC is typically a multidisciplinary committee of representatives from a specific medical or clinical area, biostatistics, epidemiology, data management, laboratory, clinical trials, and/or bioethics. Here are examples of skills that committee members should have:

- **Clinical expertise in the disease being treated**, including knowledge of its natural history, patient population treatment options, and common adverse events: For example, in a trial for Alzheimer's disease, a practicing neurologist with a focus in Alzheimer's should be chosen, as opposed to a neurologist who specializes in movement disorders.
- **Scientific expertise in the test article** (drug, biologic, device, or intervention): For example, if the test article is a new vaccine for children, a vaccinologist or infectious disease specialist who understands vaccine safety and immune responses would be preferred over a pediatrician without that specific experience.
- **Safety expertise with knowledge of specific safety issues and analyses**: Toxicologists or clinical pharmacologists could be included if their laboratory expertise is relevant.
- **Regulatory expertise**: The committee should include expertise in how the DMC operates and any regulatory requirements that should be considered.
- **Clinical trial expertise**, including familiarity with how operational and design aspects of clinical trials can affect data quality, scientific integrity, and study resources
- **Statistical expertise**, including familiarity with statistical tests used to evaluate clinical trial events, stopping rules, and decision making
- **Expertise of ethicists and patient advocates** may be needed depending on the study population, the potential political sensitivity of the trial, the novelty of the compound, or the complexity of the protocol
- **Data management expertise**, including data storage and transfer of data information, security and confidentiality of data, and data management strategies.[10]

Typically, a DMC has three to five voting members, but there is no required number. The final composition will depend on the study and the type of expertise needed. The experience of the members on a DMC should be considered during the selection process. This ensures that at least some of the DMC members have previously served on a DMC. What is most important is that the combined skill set of DMC members exhibits expertise in all relevant areas of the study, particularly those areas related to risk.

Independence and Confidentiality

A key element in the selection of DMC voting members is independence from the clinical trial. No member of the DMC can play other roles in the clinical trial. For example, investigators, executive committee members, and steering committee members would be ineligible to serve on the DMC. A general rule to follow is that if someone is a consultant to a program, serves on a trial committee, or is an investigator, that person cannot serve on the DMC unless they forego the other position within the trial. Likewise, a consultant or investigator on a different trial of the same compound would be prohibited from serving on the DMC (*e.g.*, if an anti-infective is being tested in one trial for skin infections and another for bronchitis). This general rule is not applicable to the study statistician or someone who presents data reports to the DMC, because that person is often involved in the randomization and integrity of the data. Individuals who serve on the DMC should be free of apparent significant conflicts of interest, whether they are financial, intellectual, professional, or regulatory in nature. For example, anyone with a significant financial interest in the outcome of a study, either positive or negative, should not serve on the DMC. Other types of non-financial conflicts may be harder to define and measure. Many of the individuals qualified to serve on a DMC may have other research activities, some of which may have the appearance of a conflict of interest. These may be scientific (*e.g.*, they are working on the same problem) or academic advancement (desire publication out of the activity). Perhaps the most common conflict is that members are often too busy and cannot give the program the time it deserves.

Management of conflict of interest must be specifically and repeatedly addressed by the DMC during the course of a trial. Typically, an initial disclosure of potential conflicts is submitted by each committee member. If a potential conflict is considered to be too significant, members may recuse themselves from the DMC or divest themselves of that interest. Because trials often continue for more than a year and because DMC members have unique expertise in their field, it is not uncommon for new conflicts to arise. The DMC should be alert to finding these perceived or actual conflicts and move quickly to manage them.

In addition to addressing externality and conflicts of interest, a DMC places high value on confidentiality. All members of the DMC need to be familiar with the strict confidentiality requirements surrounding this activity. This is not the "informal confidentiality" that often accompanies academic discussions; there are potentially serious repercussions from a breach. Even the mention of unblinded study information to a professional colleague unconnected with the study is not permitted. A breach of confidentiality could potentially find its way back to investigators or others directly involved with the trial. This would ultimately lead to the perceived introduction of bias and could invalidate the trial results.

A breach of confidentiality may have other, non-scientific negative effects. For instance, non-confidential disclosure of unblinded trial information could be used to inform financial decision-making. Use of confidential information may be considered "inside information" and could subject those involved to criminal penalties.

The DMC should have a chairperson who makes sure the DMC conducts a thorough review and that their discussions and conclusions are accurately documented. It is highly recommended that the DMC chair has previous experience as a member of a DMC and is aware of the regulatory responsibilities for ensuring safety of clinical trial subjects. It's also important that the DMC chair exhibits "chairperson skills," such as running an efficient meeting and making sure input is gathered from all members prior to making decisions according to the committee's responsibilities.

Each DMC member should sign an agreement describing their obligations, confidentiality requirements, and remuneration, as well as a conflict of interest disclosure. In addition, the agreement should explain that the DMC may include non-voting members, such as medical and scientific experts, administrators, or other liaisons. These individuals may contribute to the committee during certain open discussions as long as they agree to the same terms for confidentiality and independence.

DMC Charter

The first task of the DMC is to develop a charter documenting the committee's purpose, responsibilities, study description, operational principles, and procedures. The charter provides information for the sponsor and regulatory agencies to inform them of the activities of the DMC. A charter documents that procedures are pre-specified and operations will not be inappropriately influenced by interim data, which could bias the committee's interpretation of the study's results. The charter should include statements regarding the elements of independence, as well as a process for continuing review of potential conflicts of interest.

The committee charter should also be explicit about how the DMC will function. For instance, it needs to define the various roles and responsibilities of those involved in the clinical trial, not just the DMC members. Include the responsibilities of the sponsor, other committees (*e.g.*, steering committee), and other participants (*e.g.*, data center or labs), as well as how they will interact with the DMC.

With regard to data, the charter should specify how and when the data will be delivered to the DMC. Varied sources of data may contribute to the analyses, including demographics, adverse events, diagnostic laboratory values, ECGs, radiological images, regulatory reports, or other measures of importance. On-time data delivery, quality control, and archiving procedures are critical to the data analysis function and should be described in the charter.

The charter should also describe the DMC meetings, including their frequency, composition, permitted attendees, voting members, meeting organization and proceedings, venue (in person or electronic), handling of meeting minutes, definition of a quorum, and what happens when a member needs to be replaced. In addition, include a description of what happens during different sessions, such as:

1. Open sessions are where the committee discusses study operations, safety concerns, and other issues that do not involve unblinded data. Data is usually presented in aggregate and the focus is on trial accrual and drop-out rates, patient eligibility rates and reasons for ineligibility, protocol violations, adverse events, study resource management, and the timeliness of data submission. Information from open sessions may be shared with the study sponsor.
2. Closed sessions are where attendance is more restricted, issues surrounding unblinded data are discussed, potential protocol modifications are deliberated, evaluation of relationship between adverse events and intervention, treatment compliance, and the proceedings and results are confidential.[11]

DMC Analysis Plan

In addition to defining the operations of the DMC, a data analysis plan should accompany or be incorporated into the DMC charter. The analysis plan should be prospectively designed prior to the first interim review of the data. The plan may include templates of tables, listings, and figures that can be populated once the data are submitted. These templates are just a starting place and may require modification once experience with the trial data is gained.

Typically, templates show that the data will be reported using study codes (for example Group A and Group B) to maintain blinding of the treatment groups (until the time the DMC agrees to view unblinded data). The unblinded randomization data is supervised by the study statistician and only released in a closed session. The FDA recommends that a DMC have access to the actual treatment assignments for each study group at any given time.[12] However, the guidance acknowledges an alternate viewpoint—that DMCs should only have access to data that allows comparison between study arms, without knowing the treatment assignment. The guidance explains further: "This approach, however, could lead to problems in balancing risks against potential benefits in some cases. For example, to maintain blinding of the actual treatment assignments, safety outcomes would have to be coded differently from effectiveness outcomes when adverse effects would reveal the assigned intervention. This would prevent the DMC from evaluating the balance of risks and benefits of the active interventions, its most critical responsibility."[13] The analysis plan should include a description of the statistical methods that will be used to analyze the trial data. Statistical approaches are addressed in the ICH guidance titled *ICH Topic E 9 Statistical Principles for Clinical Trials*.[14] The most common methods are those used for classical hypothesis testing.

Specify in the plan when interim looks at the data will be performed. These interim looks require carefully considered statistical methods, as outlined in the FDA *Guidance for Clinical Trial Sponsors: Establishment and Operation of Clinical Trial Data Monitoring Committees*: "A major concern when data on group differences are assessed repeatedly as they accumulate is that the Type I error (false positive) rate may be inflated if adjustment is not made for the multiple looks at the data. Typically, the monitoring plan will specify a statistical approach that permits multiple interim reviews while maintaining the Type I error rate at the desired level."[15] As noted above, the DMC's task is to evaluate relative treatment effects based on protocol-specified endpoints to determine if the trial is meeting its objectives. Therefore, the analysis plan should address distinct safety and effectiveness thresholds that the DMC will use to determine continued accrual and conduct of the trial. The process of making the determination could be complex, especially if there is conflicting trial data. For example, interim analysis may show that the effectiveness data is strong, but emerging safety data is of concern. It is also possible that the interim assessment will demonstrate that the trial is unable to demonstrate the efficacy of one of the treatments. Special statistical methods are available to determine whether or not a trial should be stopped for futility—when the likelihood that the treatment effect being sought, based on interim data, is unlikely to be established.

The analysis plan should describe all potential stopping rules. These are automatic actions for stopping or altering a study intervention based on an analysis of the data from a prespecified time point. A statistical difference in previously defined outcomes that exceeds a specific threshold results in cessation of the trial or one of the study treatments. Developing stopping rules at the outset of a trial is not an easy process, given that it is difficult to anticipate all contingencies that could arise during the course of the trial. In addition, there may be extenuating considerations if the investigational treatment is the only therapeutic alternative for a serious medical condition. Some plans use the term "stopping guidelines" because it is less binding and allows for consideration of other factors.

In designing the analysis plan, consider the possibility of demonstrating a clear positive result prior to the end of the planned trial. Determining how long a trial should continue once a positive result is demonstrated is based on the statistical strength of the treatment difference, the length of the trial before the treatment difference was achieved, and the confidence of investigators and the DMS have about the stability of the results.

DMC Communications

Communication to and from the DMC should be planned and documented in advance. The communication plan is important for protecting data and committee proceeding confidentiality s, preserving committee independence, and avoiding premature release of findings. The nature and flow of communication between the DMC and sponsor is of primary interest. It is recommended that for substantive issues, only one DMC member (often the chairman or the chairman's agent) speaks directly with the sponsor or the sponsor's agent (*e.g.*, steering committee). If this is the case, the charter should document that the other DMC members agree to not speak directly with the sponsor about any non-administrative issues.

The communication plan is not limited to only verbal communication. Written communication should be formalized and sent under the supervision of the chairman. The most common elements of written communication are: 1) the letter of recommendation following a DMC meeting, and 2) the minutes of the meeting.

The DMC letter of recommendation describes the committee's decision. If the DMC suggests taking any action, rationale should also be provided (as long as doing so does not unblind the data). The letter should be delivered within a reasonably prompt time after completion of the meeting. This time frame can be specified in the charter. The recipient of the recommendation letter should also be specified. Typically, copies of the recommendation letter are submitted to the IRBs of the participating institutions. Similarly, minutes of the open session are delivered to the sponsor in a timely fashion. The minutes of the closed session, however, are delivered only to the members of the DMC.

The DMC does not typically communicate with anyone except the sponsor representative. If the DMC recommends changes that necessitate communication with an IRB or regulatory agency, the sponsor should initiate the communication.

The DMC generates records, which consist of letters of recommendation, open and closed minutes, and serial interim analyses. In addition, the DMC may request additional clinical information as well as outside expert analysis. The charter should also specify security provisions used to protect confidential data and back-up the data in case of inadvertent destruction, and plans for archiving and transferring these records upon completion of the clinical trial. Also, if confidential records are physically sent to DMC members, documentation of return of those records or record destruction is needed.

Conclusion

All clinical trials require monitoring commensurate with the degree of risk involved in participation, as well as the study's size and complexity. Many different individuals and groups contribute to monitoring, including the PI, sponsor, contract research organization (CRO), steering committees, institution, IRB, and oversight committees. Each plays an important role in ensuring the safety of study participants.

The type of monitoring described in this chapter is functionally distinct from other types of oversight. Data and safety monitoring is based on a planned review and analysis of data that accumulates during a trial's course, using pre-determined data points and intervals to determine continuation, modification, or stopping of the trial. The analyses and resulting recommendations are aimed at protecting the trial participants' safety and ensuring the study results' integrity and validity. The more complex and high-risk the trial, the greater the need to create a credible monitoring plan that is independent from potential interests and biases of trial organizers.

DMCs are the most independent and formal options for data and safety monitoring. Their primary purpose is to examine data for signals that might indicate harm to a certain subject cohort. Another purpose is to review the need for continued enrollment in a clinical trial and the likelihood that the proposed experiment will yield results important enough to balance the study's risks. A DMC may also provide suggestions to the sponsor about trial protocol, and offer views on emerging design issues, data quality, and patient recruitment with respect to ensuring study subjects' safety.

The factors relevant to determining whether or not to establish a DMC are safety, practicality, and scientific validity. The NIH makes DMCs a precondition of funding, but regulatory agencies and IRBs have also been requesting DMCs with increasing frequency. The ICH and FDA guidance give detailed suggestions regarding a DMC's operation and establishment. Important features of the guidance are the requirement for a DMC charter, the appointment of a qualified committee, and the processes that ensure a study's independence and confidentiality.

References

European Medicines Agency, *Committee for Medical Products for Human Use (CHMP), Guideline on Data Monitoring Committees*, July 2005, https://www.ema.europa.eu/documents/scientific-guideline/guideline-data-monitoring-committees_en.pdf.

National Institutes of Health, *Further Guidance on a Data and Safety Monitoring for Phase I and Phase II Trials*, 5 Jun. 2000, https://grants.nih.gov/grants/guide/notice-files/not-od-00-038.html .

National Institutes of Health, *NIH Policy for Data and Safety Monitoring*, June 10, 1998, http://grants.nih.gov/grants/guide/notice-files/not98-084.html.

National Cancer Institute Division of Extramural Activities—Grant Policies and Guidelines. Policy of the National Cancer Institute for Data and Safety Monitoring of Clinical Trials, September 30, 2014, https://deainfo.nci.nih.gov/grantspolicies/datasafety.pdf.

U.S. Department of Health and Human Services Food and Drug Administration, et al., *Guidance for Clinical Trial Sponsors; Establishment and Operation of Clinical Trial Data Monitoring Committees*, March 2006, https://www.fda.gov/downloads/regulatoryinformation/guidances/ucm127073.pdf.

NIH Guide for Grants and Contracts. (8:8) 5 June 1979 pg. 29, https://grants.nih.gov/grants/guide/historical/1979_06_05_Vol_08_No_08.pdf.

Greenberg, B. et al. Organization, Review, and Administration of Cooperative Studies: A Report from the Heart Special Project Committee to the National Advisory Heart Council, May 1967.

Curtis L. Meinert, *Clinical Trials: Design, Conduct and Analysis, Second Edition* (New York: Oxford University Press, 2012).

Steven Piantadosi, *Clinical Trials: A Methodological Perspective* (Hoboken, NJ: John Wiley & Sons, 1997), p. 255-265.

Chapter 10 Endnotes

1. **Susan Partridge, BSN, MBA, CCRC**, is Vice President, Research Administration for Parkland Health and Hospital System in Dallas, TX; **L. Steven Brown, MS, CPH**, is Biostatistician for Parkland Health.
2. The National Heart Institute (NHI) is now called the National Heart, Lung, and Blood Institute (NHLBI).
3. Greenberg, B. et al. Organization, Review, and Administration of Cooperative Studies: A Report from the Heart Special Project Committee to the National Advisory Heart Council, May 1967.
4. "Organization, review, and administration of cooperative studies (Greenberg Report): a report from the Heart Special Project Committee to the National Advisory Heart Council, May 1967," *Control Clinical Trials*. 1988 Jun; 9(2):137-48.
5. U.S. Dep't of Health and Human Services, NIH Guide for Grants and Contracts Vol. 8, No. 8, June 5, 1979 p.29, https://grants.nih.gov/grants/guide/historical/1979_06_05_Vol_08_No_08.pdf.
6. U.S. Department of Health and Human Services Food and Drug Administration, et al., *Guidance for Clinical Trial Sponsors; Establishment and Operation of Clinical Trial Data Monitoring Committees*, March 2006, https://www.fda.gov/downloads/regulatoryinformation/guidances/ucm127073.pdf.
7. European Medicines Agency, *Committee for Medical Products for Human Use (CHMP),Guideline on Data Monitoring Committees*, July 2005, https://www.ema.europa.eu/documents/scientific-guideline/guideline-data-monitoring-committees_en.pdf.
8. US Dep't of Health and Human Services, *NIH Policy for Data and Safety Monitoring* (June 10, 1998), https://grants.nih.gov/grants/guide/notice-files/not98-084.html.
9. US Dep't of Health and Human Services, National Cancer Institute, Essential Elements of a Data and Safety Monitoring Plan for Clinical Trials Funded by the National Cancer Institute (April 2001), https://rrp.cancer.gov/clinicalTrials/data_safety_monitoring_plan.htm.
10. Steven Piantadosi, MD, PhD, *Clinical Trials: A Methodologic Perspective, 3rd Edition*, (Hoboken, NJ: Wiley & Sons, 2017).
11. Steven Piantadosi, MD, PhD, *Clinical Trials: A Methodologic Perspective, 3rd Edition*, (Hoboken, NJ: Wiley & Sons, 2017).
12. Food and Drug Administration, Guidance for Clinical Trial Sponsors: Establishment and Operation of Clinical Trial Data Monitoring Committees (March 2006), https://www.fda.gov/RegulatoryInformation/Guidances/ucm127069.htm.
13. U.S. Department of Health and Human Services Food and Drug Administration, et al., *Guidance for Clinical Trial Sponsors; Establishment and Operation of Clinical Trial Data Monitoring Committees*, March 2006, https://www.fda.gov/downloads/regulatoryinformation/guidances/ucm127073.pdf.
14. International Conference on Harmonisation of Technical Requirements for Registration of Pharmaceuticals for Human Use, ICH Harmonised Tripartite Guideline:ICH Topic E 9 Statistical Principles for Clinical Trials, Step 4 version (February 5, 1998), https://www.ich.org/fileadmin/Public_Web_Site/ICH_Products/Guidelines/Efficacy/E9/Step4/E9_Guideline.pdf.
15. U.S. Department of Health and Human Services Food and Drug Administration, et al., *Guidance for Clinical Trial Sponsors; Establishment and Operation of Clinical Trial Data Monitoring Committees*, March 2006, https://www.fda.gov/downloads/regulatoryinformation/guidances/ucm127073.pdf.

11
Clinical Research Billing Compliance

By Ryan Meade, JD[1]

Introduction

The goal of this chapter is to discuss clinical research billing compliance. The regulations and reimbursement rules associated with billing third-party payors are not static and providers should consult federal, state and individual commercial insurance contracts to ensure the most up to date rules are applied to their claims for services. The regulations and rules are also heavily subject to interpretation due to lack of published commentary by federal and state governments.

The Medicare Program's July 2007 version of the Clinical Trial Policy (CTP)[2] provides much of the conceptual framework for research billing compliance. The CTP is a "national coverage determination" by the Centers for Medicare & Medicaid Services (CMS) and not a formal regulation published in the Code of Federal Regulations. The CTP interprets circumstances during clinical research studies in which CMS believes items and services may be "reasonable and necessary," the statutory criteria for Medicare coverage. CMS also issued a "clarification" to the CTP on September 30, 2008 in the form of a "Special Edition Article."[3] The Special Edition Article discusses how a provider's pursuit of collections against non-Medicare enrollees in research could have an impact on billing Medicare for the same services.

While the CTP only applies to clinical research services provided to Medicare beneficiaries, and is specifically written for only a sub-set of research studies (government-funded studies and drug studies), it nevertheless contains the most advanced framework for analyzing clinical research services for reimbursement. For some studies which are not covered by the CTP, including device studies, CMS defers to certain definitions and rules within the CTP. Likewise, some States have modeled their commercial insurance laws on the CTP and their Medicaid program clinical research services rules. Every third-party payor may have its own rules for coverage of services during clinical research studies, but many rely on the CTP's conceptual framework.

Since most healthcare providers participate in the Medicare Program and Medicare's CTP is the driver for much of the discussion and foundation for clinical research reimbursement rules in the United States, this chapter will focus on Medicare rules. The goal of the chapter is to provide a broad discussion of Medicare's clinical research coverage rules and does not seek to be an exhaustive review of the many ambiguities and interpretations of the CTP nor a review of the CTP's interaction with other frequently changing Medicare rules. A review such as that would be outdated as soon as it would be printed.

Basic Framework of Billing for Clinical Research Services

Clinical Research Services

Understanding terms is critical in any compliance program, but especially so in research billing compliance because numerous regulatory schemes, rules and agencies cover the same thing or activity. They do not all use the same terms. To complicate the situation, the clinical research community has spent several decades mostly isolated from reimbursement rules and terms. Establishing clear definitions of terms in a research billing compliance program is key to its success and essential for successful training and education on research compliance policies.

The very first question research billing compliance must deal with is which items and services should be covered by a clinical research billing compliance program and the billing safeguards that the provider should design. The terms "clinical trial" and "clinical research" are often used interchangeably to mean a research study that enrolls a human person. A provider should avoid taking the CTP reference to "clinical trials" literally to mean only a drug or device trial. CMS attempted to clarify this in its 2007 reconsiderations of the CTP by noting that the rule applies to "clinical research" in general, and accordingly proposed to change the name of the CTP to the Clinical Research Policy.[4] The name change was not adopted by CMS but this appears to be more the result that virtually all the proposed 2007 changes were not adopted by CMS in order to study the CTP's potential interaction with legislation that was passed during the time of the CTP's reconsideration period.

This chapter uses the term "clinical research" instead of "clinical trial" to impress the reader that when a patient is enrolled in a research study of any kind, compliance safeguards should address whether the services being provided can be billed to third-party payors. While the CTP does not address all types of clinical research studies, a provider's compliance program should consider the reimbursement status of clinical research services once a patient has signed an informed consent and formally begin participating in a clinical research study.

This chapter also uses the term "clinical research services" to denote any item or service that is scheduled to be provided to the patient by the study's protocol. Some of these services will be used for the clinical management of the patient's disease or condition, while others will be used only for research services. However, since any scheduled service is used at base for research purposes (even if merely to provide a reliable control for therapy), the services are research-related. There can sometimes be a misconception among personnel at healthcare providers that clinical research services are only those services which are used for research purposes only, without any clinical value. However, any service scheduled by the protocol is research-related in some fashion or it would not be required by the protocol. Services required to be provided by a protocol are by their nature not designed with a specific individual in mind and are part of the controlled study. Scheduled services during certain studies have the fortune of being dual purposed, for both the benefit of the individual patient enrolled in the research study and for use in assessing the objectives of the research study.

It is because the protocol requires specific types of services be provided at certain timepoints for all enrollees that all scheduled services must be considered by a research billing compliance risk control. While protocols are designed with a hypothetical patient in mind who meets the study's inclusion criteria, the scheduled services are not designed with an individual in mind. Third-party payors typically only pay for services that meet medical necessity, a patient-specific determination. In fact, many payors, such as Medicare, cover only a subset of medically necessary services—the subset being those services that meet that payor's rules on medical necessity and other factors that comprise the payor's coverage policy.[5] In other words, a third-party payor only pays for services that are designed to address a specific patient's disease, condition or signs and symptoms. For most payors, every service must meet medical necessity rules with adequate documentation in the medical record.

Clinical research services that are scheduled by the protocol need to be assessed not only for the individual enrollees, but fundamentally against the hypothetical patient who meets the minimum inclusion criteria. One of the critical questions for planning research billing safeguards is whether a particular scheduled service would be medically necessary for every patient enrolled in the research study. Consequently, all protocol scheduled services fall under the purview of a research billing compliance program because they are first scheduled to be performed because the protocol requires them to be performed, not as a dynamic response to the patient's immediate presentation. In a sense, there is a presumption that the service is for research purposes because that is the reason it is scheduled and then sites must overcome this presumption of the service being strictly for research by finding justification that a protocol-required service meets insurance coverage rules for every hypothetical patient eligible for the study.

As a final note, this chapter will often use the term "services" to mean any drug, device or procedure that involves interaction with a human or a biological specimen of the person. The Social Security Act sets out the terms "items and services" as a descriptor of the things and activities that the Medicare Program covers.[6] Use of the term "service" alone is merely used for convenience and includes what also may be defined as "items." When referring specifically to drugs, biologics, devices, procedures or such other discrete things and activities required by a research study, this chapter uses those discrete terms as a sub-set of "services."

The Three-part Conceptual Framework of Clinical Research Billing

Billing third-party payors for clinical research services should be analyzed within a three-part conceptual framework:

- Does the clinical research study qualify for coverage?
- Which items and services required by the research study meet the definition of "routine costs"?
- Does the third-party's reimbursement rules allow for coverage of the specific routine costs?

This three-part framework is important for a research billing initiative to adopt because it is important to counteract a common misunderstanding that services during a research study stand alone against the individual patient as to whether or not a third-party payor will cover the services. At a minimum, the services must be justified alone against the patient's disease or condition. But in addition to the individual services being medically necessary to manage or treat the patient's condition, the research study *itself* must be assessed as to whether it is a type of research study in which the third-party payor is willing to pay for services. In other words, does the study itself even "qualify" for coverage. Specifically with respect to Medicare, CMS has set out certain types of research studies which it is not willing to pay for services required by the study that may even be medically necessary. Research services involved with a device with a Category A investigational device exemption (IDE) are one type of research study in which Medicare is very reluctant to cover the routine costs unless the overall purpose of the study is to address a life-threatening condition among other strict conditions.[7]

As discussed below, it is not always clear whether a research study qualifies for coverage under the third-party payor's rules. Some of this is due to the difficulty in designing rules that contemplate all types of research studies. The Medicare Program has clear rules with respect to Category A or Category B IDE devices, and there are certain types of studies under the CTP that are clearly qualifying, but there are numerous types of research studies that third-party payors may disagree on about coverage. Early phase drug studies and investigations of experimental procedures that do not involve an investigational drug or device are types of research studies that pose the most vexing questions to healthcare providers for coverage. The safest approach for healthcare providers is to pose specific questions to payors, including the local Medicare contractors. However, understanding that the question of whether the study is qualifying or not is a critical step in a research billing compliance program.

When a study qualifies for coverage, this does not mean that all services required by the protocol are covered by Medicare. Qualifying for coverage only means that the services required by the protocol are potentially eligible for coverage. Additional layers of rules must be worked through before the clinical research service can be considered covered. Various payors set out different names for the next step in the framework, but Medicare uses the term "routine costs."[8] If an item or service required by the protocol meets the definition of a routine cost, then another step toward coverage is crossed.

The term "routine cost" is an unfortunate term because "cost" is not always recognized as equating to "item or service." CMS attempted to reform this term in the 2007 reconsiderations of the CTP, but did not adopt a change. The concept of a "routine cost" comes down to whether the item or service is being used for the clinical management of the patient. At base, a "routine cost" must be something that is being performed for the benefit of a specific individual. But this question of routine cost is not a wholesale deference to the physician; rather, the conclusion that something is a routine cost should be anchored in something objective (*e.g.*, peer review literature) to support the strongest defense and overcome the presumption that the service is for research purposes.

The clinical research community often uses the term "standard of care" to mean therapy that is akin to the CTP's "routine costs." However, the Medicare program does not use the term "standard of care." A later section of this chapter, "Routine Costs During Clinical Research," examines the specific wording of the CTP's term "routine cost," but "routine costs" arguably includes items and services that may be more than the standard of care and are justified for coverage based on the medical necessity of the item or service once the patient is enrolled in the research study. An example of this is a laboratory test to monitor the patient's kidney function during a drug study because the study drug is known to be toxic to the kidneys. This service would be a "routine cost" even though the standard therapy for the patient would not require kidney function tests.

Not all routine costs, however, are covered by third-party payors. Routine costs during qualifying research studies are only billable to third-party payors if the specific service is usually paid for outside the research study under the third-party payor's normal billing rules and meets applicable coverage criteria under a participant's benefit plan with a payer. If a commercial insurer does not cover dietician services for a particular condition, but dietary consultations meet the definition of a "routine cost," the service will not be covered because the payor normally does not cover dietary services for that condition. Likewise, the Medicare program does not cover most self-administered drugs provided in an outpatient setting,[9] and just because the self-administered drugs meet the definition of a "routine cost" during a qualifying research study does not mean that they are automatically billable to Medicare. Indeed, many self-administered drugs are medically necessary in an outpatient setting but are generally not covered by the Medicare program.

The CTP contains a powerful line after discussing the basics of qualifying clinical trials and routine costs: "All other Medicare rules apply." This statement succinctly identifies the CTP as merely an initial step for determining whether research services are covered. It also identifies the CTP as a peer coverage rule to all other Medicare coverage rules.

While specific third-party payors may differ in their specific rules as to what is or is not covered during a clinical research study, most payor rules implicitly follow the framework set out by Medicare, given that the Medicare program's CTP in the end requires medical necessity justification.

Qualifying Research Studies

The term "qualifying research study" is not a technical term found in the CTP or other Medicare rules. It is the term this chapter uses to mean a clinical research study that meets the initial consideration for whether any protocol scheduled services are eligible for coverage. Unfortunately, there is no single term used by Medicare to identify these qualifying research studies. The CTP uses the term "qualifying clinical trial" and in 2007 attempted to change to the "approved clinical research study." The 2007 reform attempts did not adopt this term. The device study coverage regulations likewise use a different term, referring to "covered device trials" or "approved device trial."

Although there is no common regulatory term, what all of these terms have in common is the concept that the study must initially qualify for coverage for scheduled services to be eligible for coverage. We have chosen to use the term "qualifying research study" to reinforce this concept of initial qualification of the study based on what is being studied and the design of the research study. Many research sites use the CTP term "qualifying clinical trial" to cover all qualifying studies and that is an operational choice. We have chosen in this chapter to use "qualifying research study" to emphasize that the qualifying concept applies to research studies that are far beyond studies with an investigational article, the classic design for a "trial."

Whether a research study is a qualifying research study turns on what is being studied. Medicare uses different rules for qualifying the study depending upon what is being studied. The Medicare rules provide qualifying rules for device studies that involve a device that is being investigated under an IDE. These rules also arguably include studies that are post-marketing approval studies as well. For all non-device studies, the CTP sets out the qualifying criteria.

The CTP, however, comes up short because it is not technically possible for a research study that is studying an investigational procedure or technique to be a qualifying research study. Nor does the CTP specifically allow coverage for an observational study of an FDA-approved device being used for its labeled purposes when the study is not mandated by the FDA. CMS is silent as to whether research studies that do not fit within the CTP or device study coverage regulations can qualify for Medicare coverage. The proposed 2007 changes to the CTP would have addressed these questions by allowing a "certification" process, but those changes were not adopted. In lieu of addressing these questions on a national level, CMS deferred to local Medicare contractors as to whether coverage exists for these types of studies.[10] Medicare contractors hold diverse opinions on coverage for these studies. Providers should consult local Medicare contractor rules for research studies that do not squarely fall within a qualifying research study rule. A trend appears to be lenient for coverage of pure observational studies as not falling within the jurisdiction of the CTP and relying on basic Medicare coverage rules; but, this stance can vary by jurisdiction.

Device Studies

The qualifying status of a device study turns on the type of device being studied. If the research study includes an investigational device that is considered a "covered device," then there is the potential for reimbursement from Medicare during the study. If the research study includes an investigational device that is considered a "noncovered device," the study is not a qualifying research study and the scheduled services would not be reimbursable.

The device study regulations state:

> Medicare payment is not made for medical and hospital services that are related to the use of a device that is not covered...These services include all services furnished in preparation for the use of a noncovered device, services furnished as necessary after-care

that are incident to recovery from the use of the device or from receiving related noncovered services.[11]

The Medicare Benefit Policy Manual (Chapter 14, Section 10) sets out a list of "covered devices:"

> Devices that may be covered under Medicare include the following categories:
>
> - Devices approved by the FDA through the Pre-Market Approval (PMA) process;
> - Devices cleared by the FDA through the 510(k) process;
> - FDA-approved Investigational Device Exemption (IDE) Category B devices; and
> - Hospital Institutional Review Board (IRB) approved non-significant risk devices[12]

The Medicare Modernization Act added by statute Category A IDE device studies to the list of qualifying research studies but CMS has disallowed coverage for the device itself (codified at 42 USC 1395y(m)).[13]

Category A IDE Device Studies. In a November 6, 2014 revision to the Medicare Benefit Policy Manual, a Category A device is defined as "...a device for which 'absolute risk' of the device type has not been established (that is, initial questions of safety and effectiveness have not been resolved) and the FDA is unsure whether the device type can be safe and effective."[14]

Category B IDE Devices. A Category B IDE device is defined as: "...a device for which the incremental risk is the primary risk in question (that is, initial questions of safety and effectiveness of that device type have been resolved), or it is known that the device type can be safe and effective because, for example, other manufacturers have obtained FDA premarket approval or clearance for that device type." [15] "

Criteria for Coverage. In the November 6, 2014 revision to Chapter 14 of the Medicare Benefit Policy Manual, CMS spells out the criteria for coverage of Category A and Category B IDE studies.

- For Category A: "Medicare covers routine care items and services furnished in an FDA-approved Category A IDE study if CMS (or its designated entity) determines that the Medicare coverage IDE study criteria are met."[16]
- For Category B: "Medicare may make payment for a Category B IDE device and routine care items and services furnished in an FDA-approved Category B IDE study if CMS (or its designated entity) determines prior to the submission of the first related claim that the Medicare coverage IDE study criteria are met."[17]

Category A and B IDE studies must meet the following criteria to warrant Medicare coverage:

1. The principal purpose of the study is to test whether the device improves health outcomes of appropriately selected patients.
2. The rationale for the study is well supported by available scientific and medical information, or it is intended to clarify or establish the health outcomes of interventions already in common clinical use.
3. The study results are not anticipated to unjustifiably duplicate existing knowledge.
4. The study design is methodologically appropriate and the anticipated number of enrolled subjects is adequate to confidently answer the research question(s) being asked in the study.
5. The study is sponsored by an organization or individual capable of successfully completing the study.
6. The study is in compliance with all applicable Federal regulations concerning the protection of human subjects found at 21 CFR parts 50, 56, and 812, and 45 CFR part 46.
7. Where appropriate, the study is not designed to exclusively test toxicity or disease pathophysiology in healthy individuals.

Studies of all medical technologies measuring therapeutic outcomes as one of the objectives may be exempt from this criterion only if the disease or condition being studied is life threatening and the patient has no other viable treatment options.

8. The study is registered with the National Institutes of Health's National Library of Medicine's ClinicalTrials.gov.
9. The study protocol describes the method and timing of release of results on all pre-specified outcomes, including release of negative outcomes, and that the release should be hastened if the study is terminated early.
10. The study protocol must describe how Medicare beneficiaries may be affected by the device under investigation, and how the study results are or are not expected to be generalizable to the Medicare beneficiary population. Generalizability to populations eligible for Medicare due to age, disability, or other eligibility status must be explicitly described.[18]

Further guidance on on categorizing IDE device studies can be found in an FDA guidance document, FDA Categorization of Investigational Device Exemption (IDE) Devices to Assist the Centers for Medicare and Medicaid Services (CMS) with Coverage Decisions: Guidance for Sponsors, Clinical Investigators, Industry, Institutional Review Boards, and Food and Drug Administration Staff.[19]

The result of whether a device study is approved (or qualifies) is at the time of this printing published on the CMS website for any study with an FDA IDE letter dated January 1, 2015 or afterwards. A submission is made to CMS, which will review the ten (10) criteria and make a determination on whether to approve the study. If the study is approved, then it is listed on the CMS website and the study qualifies for coverage across the country.[20]

Non-Device Research Studies

A non-device research must use the CTP to determine whether the study is a qualifying research study. Under the CTP, a qualifying research study is known as a "qualifying clinical trial" and must meet ten criteria. But how it meets these ten criteria is complex and not straight-forward. The ten criteria were originally designed as a certification approach—in which the investigators would certify that the study qualified under the CTP. That self-certification approach was never operationalized and the only way to meet the qualifying clinical trial status is for a provider to be sure that the research study is the type of research study that CMS considers to meet the criteria. Self-certifying with the ten criteria listed in the CTP is not a CMS-approved approach to meeting qualifying clinical trial status.

The research studies that meet the qualifying clinical trial criteria must be a study that is "deemed" by CMS to have seven of the ten criteria and meet the other three criteria. There are only four groups of studies which CMS "deems" to meet the first seven criteria. These types of studies are often referred to as "deemed" studies. The following are the studies that the CTP lists as meeting these criteria:

1. Trials funded by NIH, CDC, AHRQ, CMS, DOD, and VA;
2. Trials supported by centers or cooperative groups that are funded by the NIH, CDC, AHRQ, CMS, DOD and VA;
3. Trials conducted under an investigational new drug application (IND) reviewed by the FDA; and
4. Drug trials that are exempt from having an IND under 21 CFR 312.2(b)(1)[21]

If a research study is one of these four types of "deemed" studies then it automatically meets the seven so-called "desirable characteristics." At this time there is no other way to meet the seven desirable characteristics (*i.e.*, seven of the ten criteria) unless a study is one of these four types of studies. If a study meets one of these four types of studies, then it must also meet the following three criteria to be a qualifying clinical trial:

1. The subject or purpose of the trial must be the evaluation of an item or service that falls within a Medicare benefit category and not statutorily excluded from coverage (*e.g.*, cosmetic surgery, hearing aids).
2. The trial must have therapeutic intent.
3. Trials of therapeutic interventions must enroll patients with diagnosed disease rather than healthy volunteers.[22]

Routine Costs During Clinical Research

For a qualifying research study, the CTP allows coverage for "routine costs" that Medicare rules would cover outside of a research study. The CTP also allows approved device trials to utilize the "routine cost" definition for coverage. So, although there are different paths to coverage for device trials and non-device research studies, once a study qualifies under either approach, then there is potential coverage for any item or service required by the protocol that meets the definition of a "routine cost."

The CTP lists the following as "routine costs":

- "Items or services that are typically provided absent a clinical trial (*e.g.*, conventional care);
- "Items or services required solely for the provision of the investigational item or service (*e.g.*, administration of a noncovered chemotherapeutic agent), the clinically appropriate monitoring of the effects of the item or service, or the prevention of complications; and
- "Items or services needed for reasonable and necessary care arising from the provision of an investigational item or service—in particular, for the diagnosis or treatment of complications."

This definition is highly complex, confusing, and arguably self-contradictory. It also appears to erroneously use an "and" to connect the third bullet point. Read literally, particularly when including the "and," the definition is not achievable. The definition only makes sense if the "and" is treated as a scrivener's error and should be an "or" and the remaining definitions are distilled. A common approach to applying these definitions of "routine cost" is to consider them to cover: (a) conventional care items and service; (b) items and services to detect or prevent complications; or (c) the administration of the investigational article.

Just meeting of these three permutations of "routine cost" is not sufficient in itself. The item or service must not be excluded from coverage generally from Medicare. The CTP states that "all other Medicare rules apply." As discussed above, a self-administered drug in an outpatient setting may meet the definition of "routine cost" but that does not allow coverage because a peer Medicare rule prohibits coverage of a self-administered drug in the outpatient (inside or outside a research study) unless it meets one of a handful of narrow exceptions.

Application of Study Documents to Research Billing

As important as the Medicare rules are, so also are the study documents. The study documents can influence whether an item or service is billable or will be considered to be for research purposes only. Also, if the research billing is ever audited by government authorities, the study documents will be used, so it is critical that how the study services are described in the study documents be taken into account. The most relevant study documents are the clinical trial agreement, the protocol, the coverage analysis and the IRB-approved research informed consent form.

Clinical Trial Agreement

1. Parties. The clinical trial agreement is a contract usually between an institution, such as a university, and the sponsor. Sometimes the clinical trial agreement also has the hospital (provider) as the main party to the contract or as a third-party to the contract. The parties will vary based on the study and the legal relationships between the parties involved in research. In community provider settings, the physician may be the main party to the clinical trial agreement.

The principal investigator is usually also a signatory to the clinical trial agreement. How the investigator signs this document and in what capacity he or she signs the document is important to understand. If the investigator signs the clinical trial agreement to note that the investigator has read and understands the protocol and accepts responsibility for conducting the research, then the investigator may not necessarily be a contractual party. However, the wording of the signature may make the investigator a person party to the contract. Most institutions try to avoid the investigator being seen as a party to the contract.

In what capacity the investigator signs the clinical trial agreement can determine what party is liable for any actions of the investigator. If the investigator signs in his or her name alone, then the investigator may be personally liable. If the investigator signs as an employee of the investigator's practice group, then the practice group may be liable. If the investigator signs in the investigator's capacity as an employee of the university (under his or her faculty position), then the university may be liable.

2. Relevant Parts of the Clinical Trial Agreement for Billing. From a billing compliance perspective, the three most important parts of the clinical trial agreement are a) any parts of the main body of the contract that discusses compensation or financial terms; b) the exhibit incorporating the protocol; c) the compensation arrangement of "sponsor budget" that is usually an exhibit to the contract.

3. Terms in the Main Body of the Contract. What financial terms the main body of the contract commits the parties to are as varied as there are contracts. An important goal in clinical trial agreement contracting is to be as simple and straightforward as possible. This usually suggests that the main part of the contract should discuss as little as possible about compensation and financial terms and rather should refer all financial terms to the exhibit that sets out the budget compensation terms.

Problematic language in the main body of the contract includes such statements as "the compensation provided under this agreement constitutes payment to the institution for all costs associated with conducting the research study," or "the compensation covers the costs for all Services required by this agreement" (note that "Services" is often defined to be the protocol services that are set out in a separate exhibit.

The financial terms set out in the main body of the contract must be reconciled with any terms set out in the budget exhibit.

4. Protocol as Part of Clinical Trial Agreement. The protocol is usually always incorporated into the contract through an exhibit. Protocol activities often are defined as the "Services" in a clinical trial agreement; in other words, the protocol activities are what the institution is committing itself to do. Since the "Services" under a clinical trial agreement are rarely distinguished as "for research purposes only" services and "clinical care" services, any activity required by the protocol can become a "Service" under the contract.

It is important to keep in mind that the protocol is not merely a scientific document. Because the protocol *in toto* is usually incorporated by reference into the clinical trial agreement, the protocol is a contractual document as well. How the investigator performs under the protocol and what services are required by the protocol (whether they be "for research purposes only" or are "standard of care"), they are still contractual services and carry all obligations of a valid contract.

5. Sponsorship Budget/Compensation Exhibit. The sponsorship budget is usually set out as an exhibit in the clinical trial agreement. It is critical to understand that the budget/compensation exhibit is part of the contract. The sponsorship budget is every bit a part of most contracts as is the main body of the contract. Keeping the sponsorship budget and the main body of the contract harmonized—recognizing that the protocol are the services—is vital to successfully negotiating a clinical trial agreement with as few ambiguities as possible.

The sponsorship budget can have many methods for providing compensation. The budget may set out a "lump sum" that is paid at certain milestones, or the budget may set out payment for specific services. There may be a combination of both. There also may be inadvertent ambiguities in the budget as to what the payments pay for.

6. Interpreting the Clinical Trial Agreement. The following are basic points that apply to interpreting a clinical trial agreement:

- The clinical trial agreement is interpreted as a whole—the main body of the contract, the incorporated protocol, the budget exhibit are one, singular contract.
- The plain language of the contract will be considered to mean what it says. This is particularly so when two highly sophisticated parties (universities and drug/device companies) negotiate contracts.
- If the parties disagree on the meaning of the terms, then ancillary evidence can be used to show that the words did not mean what was written—based on actions of the parties or based on evidence/material from the time of executing the contract that shows what the real intent of the parties are. It is rarely sufficient for one party to take plain language interpretations and assert they mean something different without evidence that the other party also understood the terms to be different.
- If terms are ambiguous, then the general rules of contract interpretation instruct courts to interpret the language against the drafter of the agreement and in favor of the party that took the words to mean something different than what the drafter wrote. This is usually used when the parties disagree on the meaning of the term and the terms are ambiguous. Clear, plain words rarely can utilize this canon of interpretation.
- If the terms in the main body of the contract are not in sync with the budget exhibit (or if the terms within the exhibit contradict themselves), then the words must be interpreted together to determine the meaning of the words. The plainest words in the contradictory statements would be used to harmonize the contradictions. In other words, the language that most easily and readily conveys an understanding of what the terms mean would be used.
- If two statements exist that cannot be reconciled: $X=3$ and $X=4$, then there may be no way to reconcile these statements except to either amend the contract so that the parties agree on what was meant, or if disputes occur, then to look to the actions of the parties to determine if those will help inform the meaning of the terms.

7. CMS "Clarification" of September 30, 2008. On September 30, 2008, CMS issued a Special Edition Article which discussed clauses in clinical trial agreements that have long been debated. So-called "conditional payment clauses" or "contingency payment clauses" were addressed in which the sponsor agreed to pay for a service only after the enrollee's insurer denied coverage for the service. These clauses had been debated for several years under the Medicare Secondary Payer statute, particularly with respect to treatment of research-related injuries, but the Special Edition Article tackled the question of whether the contingency payment clauses operated to provide services "free of charge" to enrollees and therefore disallowed billing Medicare.

The Special Edition Article utilized Chapter 16, Section 40 of the Medicare Benefit Policy Manual to argue that when the sponsor (or anyone else) has a legal obligation to pay for a service and the provider does not pursue collection against an enrollee after the patient's insurance denies coverage, then that clause triggers the CTP's provision that services paid for by the sponsor cannot be billed to the Medicare Program.

The Special Edition Article has caused certain controversy because it went beyond commenting on the contingency payment clauses and focused on when a provider decides not to pursue collection against a research subject. If the provider decided not to pursue payment from a non-Medicare research subject, then a Medicare enrollee in the study must also received the service free of charge.

The Special Edition Article stated:

> If the routine costs of the clinical trial are furnished gratuitously (*i.e.*, without regard to the beneficiary's ability to pay and without expectation of payment from any other source), then Medicare payment cannot be made and the beneficiary cannot be charged. If private insurers deny the routine costs and the provider of services does not pursue the non-Medicare patients for payment after the denials (even though the non-Medicare patient has the ability to pay), Medicare payment cannot be made and the beneficiary cannot be charged for the routine costs.[23]

CMS offered an exception to this application of the Special Edition Article if the patient is indigent. If the patient is indigent pursuant to the provider's indigency policy, then the sponsor may pay the provider for the service and it will not disturb Medicare billing for the same service.

With respect to indigency, the Special Edition Article stated:

> If the routine costs of the clinical trial are not billed to indigent non-Medicare patients because of their inability to pay (but are being billed to all the other patients in the clinical trial who have the financial means to pay even when his/her private insurer denies payment for the routine costs), then a legal obligation to pay exists. Therefore, Medicare payment may be made and the beneficiary (who is not indigent) will be responsible for the applicable Medicare deductible and coinsurance amounts.[24]

The Special Edition Article also clarified that sponsors may not pay enrollees' co-payments and deductible without risking violations of fraud and abuse laws:

> If a research sponsor offers to pay cost-sharing amounts owed by the beneficiary, this could be a fraud and abuse problem. In addition to CMS' policy, the Office of Inspector General (OIG) advises that nothing in OIG rules or regulations under the Federal anti-kickback statute prohibits hospitals from waiving collection of charges to uninsured patients of limited means, so long as the waiver is not linked in any manner to the generation of business payable by a Federal healthcare program.[25]

Coverage Analysis

A coverage analysis is best practice to ensure that the protocol-related services are outlined and, if the services will be billed to insurance, that a rationale is given which overcomes the implicit presumption that a service required by the protocol is medically necessary for all possible eligible subjects. The coverage analysis allows commentary to anchor the rationale for coverage in national guidelines, national and local CMS rules and not just what a physician performs as local practice or the physician's intuitive sense of what needs to be done for the patient. Just as a medical record must document medical necessity for insurance coverage and not simply record a physician's order, so too, a coverage analysis provides rationale that articulates why a service is not for research purposes only but meets one of the definitions of "routine cost." A coverage analysis is a formalized review of what is within the protocol and study event calendar to ensure that a site has validated where it intends to send charges once a participant is registered onto a study that has services that generate charges within a facility's charge capture system. If the research study will generate a charge in the research site's charge capture system, then it is industry standard to develop a coverage analysis.

It has become industry standard to have the coverage analysis developed by offices other than the study team's, though in dialogue and concert with the Principal Investigator and study team. Industry experience has shown that development of a coverage analysis by individuals other than the study team minimizes bias and allows incorporation of specialized insurance rule knowledge that the study team may not possess.

Informed Consent Form

1. Basic Interpretation of Informed Consent Form. The OHRP and FDA regulations for protection of human subjects require that the informed consent be written in language that it is understandable to the subject. Many organizations set this level at an 8th grade reading level; some require a lower reading level. Consequently, interpreting the informed consent document is different from the clinical trial agreement because there is an assumption that the two parties are not on equal footing.

The critical component of interpreting an informed consent form is to remember that the words must be taken at face value. The perspective the government uses to interpret an informed consent is the perspective of the patient. A question to always ask when interpreting a research informed consent form is, "what would the patient understand this language to mean?"

The informed consent form becomes relevant for billing compliance in at least three ways: a) the expression of therapeutic benefit; b) the disclosure of added costs to the patient (which often becomes a recitation of what services are provided free or at no cost to the subject); and c) what services are the responsibility of the patient after a research related injury.

2. Expression of Therapeutic Benefit. The informed consent must describe what benefits the patient could receive as a result of participating in the research study. If the informed consent states that the patient will not receive benefit from participating in the study (but rather benefit may be derived for future patients), then the government would likely interpret that statement to mean that the study is not designed with therapeutic intent in mind. No undocumented oral statements will likely be able to override clear language in the informed consent in which the patient has been told that participating in the study will not benefit the patient.

If the benefit section of the informed consent contains language that identifies that the investigator hopes the study benefits the patient but cannot guarantee benefit, then that language supports the idea that the study has been designed with therapeutic intent in mind.

3. Added Costs Section. The research informed consent must disclose what added costs the patient will incur by enrolling in the research study. The OHRP and FDA regulations do not require that free services be listed in this section, but informed consents often list the free services for any number of reasons (some IRBs require this).

Any service that is promised free or at no cost to the participant in the research study cannot be billed. The words will be interpreted from the perspective of the patient. What would a patient (without the aide of oral interpretation) understand these words to mean? In other words, what is the plain language of the words?

If the language states that there will be "no costs to you for participating in the research study," keep in mind what services are required by the research study—all activities required by the protocol. When the patient is told he or she has "no costs" for participating, this means that the patient cannot be billed for any protocol-required services, whether those services are "for research purposes only" or also carry a clinical dimension to them.

If the language indicates that certain services are free, then those services cannot be billed. For instance, the informed consent document may indicate that the "CT scans conducted during screening will be at no cost." This only requires the CT scans that are done at the start of the enrollment process during screening to be provided without charge to the patient. However, if the language states that "all imaging services that are part of this research study" will be provided free, then no imaging services (whether X-Rays, CTs or MRIs) can be billed to the patient if the imaging service is required by the protocol.

If the language of the informed consent states that "there will be no costs for services that are performed only because you are enrolled in this study," then that can be interpreted to mean the services that are done only for research purposes and not the services that the patient would receive as part of standard of care or part of the normal care the patient would receive if he or she was not enrolled in the research study.

If the language of the informed consent contradicts itself, then the force of the contradiction must be weighed. This is the hardest aspect of informed consent language to interpret and it occurs not infrequently. An informed consent may state that "There are no costs to you for participating in this research study. Standard of care services will be billed to you or your insurer in the normal way." Keep in mind: what would the patient understand this language to mean? Would the patient understand this to mean that all study-required services are free but any services that are outside the study will be billed? Would the patient understand this to mean that the "for research only" services during a study are not billable but that any services required by the study but for clinical care will be billed? There is no clear answer to this. Patterns of behavior and actions could be used to interpret this one way or another; conversations with the patient at the time of consenting could also be used to interpret this.

When the language of the informed consent contradicts itself as written above, then surrounding language should be used to interpret the contradictory language. In the example above, there are merely two sentences written out. If the language occurs in the context of a longer paragraph in which the language has multiple permutations of "there are no costs to you," followed by a brief line discussing standard of care as billable, then the language would likely be construed in favor of the patient. If the opposite is true, then the weight may be on the side of billing for the standard of care services.

Protocol

The protocol is often overlooked as making up a contractual document. The activities required by the protocol are often the "Services" in the clinical trial agreement. Obligations of the institution or provider or investigator that are set out in the protocol can be construed as contractual obligations.

The protocol is subject to all interpretations that apply to the clinical trial agreement. Language that is plainly stated in the protocol must be taken at face value unless shown to be otherwise.

The interpretation of the protocol often comes into play for billing purposes in attempting to determine whether a protocol-required service is for research purposes only or may be done for both research purposes and the clinical care of the patient. Budgeting must be done based on the patient who minimally meets the inclusion criteria. A question that must be asked is whether every patient who will receive a service will receive the service for their clinical care. If the protocol states that a service is being done for research purposes only, then the protocol must be assumed to mean that it is done for research purposes only unless the physician can demonstrate that every patient who possibly meets the inclusion criteria would receive that service for their clinical care.

Statements in the protocol that usually affect billing are those statements that indicate something is being required by the protocol only for research purposes or for data collection purposes. In conducting a coverage analysis, these statements must be taken at face value until the investigator indicates otherwise.

Appendix

The following is a re-print of the July 2007 Medicare Clinical Trial Policy (National Coverage Determination 310.1)

Indications and Limitations of Coverage

Effective for items and services furnished on or after July 9, 2007, Medicare covers the routine costs of qualifying clinical trials, as such costs are defined below, as well as reasonable and necessary items and services used to diagnose and treat complications arising from participation in all clinical trials. All other Medicare rules apply.

Routine costs of a clinical trial include all items and services that are otherwise generally available to Medicare beneficiaries (*i.e.*, there exists a benefit category, it is not statutorily excluded, and there is not a national non-coverage decision) that are provided in either the experimental or the control arms of a clinical trial except:

- The investigational item or service, itself unless otherwise covered outside of the clinical trial;
- Items and services provided solely to satisfy data collection and analysis needs and that are not used in the direct clinical management of the patient (*e.g.*, monthly CT scans for a condition usually requiring only a single scan); and
- Items and services customarily provided by the research sponsors free of charge for any enrollee in the trial.

Routine costs in clinical trials include:

- Items or services that are typically provided absent a clinical trial (*e.g.*, conventional care);
- Items or services required solely for the provision of the investigational item or service (*e.g.*, administration of a noncovered chemotherapeutic agent), the clinically appropriate monitoring of the effects of the item or service, or the prevention of complications; and
- Items or services needed for reasonable and necessary care arising from the provision of an investigational item or service—in particular, for the diagnosis or treatment of complications.

This policy does not withdraw Medicare coverage for items and services that may be covered according to local medical review policies (LMRPs) or the regulations on category B investigational device exemptions (IDE) found in 42 CFR 405.201-405.215, 411.15, and 411.406. For information about LMRPs, refer to www.lmrp.net, a searchable database of Medicare contractors' local policies.

For noncovered items and services, including items and services for which Medicare payment is statutorily prohibited, Medicare only covers the treatment of complications arising from the delivery of the noncovered item or service and unrelated reasonable and necessary care. However, if the item or service is not covered by virtue of a national noncoverage policy in Pub. 100-03, NCD Manual and is the focus of a qualifying clinical trial, the routine costs of the clinical trial (as defined above) will be covered by Medicare but the noncovered item or service, itself, will not.

A. Requirements for Medicare Coverage of Routine Costs

Any clinical trial receiving Medicare coverage of routine costs must meet the following three requirements:

- The subject or purpose of the trial must be the evaluation of an item or service that falls

within a Medicare benefit category (*e.g.*, physicians' service, durable medical equipment, diagnostic test) and is not statutorily excluded from coverage (*e.g.*, cosmetic surgery, hearing aids).
- The trial must not be designed exclusively to test toxicity or disease pathophysiology. It must have therapeutic intent.
- Trials of therapeutic interventions must enroll patients with diagnosed disease rather than healthy volunteers. Trials of diagnostic interventions may enroll healthy patients in order to have a proper control group.

The three requirements above are insufficient by themselves to qualify a clinical trial for Medicare coverage of routine costs. Clinical trials also should have the following desirable characteristics; however, some trials, as described below, are presumed to meet these characteristics and are automatically qualified to receive Medicare coverage:

1. The principal purpose of the trial is to test whether the intervention potentially improves the participants' health outcomes;
2. The trial is well-supported by available scientific and medical information or it is intended to clarify or establish the health outcomes of interventions already in common clinical use;
3. The trial does not unjustifiably duplicate existing studies;
4. The trial design is appropriate to answer the research question being asked in the trial;
5. The trial is sponsored by a credible organization or individual capable of executing the proposed trial successfully;
6. The trial is in compliance with Federal regulations relating to the protection of human subjects; and
7. All aspects of the trial are conducted according to the appropriate standards of scientific integrity.

B. Qualification Process for Clinical Trials

Using the authority found in §1142 of the Act (cross-referenced in §1862(a)(1)(E) of the Act), the Agency for Healthcare Research and Quality (AHRQ) will convene a multi-agency Federal panel (the "panel") composed of representatives of the Department of Health and Human Services research agencies (National Institutes of Health (NIH), Centers for Disease Control and Prevention (CDC), the Food and Drug Administration (FDA), AHRQ, and the Office of Human Research Protection), and the research arms of the Department of Defense (DOD) and the Department of Veterans Affairs (VA) to develop qualifying criteria that will indicate a strong probability that a trial exhibits the desirable characteristics listed above. These criteria will be easily verifiable, and where possible, dichotomous. Trials that meet these qualifying criteria will receive Medicare coverage of their associated routine costs. This panel is not reviewing or approving individual trials. The multi-agency panel will meet periodically to review and evaluate the program and recommend any necessary refinements to CMS.

Clinical trials that meet the qualifying criteria will receive Medicare coverage of routine costs after the trial's lead principal investigator certifies that the trial meets the criteria. This process will require the principal investigator to enroll the trial in a Medicare clinical trials registry, currently under development.

Some clinical trials are automatically qualified to receive Medicare coverage of their routine costs because they have been deemed by AHRQ, in consultation with the other agencies represented on the multi-agency panel to be highly likely to have the above-listed seven desirable characteristics of clinical trials. The principal investigators of these automatically qualified trials do not need to certify that the trials meet the qualifying criteria, but must enroll the trials in the Medicare clinical trials registry for administrative purposes, once the registry is established.

Effective September 19, 2000, clinical trials that are deemed to be automatically qualified are:

1. Trials funded by NIH, CDC, AHRQ, CMS, DOD, and VA;
2. Trials supported by centers or cooperative groups that are funded by the NIH, CDC, AHRQ, CMS, DOD and VA;
3. Trials conducted under an investigational new drug application (IND) reviewed by the FDA; and
4. Drug trials that are exempt from having an IND under 21 CFR 312.2(b)(1) will be deemed automatically qualified until the qualifying criteria are developed and the certification process is in place. At that time the principal investigators of these trials must certify that the trials meet the qualifying criteria in order to maintain Medicare coverage of routine costs. This certification process will only affect the future status of the trial and will not be used to retroactively change the earlier deemed status.

The CMS, through the national coverage determination (NCD) process, through an individualized assessment of benefits, risks, and research potential, may determine that certain items and services for which there is some evidence of significant medical benefit, but for which there is insufficient evidence to support a "reasonable and necessary" determination, are only reasonable and necessary when provided in a clinical trial that meets the requirements defined in that NCD.[26]

Medicare will cover the routine costs of qualifying trials that either have been deemed to be automatically qualified, have certified that they meet the qualifying criteria, or are required through the NCD process, unless CMS's Chief Clinical Officer subsequently finds that a clinical trial does not meet the qualifying criteria or jeopardizes the safety or welfare of Medicare beneficiaries.

Should CMS find that a trial's principal investigator misrepresented that the trial met the necessary qualifying criteria in order to gain Medicare coverage of routine costs, Medicare coverage of the routine costs would be denied under §1862(a)(1)(E) of the Act. In the case of such a denial, the Medicare beneficiaries enrolled in the trial would not be held liable (i.e., would be held harmless from collection) for the costs consistent with the provisions of §§1879, 1842(l), or 1834(j)(4) of the Act, as applicable. Where appropriate, the billing providers would be held liable for the costs and fraud investigations of the billing providers and the trial's principal investigator may be pursued.

Medicare regulations require Medicare+Choice (M+C) organizations[27] to follow CMS's national coverage decisions. This NCD raises special issues that require some modification of most M+C organizations' rules governing provision of items and services in and out of network. The items and services covered under this NCD are inextricably linked to the clinical trials with which they are associated and cannot be covered outside of the context of those clinical trials. M+C organizations therefore must cover these services regardless of whether they are available through in-network providers. M+C organizations may have reporting requirements when enrollees participate in clinical trials, in order to track and coordinate their members' care, but cannot require prior authorization or approval.[28]

Chapter 11 Endnotes

1. **Ryan Meade, JD**, is a Senior Managing Director at Ankura Consulting in Chicago, IL, and also serves as Director of the Regulatory Compliance Studies Program in the Center for Compliance Studies at Loyola University Chicago School of Law.
2. US Department of Health and Human Services, Centers for Medicare and Medicaid Services, National Coverage Determination for Routine Costs in Clinical Trials, 310.1 (July 2007).
3. US Department of Health and Human Services, Centers for Medicare and Medicaid Services, MLN Matters Special Edition SE0822 (September 30, 2008, revised May 16, 2018).
4. US Department of Health and Human Services, Centers for Medicare and Medicaid Services, Decision Memo for Clinical Trial Policy (CAG-00071R2) (October 17, 2007).
5. "Physician practices should remember that 'necessary' does not always constitute 'covered'...." OIG Compliance Program for Individual and Small Group Physician Practices, 59 Fed. Reg. 59,439 ((October 20, 2000).
6. Social Security Act §1862 (42 U.S.C. 1395y).
7. Social Security Act §1862(m).(42 U.S.C. 1395y).
8. US Department of Health and Human Services, Centers for Medicare and Medicaid Services, National Coverage Determination for Routine Costs in Clinical Trials, 310.1 (July 2007).
9. US Department of Health and Human Services, Centers for Medicare and Medicaid Services, Medicare Benefit Policy Manual, Chapter 15, Section 50.
10. US Department of Health and Human Services, Centers for Medicare and Medicaid Services, Final Decision on Clinical Trial Policy Q's and A's (October 17, 2007).
11. 42 CFR 405.207(a).
12. US Department of Health and Human Services, Centers for Medicare and Medicaid Services, Medicare Benefit Policy Manual, Chapter 14 – Medical Devices (Rev. 198, 11-06-14).
13. 42 USC 1395y(m)(2)(C).
14. US Department of Health and Human Services, Centers for Medicare and Medicaid Services, Pub 100-02 Medicare Benefit Policy, Transmittal 198, (November 6, 2014).
15. US Department of Health and Human Services, Centers for Medicare and Medicaid Services, Medicare Benefit Policy Manual, Chapter 14 – Medical Devices (Rev. 198, 11-06-14).
16. Id.
17. Id.
18. US Department of Health and Human Services, Centers for Medicare and Medicaid Services, Pub 100-02 Medicare Benefit Policy, Transmittal 198, (November 6, 2014).
19. Food and Drug Administration, FDA Categorization of Investigational Device Exemption (IDE) Devices to Assist the Centers for Medicare and Medicaid Services (CMS) with Coverage Decisions: Guidance for Sponsors, Clinical Investigators, Industry, Institutional Review Boards, and Food and Drug Administration Staff (December 5, 2017).
20. https://www.cms.gov/Medicare/Coverage/IDE/Approved-IDE-Studies.html.
21. US Department of Health and Human Services, Centers for Medicare and Medicaid Services, National Coverage Determination for Routine Costs in Clinical Trials, 310.1 (July 2007).
22. US Department of Health and Human Services, Centers for Medicare and Medicaid Services, National Coverage Determination for Routine Costs in Clinical Trials, 310.1 (July 2007).
23. US Department of Health and Human Services, Centers for Medicare and Medicaid Services, MLN Matters Special Edition, SE0822, Clarification of Medicare Payment for Routine Costs in a Clinical Trial, (revised May 16, 2018).
24. Id.
25. Id.
26. Author's note: This is a reference to the CMS coverage with evidence development process which can establish special National Coverage Determinations for unique trials.
27. *Author's note:* The reference to "M+C organizations" are references to what are now called Medicare Advantage Plans (MAPs); that is, private health plans with contracts with CMS to provide equivalent Part A and Part B benefits, plus possibly more, under the Medicare Part C legal structure.
28. *Author's note:* Services during approved device studies are paid for by MAPs routine costs for non-device qualifying clinical trials are paid by MAPs. As discussed in Chapter 1, this process is tedious and takes numerous areas of a hospital or practice to ensure billing compliance.

12
Grant Management

By Tammie Bain, BS, JD, and Jennifer Laporte, MPA, CRA[1]

Introduction

What does it mean to be compliant in grants management? It means an institution is fulfilling its sponsor-required obligations as part of accepting a sponsor's funds to conduct research or perform an activity. Institution-wide solutions to ensure grant management compliance may include all areas from grant personnel to institutional support functions (such as payroll services) to upper leadership (such as conflict of interest committees). A successful compliance program requires careful documentation and cohesiveness of policies, practices, procedures, and controls, as well as a strong sense of who is responsible for various activities and role delineation.

To understand which laws, rules, and regulations apply to any sponsored study, we must understand the nature of the various funding mechanisms. Grants from government entities are considered public assistance. The funding agency does not direct the science and expects very little in return for the funds—primarily financial and technical reports, as well as disclosure of patents and listing any publication resulting from the sponsored study. The goal of a study funded by a grant is not to provide a specific outcome, but to increase knowledge. Contracts are mechanisms under which the funding entity acquires specific goods, services, and/or technology. Unlike grants and cooperative agreements, and in addition to other laws, rules, and regulations, federal contracts are subject to Federal Acquisition Regulations (FARs), which are addressed in the chapter covering contracts. When a contract is issued, the funding agency is very much involved in developing the research plan, scope of work, and/or protocol as well as management/oversight of the institution's performance. The contract sets specific deliverables and schedules. Federal cooperative agreements are a hybrid of grants and contracts. With these cooperative agreements, the government has a more hands-on approach than with grants, but without the same level of control under a contract. These agreements do set specific deliverables, but the recipient has greater control in how to meet the objectives. Further, these mechanisms are considered public assistance, rather than acquisitions, and are not subject to the FARs. The primary goal of a cooperative agreement is to increase knowledge, but with a higher expectation for a specific outcome than what is expected under a grant. For the purposes of this chapter, the term "grant" will include cooperative agreements.

The vast majority of federal funding provided by grants is issued by the National Institutes of Health (NIH) under the U.S. Department of Health and Human Services (HHS). Therefore, NIH has played a significant role in establishing rules governing studies funded with federal dollars. The NIH is referenced frequently throughout this chapter.

Because consequences for non-compliance associated with non-governmental funding do not typically include penalties mandated by state or federal law, this chapter focuses on grants issued by governmental bodies, primarily federal. This is not to undermine the importance of complying with the rules, guidelines, and policies of our generous non-governmental partners. Many non-governmental sponsors require funding recipients to comply with all NIH requirements; therefore, the requirements discussed in this chapter may be applicable to awards made by state, local, commercial, and nonprofit entities. Even though there might not be legal penalties for non-compliance with the terms of these awards, institutions may have other consequences that are almost as serious (*i.e.*, destroying your relationship with the sponsors).

Grant awards are made to institutions, not individuals. All recipients of government grant funds must comply with all applicable federal laws, regulations, rules, guidelines, and policies. In addition, grantees must comply with all terms and conditions stated in the NIH Notice of Award (NOA), which may include both standard and special conditions. With NIH awards, pay particular attention to Section IV of the NOA which contains any special terms and conditions. Further, the activities, regardless of funding source, must comply with state and local laws and regulations applicable to the institution, individuals working on the study, and the activity itself. Rarely is an institution required to sign an NOA; however, it is still a legally binding document. In particular, drawing funds from the HHS Payment Management System means that grantees agree to the terms and conditions of the grant award, thereby establishing the legal rights and obligations of the parties.

OMB Circulars, Uniform Guidance, and the Code of Federal Regulations

Historically, the laws, rules, and regulations governing federal funding provided under grants were codified in OMB Circulars. These documents, issued by the federal Office of Management and Budget (OMB), provide the rules applicable to all federal funding agencies each time they distribute public assistance (*i.e.*, issue grants). The funding agencies in turn flow these requirements to all grant recipients. In an effort to streamline funding requirements and make terms consistent among many federal agencies, the requirements in OMB Circulars are now consolidated into a single set of requirements within the Code of Federal Regulations (CFR), namely, 2 C.F.R. § 200. This set of regulations is referred to as the Uniform Guidance and became effective December 26, 2014. Unlike the OMB Circulars, the CFRs are directly enforceable against institutions and individuals.

According to the Government Publishing Office (GPO) website, which houses federal documents, "The Code of Federal Regulations (CFR) annual edition is the codification of the general and permanent rules published in the Federal Register by the departments and agencies of the Federal Government. It is divided into 50 titles that represent broad areas subject to federal regulation."[2] The Uniform Guidance, cited as 2 C.F.R. § 200, means that the information is in Title 2, Part 200.

The Uniform Guidance is applicable to all grants awarded after the effective date of the Uniform Guidance, as well as those preexisting awards that have since been amended to add incremental funding. In the rare event an institution has an award issued prior to the effective date (which has not been amended to state that the Uniform Guidance will govern), the OMB Circulars still apply. For the vast majority of awards now in effect, the Uniform Guidance is the roadmap grant recipients use to ensure successful stewardship of their federal funds. Under particular grants, some federal agencies may have more specific rules and/or exceptions, but the Uniform Guidance contains the basic guidelines for any and all federal funding under grants, as well as some rules for federal contracts.

Don't forget that the funding announcement and notice of award often contain requirements applicable after receiving an award. For instance, the Uniform Guidance and Federal Acquisition Regulations (FARs) both govern federal funding through contracts. Recipients of funding provided under cooperative agreements should follow both the Uniform Guidance and any other regulations and policies issued by the funding entity. For instance, cooperative agreements with the U.S. Department of Defense (DoD) are also governed by the DoD Grant and Agreement Regulations (DoDGARs), codified in Title 32 of the CFR.

Note that the federal government provides separate rules for specific types of entities, broken into broad categories such as federal, state, and local governments; tribal governments; institutions of higher education; and for-profit and nonprofit entities. Therefore, it is important that you understand whether your institution is a for-profit, nonprofit, higher education, or governmental entity to determine which subparts of the Uniform Guidance govern federal funds received by your institution. If in doubt, ask your office of general counsel to provide you with more information.

Risk Areas

Grants management compliance has some risk areas. The Uniform Guidance lists these risk areas as (not an exhaustive list):

1. Facilities and administrative costs
2. Salary administration (effort reporting, institutional base salary, and salary cap)
3. Cost considerations (administrative and clerical costs, allowable costs, and service/recharge centers)
4. Cost transfers
5. Subrecipient monitoring
6. Cost sharing
7. Accounting procedures
8. Noncompliance with assurances and special terms and conditions of award
9. Financial reporting
10. Cost accounting standards
11. Documentation/permission

Facilities and Administrative Costs

Facilities and administrative (F&A) costs are often referred to as overhead or indirect costs. They are the very real costs of conducting studies funded by external parties. These costs are typically very difficult to allocate to any particular study underway at an institution. Therefore, the costs are pooled and a set rate or percentage of direct costs is calculated and applied to all sponsored studies. Please note that most higher education institutions use the percentage of direct costs methodology.

The Uniform Guidance defines F&A costs as "those that are incurred for common or joint objectives and therefore cannot be identified readily and specifically with a particular sponsored study, an instructional activity, or any other institutional activity."[3] More specifically, the Uniform Guidance defines facilities as "depreciation on buildings, equipment and capital improvement, interest on debt associated with certain buildings, equipment and capital improvements, and operations and maintenance expenses."[4] It defines administrative as "general administration and general expenses such as the director's office, accounting, personnel and all other types of expenditures not listed specifically under one of the subcategories of "Facilities" (including cross allocations from other pools, where applicable)."[5] Where you capture your F&A costs depends upon the category of your institution. For example, library costs may be captured under facilities or administrative, nonprofit organizations would capture them under administrative costs, and institutions of higher education would capture library costs under facilities. This is important in that the facilities cost is capped at 26%; therefore, it is advantageous to capture library costs under administrative costs.

These rates are negotiated with the federal government through either the U.S. Department of Health and Human Services (DHHS) or the DoD Office of Naval Research (ONR). The correct agency is often referred to as the "cognizant agency." The cognizant agency is typically determined by the institution identifying which one provides the most funds to the institution in the three years prior to negotiation, with DHHS as the default agency when this cannot be determined (i.e., the institution does not receive funding from either agency). The negotiated rates must be accepted by all federal agencies with some exceptions due to special circumstances (i.e., required by law or regulation).

Many institutions have separate F&A rates negotiated for broad categories of research, instruction, and public service. Some of these categories are frequently subdivided into on- and off-campus rates. Off-campus rates are reduced, as campus facilities will either not be used or minimally used; therefore, the F&A rate captures only the administrative costs. Institutions may also have separate negotiated rates for general research and clinical trials. Because the work performed in clinical trials is so specific, an institution is able to directly budget some costs that might otherwise be considered administrative (recruitment efforts, screening efforts, nursing staff, etc.), and the rate is reduced in proportion. Furthermore, because many state or local government entities receive state funding to cover facilities, they may have reduced rates, covering only the administrative portion, for studies funded by state agencies.

The Uniform Guidance, under Appendix III to Part 200, provides guidelines for establishing an F&A rate for institutions of higher education. For nonprofit organizations, guidelines are in Appendix IV.

While a simplified method to calculate the F&A rate exists for smaller institutions, typical institutions of higher education calculate the F&A rate by adding all allowable but not readily allocable facilities and administrative costs associated with the sponsored activity, and then divide that total by all direct costs of the sponsored activity. For certain institutions that do not have an F&A rate established with the federal government, the Uniform Guidance now allows a de minimis rate of 10%.

It is important to be consistent across all funding mechanisms and all categories of sponsors when determining whether certain expenses will be recovered as direct or indirect costs. If a category of costs is used to calculate the indirect cost rate, with rare exceptions, that category of costs cannot be charged to any grant as direct costs, even when an institution is able to clearly allocate such costs to a specific study. For instance, if an institution captures office supplies in their F&A rate, no office supplies may be charged to a grant, even if they can clearly show that the supplies were used solely for one specific study. An institution may be able to obtain an exception to this by clearly explaining the items purchased were not in fact general office supplies, but special products required for that study (i.e., beaker labels that can withstand experimental conditions, such as high heat, which general supply labels cannot do).

Unallowable Costs in F&A Proposals

Although this may vary by type of entity seeking an F&A rate, the following is a non-exhaustive, general list of costs not allowed in calculating F&A rates for institutions of higher education:

1. Advertising, with some exceptions (such as personnel recruitment, procurement of goods and services, and disposal of surplus materials)
2. Alcoholic beverages
3. Bad debt expenses
4. Commencement and convocation costs
5. Direct costs
6. Goods or services for personal use, including housing and personal living expenses
7. Insurance against defects and/or medical liability
8. Losses on other sponsored agreements or contracts, including cost-sharing agreements or any under-recovery through negotiation of flat amounts for F&A costs

9. Memberships, subscriptions, and professional activity costs
10. Pre-award costs, except as may be authorized by the funding entity
11. Student activity costs, with limited exceptions
12. Travel costs

Supersession

The Uniform Guidance, as stated in §200.104, clearly supersedes the OMB Circulars. "As described in §200.110 Effective/applicability date, this part supersedes the following OMB guidance documents and regulations under Title 2 of the Code of Federal Regulations.

OMB Guidance Documents

a. A-21, "Cost Principles for Educational Institutions" (2 CFR part 220);
b. A-87, "Cost Principles for State, Local and Indian Tribal Governments" (2 CFR part 225) and also FEDERAL REGISTER notice 51 FR 552 (January 6, 1986);
c. A-89, "Federal Domestic Assistance Program Information";
d. A-102, "Grant Awards and Cooperative Agreements with State and Local Governments";
e. A-110, "Uniform Administrative Requirements for Awards and Other Agreements with Institutions of Higher Education, Hospitals, and Other Nonprofit Organizations" (codified at 2 CFR 215);
f. A-122, "Cost Principles for Non- Profit Organizations" (2 CFR part 230);
g. A-133, "Audits of States, Local Governments and Non-Profit Organizations,"; and
h. Those sections of A-50 related to audits performed under Subpart F— Audit Requirements of this part."

2 CFR 200 Subsection E (200.400 through 200.520) (Previously A-21: Cost Principles for Educational Institutions)

This is one of the most important sections of the Uniform Guidance and contains the Cost Principles for grant funding. These principles address the general grant 'mantra' – reasonable, allowable and allocable expenses. They also address direct costs, indirect costs, provisions for selected cost items, and audit requirements.

Subrecipient Monitoring

When an award is granted to an institution, the applicant institution receiving the award is referred to as an awardee, or pass-through entity (PTE) (per the Uniform Guidance). As a recipient of federal funds, the PTE is fully responsible for meeting all obligations described in the proposal and award. The proposal itself becomes part of the award; therefore, the PTE is legally obligated to do everything promised in the proposal.

A proposal budget can include costs that will be distributed to another entity. There are two ways that costs can be distributed: either to a subrecipient or contractor. The Uniform Guidance draws a distinction between these two. The relationship between awardee and contractor is one of procurement. A contractor provides goods or services through their normal business. Such goods or services benefit the study, but are ancillary to it. Federal award compliance requirements are not passed-through to contractors.

A subrecipient's performance is measured according to whether the federal award's objectives are met. Applicable federal program requirements from a federal award flow down to subrecipients and are identified in subaward agreements. The PTE is fully responsible for its subrecipients' activity (or lack thereof) during the study. Subpart D of the Uniform Guidance requires a PTE to perform a risk assessment of and monitor its subrecipient, and also follow up on audit findings.

An awardee is referred to as a PTE because it receives federal funds and passes-through a portion of those funds to another entity—the subrecipient. The PTE should examine the subrecipient, determine the overall level of risk the subrecipient presents, and develop an appropriate monitoring plan based on the level of risk. As part of a subrecipient monitoring plan, it is imperative that the PTE and the subrecipient enter into a contractual relationship once an award is made. The contract (often referred to as a subaward, or subgrant) should always include the appropriate federal award information as required by the Uniform Guidance, any specific requirements required by the federal award itself to be flowed down, as well as specific terms or conditions as determined by the risk assessment. The subaward agreement should identify the source of funds as well as regulations applicable to the study. The terms and conditions of the subaward should make clear the following (and note that this list is not exhaustive):

1. If applicable, no study should ever begin without approval(s) of a subrecipient's IRB, Institutional Animal Care and Use Committee (IACUC), and/or its committee governing hazardous materials. And note that any DoD funding obligates an institution to also obtain approval of the Human Research Protection Office (HRPO) (DoD's IRB) if human subjects are involved in a study and approval of Animal Care and Use Review Office (ACURO) (DoD's IACUC) if any vertebrate animals will be involved in a study. Even if an IRB and/or IACUC have approved a study, an institution cannot spend DoD funds until its oversight committees have also approved the study or any changes to the protocol. Further, any serious adverse events or information which may affect a study subject's participation in the study, should be reported to the appropriate oversight committee of the awardee.
2. A subrecipient should provide its audit certifications on an annual basis during the study period.
3. A PTE should have access to all records and financial statements related to the study to ensure that subrecipient is in compliance with the Uniform Guidance.
4. A PTE should be allowed to inspect subrecipient facilities to ensure the study is progressing as agreed upon by reviewing information, facilities and equipment, and/or operations.(Failure of the subrecipient to meet its obligations and conduct the study in accordance with the timeframe set forth in the proposal and award does not relieve the PTE from meeting its obligations.)
5. A subrecipient may only use its federally negotiated F&A rate and provide documentation evidencing its current rate. Additionally, if the subrecipient does not have a negotiated rate, they can use the Uniform Guidance de minimus rate of 10%.
6. Any and all payments to the subrecipient are subject to the PTE's review and approval, and if any costs are not in agreement with the budget and/or deemed not to be reasonable, allocable and allowable, the PTE has the right to refuse payment for such costs. In addition, if the costs are not incurred during the period of performance, the PTE has the right to refuse payment for such costs, unless approval has been obtained from the funding agency. (If the federal agency determines that a cost is not reasonable, allocable, and/or allowable, at minimum, that amount must be refunded by the PTE regardless of whether the subrecipient reimburses the PTE; therefore, strong language in the subcontract is advisable.)
7. Payments should further be tied to the timely progress of the study and submission of reports to the PTE in accordance with the proposal and award. (Failure of the subrecipient to provide progress/final reports does not relieve the PTE from the duty of submitting its own reports to the agency in a timely manner.)
8. A subrecipient should document any cost share commitments made. The final invoice should be tied to adequate proof of such cost share.
9. A subrecipient should make assurances that neither it nor any key personnel

working on the study has/have been debarred or suspended from receiving federal assistance.
10. All reports that a subrecipient provides to the PTE should be clearly identified in the subaward. Reports could include: technical/progress, financial, and Invention Statement reports. Reports could be required on a regular basis, such as annual, quarterly, monthly, as-needed basis, or at the end as a final report.

An important part of federal award compliance is the ongoing monitoring of the subrecipient by the PTE. Ongoing monitoring includes actions such as crosschecking the subrecipient against federal debarment/suspension lists to confirm the subrecipient is not on them, requiring regular progress reports, and performing desk or site reviews. Additionally, the Uniform Guidance requires the PTE to review annual audit findings and issue timely management decisions about the findings.

Review of Proposals

Proposal review prior to submission is the first line of defense when it comes to compliance. It is imperative that the individual reviewing the proposal be familiar with the funding opportunity announcement, sponsor's guidelines, Uniform Guidance, and other applicable CFRs, as well as the grant applicant's institutional policies and procedures. Here's the basic information that should always be reviewed from an institutional perspective:

1. Narrative

The proposal narrative should not include commitments that do not match the budget. These may be easy to miss when preparing the budget or making final revisions to the text. For example, the narrative may include a specified level of institutional commitment, such as cost sharing, equipment purchase, salary support, or travel costs, which are not shown in the budget. Regardless of whether a commitment is in the budget, the applicant institution is responsible for providing the commitment promised upon award. Therefore, no review is complete if every portion of the proposal has not been read. While it may be possible to renegotiate with the sponsor at award time, the likelihood of the sponsor awarding additional funds is remote and an institution cannot be assured the sponsor will reduce the promised commitment in the proposal.

2. Budget

The budget is the most likely location for issues that could become compliance concerns upon award. These are the areas to closely review:

a. **Costs:** All costs must be allowable, reasonable, and allocable, as described in the Uniform Guidance Subpart E Cost Principles.
   i. **Allowable:** According to 2 C.F.R. § 200.403, allowable costs must be necessary and reasonable for the study, conform to any limitations or exclusions of the award, be consistently treated, be determined according to generally accepted accounting principles, not be used as cost share for another federal study, and be adequately documented. It is a good idea to remember that you start with the Uniform Guidance, CFRs, the agency guidelines, and the Funding Opportunity Announcement (which will prevail if there are any discrepancies). The funding announcement should be reviewed for restrictions on which specific costs are allowable. While every rule has its exceptions, costs for items such as administrative support (recovered in F&A rate), alcohol, meals, electronic devices (especially if for student use), capital improvement, etc., should be reviewed carefully.
   ii. **Reasonable:** Cost reasonableness is addressed in 2 C.F.R. § 200.404, where it notes that costs should not exceed what

a prudent person would incur under the same circumstances.

 iii. **Allocable:** According to 2 C.F.R. § 200.405, costs are allocable when they can be assigned to the award in proportion to the benefit received by the study. Be sure it is possible to clearly ascertain that the costs are directly related to the advancement of the study. Any costs not allocable to the study (in whole or in part) are captured in the institutional F&A return. An example of an easy mistake is charging 100% of the cost of equipment to a study and then using that equipment for general purposes, teaching, or another sponsored study. If equipment purchased under an externally funded study will be used for any purpose other than the study funding the purchase, you must charge to that study only the percentage you will use the equipment on that study.

b. **Salaries:** Salary should be an appropriate percentage of the employee's institutional base salary. If it is the policy of the applicant institution to show any stipends received by the investigator or other personnel outside the base salary (*i.e.*, increases for serving as department chair or other administrative duties), only the base salary should be used. While a reasonable inflation each year to capture salary increases is often allowable (as is inflation to capture any anticipated increase due to promotion, tenure, etc.), sponsor guidelines should be reviewed for limits. Additionally, some sponsors (NIH, for example) have a policy of only reimbursing up to a specified salary cap. Review sponsor guidelines for instructions on how to budget employees who have institutional base salaries over the sponsor's cap.

For investigators at academic institutions, determine if their salary is paid based on a 9-month (academic) or 12-month (calendar) contract year. If paid on a 9-month year, it is acceptable to budget for funds to cover their effort during the summer, providing the applicant institute's policy regarding summer salary is followed as well as any sponsor limits.

In addition, include fringe benefits, unless they are captured in the applicant institution's F&A rate. Some institutions have a policy to use a percentage calculation; others use actual costs. Whichever method the applicant institution uses to determine the fringe rate, it should be used consistently. An institution should not use one calculation that would provide a higher rate for federal budgets and a second calculation that would produce a lower rate for non-federal budgets.

c. **Cost Share:** In the budget, cost share refers to costs identified as part of the study covered by the applicant institution or a third party. Most institutions have a policy requiring multiple levels of approval and possibly limits cost sharing. While many investigators believe that cost sharing makes their proposals more competitive, this is rarely the case. The funding opportunity announcement should be reviewed for information on whether cost share is counted in proposal evaluation. It is important to follow institutional policy and see that all requisite approvals are obtained. In the event that cost share is approved, it is important to communicate with the investigator and/or departmental staff all of their responsibilities once the award is made. If there are any subrecipients proposing cost share in the proposal, the applicant institution will be responsible for meeting the full commitment, even if the subrecipient fails to meet its obligations. It is imperative that all documentation is received in accordance with all institutional policies, evidencing the required cost share by the subrecipient.

d. **F&A Rate:** Once an F&A rate is established with a cognizant federal agency, your institution must use that rate for all federal proposals, unless otherwise stated in the funding opportunity announcement or that agency's guidelines. Any deviation from the institution's negotiated rate should require approval by the appropriate institutional authority. Many investigators believe that a lower F&A rate will make their proposal more appealing to the agency—this is not necessarily true, and definitely not true for federal agencies. As some institutions have multiple rates, make certain the budget uses the correct institutional rate—research, instruction, community service, as well as on-campus or off-campus. When it comes to compliance, consistency is of utmost importance.

e. **Tuition:** For most federal agencies, tuition is an allowable expense. However, there are some specific federal and non-federal programs that do not allow this expense. The Funding Opportunity Announcement (FOA) should be reviewed carefully for restrictions. In addition, follow the applicant institution's policy. Some institutions do not charge tuition to sponsors, even if it is an allowable expense. Consistency is key—so, if there is an institutional policy, apply it regardless of the source of funds.

f. **Course Buy-Out:** If the investigator's effort interferes with his/her teaching load, some agencies pay their salary during all or part of the academic year, or they pay an amount sufficient to pay an adjunct or visiting professor to cover the investigator's academic duties. If these funds are requested, it is important that it be fully described and justified in either the narrative or budget justification.

g. **Modified Total Direct Costs (MTDC) and Facilities & Administrative (F&A) Costs:** Modified total direct costs are all costs to which the F&A multiplier can be applied. For example, costs such as equipment and tuition cannot go into the base total for calculating F&A for most agencies. The proposal budget should be a best estimate of study direct costs and the F&A calculation should be done correctly.

One note of caution with regard to cost or recharge centers is that overhead costs are frequently rolled into the prices charged for the services provided by one or all of those centers. Therefore, when preparing budgets, know if your cost center or recharge center costs should be removed from the base when calculating F&A.

3. Subrecipients

Remember that the applicant institution is responsible for all aspects of the study, including those proposed to be undertaken by a subrecipient. Therefore, the applicant institution must also review the subrecipient's budget. The applicant institution will be responsible for any unallowable costs in the subrecipient's budget. In addition to ensuring compliance, this can prevent possible friction between the investigators. Watch for cost share issues and accurate F&A use. Further, it is advisable to obtain the F&A rate document from any subrecipients at the proposal stage.

Effort Reporting

It is important to remember that effort and payroll go hand in hand. Also remember that salary and fringe represent a significant portion of all federal funding. Therefore, effort reporting is one of the strongest ways for a sponsor to meet its duty to ensure the hard-earned dollars of taxpayers are spent appropriately. Accordingly, an awardee should have internal controls that ensure salaries and wages that are charged to a grant are accurate as well as allowable and allocable to the grant. Anyone who is funded on a federal grant must understand that their payroll is connected and interdependent on effort reporting and certification. The description of the roles and responsibilities for key staff is essential. The budget should include compensation only for those persons involved in the conduct of the study, and the percentage of their effort for the study should be specified accurately. Charges should be based on an appropriate percentage of their institutional base salary and applicable fringe rate. Remember, when someone certifies his/her effort, they are making a legally binding commitment to the accuracy of that statement; therefore, it is important that we impress upon our research team the need to be forthcoming with all information. Keep in mind that while salary often is the same percentage as the amount of effort an investigator puts into a study, it is possible that the percent of effort could be higher than the amount of salary charged, resulting in institutional cost share of the difference. Salary can never be higher than the percentage of effort.

Cost Transfers

Cost transfers are costs transferred between sponsored program accounts, or between an administrative account and sponsored program account. Expenditures should be charged to correct funding sources, however under certain circumstances a transfer is required to correct an incorrectly charged expense. An institutional procedure establishing regular review of expenditures helps ensure proper allocation of costs. It is important to document the reason behind a cost transfer so that the allowability, allocability, and reasonableness of an expense is clear. Simply stating that a cost transfer was made to correct a mistake is not an adequate explanation, and cost transfers done to cover budget shortfalls or for convenience should not be allowed. Cost transfers should be done in a timely way. They can occur at the end of a study, but should not occur with charges that are 90 days old or older. This is a major red flag for auditors. If you must move charges 90 days or longer after a study closes, it is imperative to provide a thorough explanation for doing so. Costs incurred toward the end of a study are highly scrutinized. They should be made for the purpose of study goals. They should not be made to spend out remaining funds. Likewise, cost transfers onto a federal grant toward the end of a study are more likely to be reviewed and questioned. Cost transfers can send up a red flag to show an organization's poor financial management of the grant. In addition, moving salary costs after effort reporting is also a red flag for auditors. If this is necessary, document the action with a full explanation of why it is required after the person has already certified his/her effort. It is also advisable to provide a statement on how this error will be avoided in the future.

Cost Sharing

Cost sharing or the provision of matching funding represents those costs of a sponsored study borne by the grantee institution, or a third party, rather than the sponsor. Certain criteria consider cost sharing allowable and view them both positively and negatively. An applicant institution should have a policy to define how cost share is handled. The policy should clearly state institutional rules relating to acceptability, approval, and documentation. Cost share can be mandatory (required by the specific program), voluntary committed (not required by the program but is quantified in the proposal), or uncommitted (not required by the program and not specifically identified in the proposal). The goal of an institutional policy should be to ensure funds are available for studies, but also that resources are allocated appropriately. Cost sharing can significantly impact your F&A rate (it goes into the denominator of the calculation), so institutions must be fully aware of the sum total of all cost sharing activities. Mandatory and voluntary committed cost share should be tracked and regularly reported to the sponsor. Resources committed as cost share to a federally funded study cannot be devoted to another.

Basic Responsibilities for Best Practices

Organizations should be certain that their current policies and procedures are clearly communicated to staff, and that their practices comply with those policies and procedures. This should include role delineation and clearly assigned and accepted roles and responsibilities for all sponsored studies. If you accept federal dollars, your institutional leadership should be knowledgeable and supportive to ensure that proper oversight is provided. Any education program must include both externally mandated and institutionally determined compliance requirements. The most successful programs create a climate that encourages compliance, including appropriate incentives and protections for employees who report noncompliance. Institutions should engage in ongoing risk assessments to monitor changes in regulations and compare them with institutional policies and procedures to evaluate the compliance program's effectiveness.

Accounting Basics

In order to maintain correct and appropriate billing, as well as compliance with policies, a separate account must be established for each study. Program income must be identified and accounted for by study. There are four alternatives: additive, deductive, combination, and matching funds.

Expenses should be charged in accordance with:

- Award terms and conditions
- Any policy statement of the funding entity
- Salary rate limitation
- Cost accounting standards
- The Uniform Guidance
- Any other terms and conditions provided by the sponsor, including contract terms within a cooperative agreement

All expenses must be appropriately documented and monitored. Any late expense submission is risky and inefficient. It should be discouraged in grants accounting. Actual expenses should be periodically compared with the budget and verified as accurate (*i.e.*, reasonable, allocable, allowable, and consistently charged). Any mischarges should be corrected in a timely manner (cost transfers) and, when required, prior approvals should be obtained. Any subrecipient's expenses should be consistently monitored, as they are the PTE's responsibility.

The bottom line for managing grant dollars is to establish a system that provides information regarding payroll and fringe benefits, and a process for reviewing and approving cost reimbursement. In order to have effective management, an institution must deal with issues regarding effort reporting, cost overruns, and cost containment, and determine if any unallowable cost has been charged to the grant.

Financial Reporting

All financial status reports (FSRs) for federal awards should be submitted to the sponsor through the appropriate mechanism (*i.e.*, NIH Commons) on a timely basis. All reporting of expenses and program income must agree with institutional accounting records. Timely report submission must adhere to the sponsor's deadlines.

NOTE: NOAs or other award documents and/or sponsor guidelines will specify if more frequent or other financial reporting is required.

Conclusion

Grants accounting and management are important elements of research compliance. Although there are many instances where the efforts to comply with regulations seem to outweigh their benefits, follow the rules and account for any expenditures and your institution can successfully and compliantly complete a grant from the letter of intent through grant closeout.

Chapter 12 Endnotes

1. **Tammie Bain, BS, JD**, is Assistant Director, Industry Contracts for Emory University Office of Technology Transfer in Atlanta, GA; **Jennifer Laporte, MPA, CRA**, is Sponsored Programs Manager for Morgridge Institute for Research in Madison, WI.
2. "About Code of Federal Regulations," U.S. Government Publishing Office, accessed November 20, 2018, https://www.gpo.gov/help/about_code_of_federal_regulations.htm.
3. 2 C.F.R. § 200 (2014).
4. 2 C.F.R. § 200 (2014).
5. 2 C.F.R. § 200 (2014).

13
Research Auditing and Monitoring

By Sheryl Vacca, CHC-F, CCEP-F, CCEP-I, CHRC, CHPC[1]

Introduction

Effective compliance programs include auditing and monitoring as key elements to their success. The Office of Inspector General (OIG) at the Department of Health and Human Services (HHS) has emphasized in several publications that an ongoing evaluation process is critical to a successful compliance program. The Federal Sentencing Guidelines (FSG) require that an organization takes reasonable steps to ensure it follows its compliance and ethics program, including auditing and monitoring to detect criminal conduct. In designing auditing and monitoring activities, it is important that the research compliance professional work closely with the organization's chief compliance professional in order to gain a clear understanding of auditing and monitoring expectations and how these activities can be leveraged together to help minimize and mitigate risks for the organization.

The research compliance professional should implement an auditing and monitoring program that periodically audits the research operation for compliance to applicable regulatory requirements, detects and prevents noncompliant behavior, and reviews that management has implemented corrective action to address noncompliance through ongoing performance management.

General Research Auditing and Monitoring Concepts

Independence and objectivity are important concepts to consider when defining auditing vs. monitoring. Commonly, monitoring is conducted as a management tool in daily operations to concurrently check on performance. This type of scenario is not considered independent due to management performing this function for their own departments. There is a real and/or perceived view of a "vested interest" in the outcomes. Monitoring is usually an informal method of self-review. Auditing is a formalized method which is always independent of the business function being audited and where the auditor has no clear interest in the findings and/or overall outcome of the audit.

Objectivity assures that auditing and monitoring attributes can be measured, and the integrity of the attributes is consistent regardless of who performs the activities. Additionally, objective measurement of the attributes provides clarity in the overall auditing and/or monitoring outcomes.

Annual auditing and monitoring plan. If a research compliance program is part of a comprehensive compliance program, it is important to consider how the research risks will be integrated into the overall programmatic elements of successful auditing and monitoring. The process for developing the plan should consider the following:

- What are the high risk research priority areas identified through the risk assessment process for inclusion in the plan? Consider:
  - Is there any other business area in the organization that is conducting an audit or monitor activity in this area?

- If yes, could you leverage this resource for assistance in completing the stated activity OR utilize their activity and integrate the results into the overall plan?
- What resources are needed? (*i.e.*, subject matter experts) Consider:
    - Is the subject matter in-house?
    - If subject matter requires outsourcing, budget considerations and overall risk priorities may need to be re-evaluated.
- How many hours are needed to complete the plan?
- What are the projected timeframes?
- What are the auditing or monitoring activity definitions and are they outcome or process-oriented?
- Is there flexibility in the plan for changes in risk priorities and possible unplanned compliance risks/crises which may need auditing or monitoring?

It is important that senior leadership participate in and agree with the determination of high risk priorities for the auditing and monitoring plan. This assures buy-in and management focus on compliance risk priorities. Also, if management is involved at the plan's development stage, they will be educated about the types of activities being planned and resources needed to conduct those activities. Then during the plan year, management will understand if there is a need for additional resources and/or change in focus in the plan as the business environment and priorities may change.

Process for conducting research compliance audits and/or monitors (each referred to as an "activity"). Each activity should have a defined framework which will provide management with an understanding of the overall expectations and approach as you execute the plan. The framework for your activities should include:

- Purpose and goal for activity (auditing or monitoring). Consider:
    - Scope will be identified from the purpose or goal, but needs to be objective, measureable, and concise
    - *Before conducting activities in high risk priority areas,* it is important to consider whether legal advice may be needed in establishing activity approach
- Initial discussion with business area for input related to audit attributes, timing, and process. Consider:
    - Concurrent vs. retrospective activity may be determined at this point. Their definitions:
        - A concurrent activity happens in "real time" and before the end point of what you are looking at has occurred
        - A retrospective activity happens after the end point has occurred, (*i.e.*, the claim has been submitted, the research has concluded, etc.) Milestones should be determined for rationale as to how far back to go (*i.e.*, when a new law passed, or a new system went into effect, etc.)
- Finalized approach and attributes. Consider:
    - That the sampling methodology will be determined largely by the scope (purpose and goal) of your activity (*e.g.*, the sample used in self-reporting a risk area to an outside enforcement agency may be predetermined by the precedent the enforcement agency has set in the industry to determine if education is needed in a risk area, etc.)
    - Audience's frame of reference when receiving activity results and developing an appropriate format for reporting
- Conduct activity
- Preliminary findings/observations
- An opportunity for findings/observations to be validated by business area
- Finalized report
- System to follow up on execution of management corrective action related to activity findings/observations
    - Data collection and tracking, which provide trend analysis and measurement of progress
- Key points of activity that may be provided to leadership and/or in board reporting

Documentation. Document the overall process of developing the auditing and monitoring plan. This includes describing how the risk assessment was conducted and the methodology for the prioritization of risks. Additionally, unless the activity is under attorney-client privilege (the attorney will direct what they want to be documented for that work product), work papers to support the audit findings, reports, and corrective action plans should be documented. Be sure to define prior to the audit activity, what should be considered in "work papers" and documented.

Annual evaluation of execution of auditing and monitoring plan. At the end of each plan year, it is important to conduct an evaluation of the overall effectiveness of the plan. Questions to consider may include: Was the plan was fully executed? Were appropriate resources utilized for plan execution? Were the activities conducted in a timely manner? Did the plan "make a difference" in regards to the organization's strategy and business? Did the plan reach the goal of detecting, deterring, and/or preventing compliance research risks from occurring? Annual evaluations may be conducted through self-reviews or independent of the compliance function by the organization's internal audit or by a third party. However, it is recommended that independent reviews are conducted on a biannual basi to determine the effectiveness of the plan.

Potential Research Risk Areas for Consideration in the Plan

Priority risk areas will evolve dependent on industry focus by other similar organizations, geographic market environment, enforcement or regulatory agencies, public visibility, etc. Examples of research risk areas may include:

- Clinical research billing. Consider:
  - Is it a "deemed" and qualifying trial? What are the routine costs?
  - Which research procedures are not reasonable and necessary, but must be paid by the sponsor?
  - Are you billing for services that were already paid by the sponsor?
  - Are you billing for services that were promised at no cost in the informed consent? Are you billing for services that are for research-purposes only? Are you billing for services that are part of a non-qualifying clinical trial?
- Conflict of interest
- Environmental health and safety
- Animal research protection
- Sponsored research requirements met
- Biosafety
- Information technology security
- IRB weaknesses in process controls, such as:
  - Human subject protection
  - Privacy
  - Follow up after initial approval of research
- Principal investigators, and their:
  - Time and effort reporting
  - Fiscal responsibility
  - Grant closeouts
- Research misconduct
- Regulatory, legal requirements

Risk areas are defined by the organization through the risk assessment process and prioritized according to established methodologies.

Conclusion

Effectiveness in the development and execution of the auditing and monitoring plan will be determined by the integrity and characteristics of the overall auditing and monitoring process. Effective auditing and monitoring activities will demonstrate continual process improvement with compliant behavior and activities. Additionally, research compliance risks will be detected, deterred, and/or prevented with an effective auditing and monitoring plan and appropriate, timely follow-up by management for mitigating risks.

Chapter 13 Endnotes

1. **Sheryl Vacca**, CHC-F, CCEP-F, CCEP-I, CHRC, CHPC, is Senior Vice President, Chief Risk Officer for Providence St Joseph Health in Providence, RI.

14
What are Export Controls?

By Kelé Piper, MS, CIP, CHRC[1]

Introduction

International research activities often involve the exchange of information or technology. It is vital to understand that export controls do not always apply to a physical shipment of a "thing," but can also be the exposure of technological knowledge to foreign persons, entities, or countries, both on foreign or domestic soil. This is called a "deemed export." While this may seem a little overwhelming, certain exclusions apply to research activity.

The intent of this section is to provide an overview of the structure and content of regulations commonly called export controls, to describe their relevance to research, and suggest some potential approaches to an export control compliance program.

Export Controls: A Brief Description

Export controls refer to federal regulations that apply to the export of oral, written, electronic, or visual disclosure; or shipment, transfer, or transmission of goods, technology, services, or information to anyone outside of the United States, a non-U.S. entity, or a non-U.S. individual (regardless of location). Export controls have existed for decades, but renewed focus on them increased dramatically after September 2001 and has been stimulated by the risk and speed with which technological advances occur.

In the export control context, the term "export" applies not only to the shipping or personal delivery of technology, information, or funds outside of the United States, but also to the deemed export or disclosure of technology or information to a foreign entity or foreign national on U.S.-soil. Examples of a deemed export could include a tour of laboratory spaces, research involvement, hosting observers or other types of visitors in laboratory or research space, or through discussions or lectures of sensitive research.

The three primary sources of export control regulations are the U.S. Department of Commerce Export Administration Regulations (EAR), the U.S. Department of State International Traffic in Arms Regulations (ITAR), and the U.S. Department of the Treasury Office of Foreign Asset Control (OFAC). There are other regulations (such as those of the U.S. Department of Transportation, International Air Transport Association (IATA), Center for Disease Control, U.S. Fish and Wildlife Services, U.S. Drug Enforcement Administration, etc.) that may also apply to shipping materials outside of the United States, but EAR, ITAR, and OFAC are the key components of federal export controls. The purpose of these regulations is to control proliferation of certain military technologies, and some non-military technologies that have the potential for military applications (called dual use because they have both commercial and military applications), protect certain U.S. commercial technology advantages, and enforce U.S. Department of State opposition to financial flows from the United States to embargoed countries, entities, and persons.

EAR is a set of U.S. government regulations on the export and import of most commercial items.[2] Many of these items are dual-use items. To determine if EAR is applicable, an item can be verified on the Commerce Control List (CCL), also known as the dual-use list.[3]

ITAR regulations apply to the export or import of defense-related articles or services listed in the U.S. Munitions List (USML) for military applications, including deemed exports.[4] Manufacturers and distributors are required to register with the Directorate of Defense Trade Controls (DDTC).

OFAC regulations govern economic and trade sanctions to support foreign policy objectives and national security.[5] Organizations should continually check the the Specially Designated Nationals and Blocked Persons List (SDN), which is published by OFAC, to ensure that they are not doing business with anyone listed. In addition, transactions with boycotted or embargoed countries or countries where trade sanctions exist are also subject to OFAC regulations.

The United States adopted two laws that seek to counteract U.S. citizens from participating in other nations' economic boycotts or embargoes. These anti-boycott laws are the Export Administration Act (EAA) and the Tax Reform Act (TRA). They were adopted to keep U.S. firms from being used to implement foreign policy that runs contrary to U.S. policy. The TRA is designed to penalize through tax benefits for certain types of boycott-related agreements.

Export control violations are serious concerns for both individuals and organizations. Depending on the circumstances, these violations can result in fines, jail time, or both. Violations can be criminal or administrative. Criminal penalties range from 10-20 years in prison and up to one million dollars in fines for individuals or one million dollars or five times the value of the exports involved for organizations. Administrative penalties can include fines to $250,000 per violation, denial of export privileges, revocation of export licenses, and/or exclusion from practice.

Export Controls and Academic Research

The conventions of modern academic research commonly involve sharing information, equipment, materials, and funds with foreign collaborators both domestic and abroad; and many of these common research transactions are subject to export controls.

Challenges for Research Organizations

Some items are clearly within the scope of covered technologies, such as nuclear- and weapon-related research. However, some items listed in the CCL are not as clear-cut. In some cases, these items are even part of another product, such as ball bearings, lasers, or even encryption software on a laptop. In these cases, it can be difficult to determine if a controlled export license is required, as you many need to contact manufacturers or even federal agencies for their determinations. Depending on the complexity, you may need to engage outside counsel with expertise in this area. Another challenge is the flow of information. Collaborators are no longer just the laboratories next door, but they are laboratories across the globe. Information and technology are easily transferred within seconds, both intentionally and unintentionally. The challenge is not just how to be compliant with export control regulations, but it's more important to know how to recognize when and where it is happening within your organization.

Regulatory Options for Export Control Management in Academic Research

There are exclusions from the export control requirements. These include:

- Fundamental Research Exclusion
- Educational Information Exclusion
- Publicly Available/ Public Domain Exclusion

National Security Decision Directive 189 (NSDD 189) defines fundamental research as "basic and applied research in science and engineering, the results of which ordinarily are published and shared broadly within the scientific community, as distinguished from proprietary research and from industrial development, design, production, and product utilization, the results of which ordinarily are restricted for proprietary or national security reasons."[6]

Research projects conducted as fundamental research, as defined above, generally meet the Fundamental Research Exclusion criteria and are not subject to export control laws and regulations unless they have other mitigating factors. For example, research results meet the exclusion criteria and would not require an export control license. However, transferring information, materials, or technology outside of the United States, even to the research collaborator, does not meet the exclusion criteria, except under limited circumstances. Research projects that do not qualify for the exclusion include those that are classified, are completed for a military application, are funded through a foreign sponsor, or have restrictions on publication or foreign national participation restrictions.

Fundamental research is essential to an open academic environment. Research institutions need to be cautious that they do not diminish the exclusions provided through fundamental research. Instances that invalidate the exclusion include contractual restrictions on foreign national participation in the research, publication restrictions, or restrictions on dissemination of the research results. Be aware of agreements outside of the formal contract that are made between the sponsor and researcher to side-step these requirements. It is recommended that these side agreements be addressed in a policy.

The Educational Information Exclusion includes information that is part of a published curriculum of commonly taught courses in mathematics, science, and engineering ,or in teaching labs connected to these courses.

The Publicly Available/Public Domain Exclusion refers to information that is available to the public through the public domain and includes technology and software. As a note, this does not apply to encrypted software. The public domain includes already published materials that can be purchased through commercial means, obtained from a library, searched on the internet, or which have been provided for public or unlimited distribution. A detailed legal definition of what the "public domain" means can be obtained at 22 C.F.R. § 120.11.

Identifying and Mitigating Risky Areas for Potential Export Control Risks

Export control regulations are complex. Educating your research community on how to identify export control issues is critical to minimize risk and exposure to government actions. In your normal course of business, some common business practices will be easier to monitor, while others might involve a little more effort.

Identified here are some of those more difficult areas, but each organization has a unique workflow with unique risk areas. As you assess your organization for export control catch points, realize that the process of getting an export control license can sometimes take months, so start early and build in time for delays. There is no guarantee a license will be granted.

Train researchers to recognize red flags that may expose their research to export control regulations and to initiate early contact for help mitigating potential problems.measures for non-compliant aspects of a research project. Here are some recommendations to stay compliant with export control regulations:

- For research that is part of a grant application, identify areas that would require an export control review, such as an international site or collaboration.
- Train personnel who draft and approve contracts to recognize export control language and negotiate on behalf of the institution to stay compliant with export control reg-

ulations and retain fundamental research *exclusions*. Work with your general counsel or outside counsel who specialize in export controls to draft templates to help facilitate this process.
- Identify high-risk research areas (*i.e.*, cutting-edge technologies, biologics, nuclear materials, space exploration and navigation, or GPS tracking technologies, etc.) within your institution for education and training purposes. This information is essential for the researchers as well as the supporting research infrastructure. The more individuals who can identify export control risk, the better chance you have to prevent violations.
- Review procedures with shipping departments likely be involved with the research community when shipping internationally. Evaluate the carriers your institution uses to validate their practices and ensure they are compliant with export control regulations.
- Additionally, require staff to obtain training through IATA or a similar course, for the proper method and packaging for transportation of materials. When we think about shipping items, we tend to only consider that items will be shipped via a professional carrier in a manner that can be somewhat monitored. However, it is recommended that you incorporate into your policy and training the dangers of carrying items subject to export control regulations in luggage or on one's person.
- Similarly, researchers who travel with data and equipment are also subject to export control regulations. Examples include traveling with high-tech equipment such as advanced GPS devices, scientific research equipment, or controlled, proprietary, or unpublished data. This can include laptops, cameras, and cell phones, depending on the destination.
- Some committees or departments that are not directly involved in the export control process, but still review research information, could flag a research project that should be considered for an export control review. For example, the Institutional Review Board (IRB) application will request information about collaborators, data storage, and material transfers, among other things, that could possible trigger notifications to key individuals within your institution.
- Partnering with your Human Resources Department as they onboard foreign researchers, students, interns, etc., may also help identify potential areas of export control violation. If a foreign national is coming to your institution for research purposes, it would be prudent to understand that person's role and function while at your institution to avoid deemed export control problems. OFAC checks of these individuals should be built into your onboarding procedures.

Conclusion

In a perfect world, it is ideal for your institution to have some sort of international or export control program or office with individuals who specialize in this complicated and challenging regulatory framework. However, not all institutions will be able to put such a program or office in place. Without these types of resources, it is then the responsibility of the institution to identify areas of risk and design mitigating measures to help reduce their risks. Develop tools and checklists to help researchers and support staff identify export control issues, as well as direct them to individuals or departments that can make export control license determinations and, if necessary, file an application for an export control license.

Information Resources

Export Administration Regulations (EAR)

- Bureau of Industry and Security (BIS): http://www.bis.doc.gov/
- BIS Export Administration Regulations Downloadable Files (Clink on link for Part 774–The Commerce Control List): https://www.bis.doc.gov/index.php/forms-documents/regulations-docs/2345-774-10-24-18/file
- BIS Export Administration Regulations Training archived Online Training Room: https://www.bis.doc.gov/index.php/2011-09-13-18-45-55
- BIS Lists of Parties of Concern: https://www.bis.doc.gov/index.php/policy-guidance/lists-of-parties-of-concern

International Traffic in Arms Regulations (ITAR)

- U.S. Department of State Directorate of Defense Trade Controls (DDTC): https://www.pmddtc.state.gov/
- DDTC Understand the ITAR and Export Controls: https://www.pmddtc.state.gov/?id=ddtc_public_portal_itar_landing

Office of Foreign Asset Control (OFAC)

- U.S. Department of Treasury Office of Foreign Assets Control (OFAC): https://www.treasury.gov/about/organizational-structure/offices/Pages/Office-of-Foreign-Assets-Control.aspx
- OFAC Consolidated Sanctions List Data Files: https://www.treasury.gov/resource-center/sanctions/SDN-List/Pages/consolidated.aspx
- OFAC Specially Designated Nationals and Blocked Persons List (SDN) Human Readable Lists: https://www.treasury.gov/resource-center/sanctions/SDN-List/Pages/default.aspx

Chapter 14 Endnotes

1. **Kelé Piper, MS, CIP, CHRC**, is Director, Research Compliance for Beth Israel Deaconess Medical Center in Boston, MA.
2. 15 C.F.R. § 700-799.
3. 15 C.F.R. § 774.
4. 22 C.F.R. § 120-130, 22 C.F.R. § 121.
5. 31 C.F.R. § 500-599.
6. S.C. Res. 189, ¶ 1 (September 21, 1985).

15
Integrating Research Compliance into the Corporate Compliance Program

By Wendy Schroeder, BSN, RN, CCRC[1]

Introduction

Defining a research compliance infrastructure and implementing standard operating procedures (SOPs) poses challenges for many institutions and hospitals. Fostering research compliance within the complexity of an Academic Medical Center (AMC), hospital or university system often ends up in silos of effort within the different facilities or institutions and can even result in conflicting SOPs between departments. Small hospital systems struggle with multiplex compliance issues so that research compliance is neither a priority nor an area of domain knowledge for most compliance officers.

Understanding risk assessments while maintaining training and education is often a challenge for the average research enterprise. This chapter will address the key areas of research risk including regulatory, financial and legal aspects of compliance. The discussion will include strategies and models to deal with policies and procedures and to "synchronize" the operations so that the reader is fully aware of the complex issues involving compliance and an informed participant in risk mitigation. Some institutions have a de-centralized process, while others have centralized systems. You will also find some semi-centralized procedures with a mix of resource support. Any way you set up to operationalize compliance, you must include policy, process, education and auditing. Some of the topics discussed may be covered in other chapters of the manual; however, this chapter will link interrelated principles with policy, procedures, and the operational relativity to highlight critical components of a research compliance strategy within a corporate compliance infrastructure.

Functional Areas of a Research Compliance Program

Human Subject Protection

As demonstrated by the evolution of laws and regulations, research and the quest for scientific discovery must never be more important than the safety and welfare of human subjects. Regulatory agencies have established and codified standards for the conduct of ethical research including specific instructions to committees charged with ensuring the rights of human subjects participating in research. We know these committees as Institutional or Independent Review Boards. The IRB reviews research protocols to assess the risks of the study to subjects and ensure those risks are not greater than the potential contribution to science, and to ensure subjects are adequately informed of those risks and have appropriate study information important to their decision to participate.

To accommodate growth and diversity in research—variations in study design (observational and cohort studies), social and behavioral research, analytics and biospecimens, electronic health and digital data records, mobile technology, etc. HHS published revisions to the Common Rule[2] on January 19, 2017. By an interim final rule published on January 22,

2018, the effective and general compliance dates were delayed for a 6-month period, until July 19, 2018.[3] On June 19, 2018, a final rule was published to delay the general compliance date until January 21, 2019.[4] The revised Common Rule, including technical amendments made by the January 22, 2018 interim final rule and the June 19, 2018 final rule, is referred to as the "2018 Requirements." FDA intends to undertake rule-making to harmonize FDA regulations 21 CFR 50 (human subject protection) and 21 CFR 56 (IRBs) with the 2018 Requirements. The FDA issued guidance to Sponsors, Investigators and IRBs in October 2018 to explain the impact of the revised Common Rule on FDA-regulated clinical investigations.

Institutional Review Boards (IRB)

An IRB is an administrative body established to protect the rights and welfare of human research subjects recruited to participate in research activity. Although conceptually modeled for local IRB review, the regulations allow review of research by IRBs in locations other than where the research is performed. Whether the IRB of record is a function within or external to the organization, institutions conducting research involving human subjects must ensure the protection of those subjects, and in the case of FDA-regulated research, provide assurance of regulatory compliance to the sponsor. In addition, the institution must certify to the sponsor that each research project or activity involving human subjects has been reviewed and approved by an IRB in accordance with the assurance given by the institution to the sponsor.

Research involving human subjects conducted or supported by federal departments or agencies should be reviewed by an IRB with a Federal Wide Assurance (FWA) on file with the Office for Human Research Protection (OHRP). FDA and HHS regulations define the scope of the IRB in terms of applicable types of studies—research involving FDA regulated products and research funded by PHS respectively. Yet, many research protocols reviewed by an IRB involve data collection from living individuals and are neither of these "types." Several reform proposals have recommended application of the Common Rule to apply to all research, yet there is controversy as to whether or not Congress should have the authority to regulate research that is not funded by the government and does not involve an FDA regulated product. Currently, many institutions (in their FWA) agree to protect the welfare of all human subjects involved in research, whether or not the research is regulated by FDA or federally funded (Titles 21, 42 and 45 may not be enforceable) and as such their policies require all human subjects research be reviewed by the IRB. In these and in most circumstances, the IRB has jurisdiction over all human subjects research —a scope broader than the regulations, and their authority to approve, require modifications in, or disapprove research is based on both law and institutional policy.

Currently, the NCI Central IRB offers a hybrid option for facilitated IRB review suggesting its use as key to reduce time, cost, redundancy, and variability, and to increase oversight and safety. The 2018 Requirements make federally funded research involving more than one institution reliant on a single IRB for that portion of the research conducted in the United States. The reviewing IRB will be identified by the Federal department or agency supporting or conducting the research. Exceptions are 1) cooperative research for which more than a single IRB is required by law (such as tribal law), and 2) research deemed inappropriate for single IRB review. In addition, studies that involve multiple sites have new requirements with earlier compliance dates: For grant applications with due dates on or after January 25, 2018, and contract solicitations published on or after January 25, 2018, NIH expects that all sites participating in multi-site studies, which involve non-exempt human subjects research funded by the NIH, will use a single Institutional Review Board (sIRB) to conduct the ethical review required for the protection of human subjects. The NCI CIRB becomes the IRB of record and is responsible for initial and continuing reviews of studies including amendments, and group distributed documents such as safety reports (adverse events or AEs) and recruitment materials, while the local IRB retains oversight for consideration of local context, performance, and locally occurring AEs.[5] Examples of the active and effective exercise of this oversight would include:

- Establishment of appropriate institution policies and procedures to ensure research is conducted in accordance with all applicable laws, rules, and regulations
- Establishment of appropriate IRB(s) to approve and monitor all research involving human subjects
- Oversight of the IRB(s)' activities to ensure they are functioning as intended
- Ensure equitable and enforceable consequences for non-compliance with policies and procedures and IRB actions.

The activities of a local IRB should be considered a part of an active institutional compliance program where complying with federal regulations is of extreme importance. While an institution may have only one or multiple IRBs, each must satisfy certain requirements and implement common functions. The discussion of the IRB is divided into the following sections:

- IRB membership and responsibilities
- Types of reviews
- Human subject informed consent
- Adverse events and protocol deviations.

An IRB often acts as a privacy board for research-related requests to approve a waiver or an alteration of the Privacy Rule's Authorization requirements when protected health information is being used for research (HIPAA). The 2018 Requirements, in the definition of a human subject, include identifiable biospecimens. HHS is expected to provide guidance documents on identifiability, privacy and confidentiality, and broad consent.

IRB Membership and Responsibilities. Each IRB must have at least five (5) members with the appropriate diversity of backgrounds to ensure complete and adequate review of research activities normally conducted by the institution. This diversity includes experience, expertise, race, gender, and cultural backgrounds. In addition, members should possess the professional competence necessary to review specific research activities from the viewpoint of institutional commitments and regulations, applicable laws, and applicable standards of professional conduct and practice. For those institutions that conduct research using vulnerable categories of subjects, consideration should be given to including at least one member on the IRB who has experience with those subjects. Vulnerable categories of subjects include children, prisoners, pregnant women, and people with physical or mental disabilities.

In addition to these general requirements, there are a series of very specific requirements for IRB composition, including:

- The IRB membership cannot be all members of one profession
- Gender cannot be a factor in selecting members, which would indicate that an IRB with all male or all female members would probably be challenged
- At least one member must be active primarily in scientific areas
- At least one member must be active primarily in non-scientific areas
- At least one member must have no affiliation with the institution or be a part of the immediate family of someone affiliated with the institution
- A majority of the members must be present to take action on all matters except expedited reviews and at least one of the members present must have primary activities in a non-scientific area.

The IRB is responsible for following documented procedures for:

- Conducting initial and continuing reviews of research
- Reporting findings and actions to both the investigator and the institution

Integrating Research Compliance into the Corporate Compliance Program **181**

- Determining which projects need review more often than annually
- Determining if projects with no material changes require verification from sources other than the investigator since the previous IRB review
- Ensuring that proposed changes in a research activity are promptly submitted to the IRB and are approved by the IRB before such changes are made, except when such changes are for the immediate safety of the subjects
- Maintaining appropriate records of all activities
- Ensuring prompt reporting to institutional officials and/or sponsor:
  - Unanticipated problems involving risks to subjects
  - Serious or continuing non-compliance with requirements or determinations of the IRB
  - Suspension or termination of IRB approval by the institution.

There are several non-compliance risks associated with IRB membership and responsibilities; namely:

- Insufficient diversity of IRB membership for types of research
- Insufficient expertise or training of members
- Failure to have required members; *i.e.*, outsider, non-scientific, vulnerable subject expert
- Failure to disclose conflict of interest
- Insufficient resources to support IRB operations, mainly recordkeeping, space, and staff
- Failure to identify high-risk projects that need frequent oversight and review
- Unusual number of expedited reviews to avoid a quorum for reviewing proposals and changes
- Failure to follow documentation procedures
- Lack of documented procedures for research projects that do not involve human subjects
- Lack of documented procedures for the operation of the IRB
- Lack of documented procedures for research involving human subjects.

There are many mitigation strategies that can be applied to reduce the probability of non-compliance in the IRB operations. Among the most common and most effective are:

- Documented and current policies and procedures for the conduct of research involving humans
- Documented and current policies and procedures for the composition and operation of the IRB(s)
- Appropriate training curriculum for IRB members and staff
- Appropriate training curriculum for investigators and their staff
- Web-based use of IRB agenda
- Oversight review by the research responsible party for the institution (such as, VP of Research) of IRB actions and operations including:
  - Meeting attendance
  - Qualifications of members
  - Quality of meeting minutes
  - Excessive or unwarranted use of expedited review
  - Quality and frequency of continuation reviews
  - Prompt reporting of adverse events and deviations from protocols
  - Completeness of documentation requirements.

Types of Reviews. A **full-board review** of a proposal for research involving human subjects is one that is conducted at a convened meeting of the IRB in which a majority of the IRB members are present, including at least one whose primary concerns are in nonscientific areas. In order for research to be approved in a full board review, it must receive the approval of a majority of those members present at the meeting. An **expedited review** of a proposal for research involving human subjects is one that is performed by only one member of the IRB, usually the chairperson or another member of the IRB designated by the chairperson. The single reviewer may exercise all of the authorities of the IRB except to disapprove the research. A research activity can only be disapproved in accordance with the full review process. To qualify for an expedited review, the research proposal must meet either of the following requirements:

> (1) Inclusion on the list of categories published in the Federal Register that may be reviewed through an expedited review procedure and (2) found by the reviewer(s) to involve no more than minimal risk (minimal risk means that the probability and magnitude of harm or discomfort anticipated in the research are not greater... than those ordinarily encountered in daily life or during the performance of routine physical or psychological examinations or tests); or minor changes in previously approved research during the period (of one year or less) for which approval was authorized.

The IRB that uses expedited reviews must establish a formal method for keeping all members advised of proposals which have been approved under the procedure.

The review criteria for both full reviews and expedited reviews are the same; namely,

- Risks to subjects are minimized
- Risks to subjects are reasonable in relation to anticipated benefits
- Selection of subjects is equitable
- Informed consent is sought from all subjects
- Informed consent is documented
- When appropriate, provision is made to monitor data collected to ensure safety of subjects
- When appropriate, there are adequate provisions to protect privacy of subjects and to maintain confidentiality of data
- When vulnerable categories of subjects are involved, additional safeguards are included.

The 2018 Requirements establish new **exempt** categories of research based on level of risk so that IRBs can focus on higher risk reviews.

Examples and criteria for an exempt determination include:

- educational testing, survey procedures where 1) identity of the subjects is not readily ascertained, 2) no identifying information will be recorded that can link subjects to the data, 3) disclosure of the data could not reasonably place the subjects at risk of civil or criminal liability or be damaging to the subjects' financial standing, employability, or reputation, and 4) an IRB makes the exempt determination
- benign behavioral interventions (brief in duration, harmless, painless, not physically invasive, not likely to have a significant adverse lasting impact on the subjects, and the investigator has no reason to think the subjects will find the interventions offensive or embarrassing) if the subject prospectively agrees and at least one of the following criteria are met: 1) identity of the subjects is not readily ascertained, 2) no identifying information will be recorded that can link subjects to the data, 3) disclosure of the data could not reasonably place the subjects at risk of civil or criminal liability or be damaging to the subjects' financial standing, employability, or reputation, and 4) an IRB makes the exempt determination
- secondary research for which consent is not required if at least one of the following criteria are met: 1) identifiable private information or biospecimens are publicly available, 2) information including information about biospecimens is recorded in a way that identify is not readily ascertained or linked with identifiers, and the investigator will not re-identify or contact the subjects, 3) research use of information for health care operations covered by HIPAA, or 4) federal agency (identifiable private information) data collection for non-research that is maintained in systems of records in compliance with HIPAA
- storage or maintenance for secondary research for which broad consent (for future research) is required (storage or maintenance of identifiable private information or identi-

fiable biospecimens for potential secondary research use) if an IRB makes an exempt determination
- secondary research for which broad consent is required (identifiable biospecimens for secondary research) if the following criteria are met: 1) broad consent was obtained in accordance with regulatory requirements, 2) documentation of informed consent (or waiver of documentation) was obtained, and 3) an IRB determines the research is within the scope of the broad consent and makes an exempt determination and the investigator does not include returning individual research results to subjects as part of the study plan
- federal research and demonstration projects
- taste and food quality evaluation and consumer acceptance studies.

It is the responsibility of the IRB to ensure that there is appropriate documentation to make determinations on all of these criteria and that the documentation is maintained in accordance with the recordkeeping requirements. The primary recordkeeping requirements are:

1. Copies of all proposals reviewed including scientific evaluations, if any, approved sample consent documents, progress reports from the investigators, and reports of injuries to subjects
2. Minutes of IRB meetings in sufficient detail to show:
   a. AttendanceActions taken
   b. Vote on each action including number for, number against, and abstentions
   c. Basis for requiring changes in or disapproving a proposal
   d. Written summary of the discussion of controversial issues and their resolution
3. Copies of all correspondence between the IRB and the investigators.

A **continuation review** is the annual (or more frequent) follow-up for each approved research project. The IRB has authority to observe both the consent and research process and to determine that approved protocols are being followed. This continuation review may include correspondence with and reports from the investigators, use of IRB staff to verify protocol adherence, and/or use of third-party verification on the conduct of the research. The 2018 Requirements now permit an exception to the continuing review requirement if 1) the research is eligible for expedited review, or 2) the research has progressed to the point that it involves only data analysis of identifiable private information or identifiable biospecimens and/or follow up is limited to data collection from procedures that subjects would undergo as routine care. HHS is expected to provide additional guidance documents on continuing review. The IRB is required to maintain records of continuing review activities. Common non-compliance issues in the review process include:

- Incomplete protocols
- Incorrect determination of risk/benefit ratio
- Incomplete maintenance of research files:
  - Protocols
  - Documentation of expedited reviews
  - IRB meeting minutes
  - Documentation of continuation reviews
- Protocols and/or consent forms not followed in practice
- Misuse or over-use of expedited review
- Failure to perform continuation reviews within specified time period
- Failure to properly record minutes of the IRB meetings to allow determination of compliance with requirement.

Once again, there are a wide variety of mitigation strategies that will work to reduce non-compliance in this area. Those that are most common and usually have an impact upon multiple risks when applied include:

- Provide multiple avenues for informing potential investigators of the requirements for proposal acceptance including:
  - Newsletters
  - Focus groups
  - Websites
  - Training sessions
- Provide checklists of required information for a proposal to be considered

- Provide detailed guidance for cost/benefit and risk/benefit determination including discussion on Medicare Advantage issues within clinical trials coverage
- Refuse to accept proposals for IRB action that are incomplete
- Perform oversight review of IRB activities (either by research management or internal audit) to ensure:
  - Proper use of expedited reviews
  - Proper documentation of waivers and alterations
  - Proper continuation reviews in accordance with initial approval time table
  - Adequacy of meeting minutes
  - Completeness of project files
  - Adequacy of resources to support the IRB operations.

Informed Consent

Informed consent is the foundation of all research involving human subjects. The 2018 Requirements emphasize the need to provide essential information a reasonable person would want to know before providing other supplemental information to the subject. As such, the informed consent form (ICF) format may change so that study details are organized in a way that highlights the critical information potential subjects will process in their voluntary decision to participate in the study. Additionally, within 60 days of a trial being closed to recruitment, Common Rule agencies will be required to post a final consent and contact information on a publicly available website. HHS is expected to provide guidance documents on the new consent requirement as well as the clinical trial consent form posting location. Requirements of informed consent will be covered under the following headings:

- General requirements
- Essential elements
- Additional elements
- Alterations and waivers
- Vulnerable categories of subjects
- Documentation of informed consent.

The general requirements for legally effective informed consent establish the conditions which must be present for a subject to even be presented with the required consent forms and information sheets. If these conditions do not exist, there is no legally effective informed consent, even though the documents signed by the subject or the subject's representative may contain all the necessary information. As of the 2018 Requirements, broad consent for the storage, maintenance and secondary research use of identifiable private information or biospecimens is permitted as an alternative to the informed consent requirements. The essential elements of broad consent are noted parenthetically below.

The general requirements are:

1. The informed consent is obtained under circumstances that provide the subject or the subject's legal representative with sufficient opportunity to consider freely and without coercion or undue influence whether or not to participate in the research project.
2. The informed consent is in the language understandable by the subject or the subject's legal representative.
3. The informed consent does not include any language (written or oral) that waives or appears to waive the subject's legal rights.
4. The informed consent does not include any language (written or oral) that releases or appears to release the investigator, the sponsor, the institution or its agents from liability for negligence.

For an informed consent to be considered legally effective, it must contain at least the following essential elements (unless applicable exceptions apply; see Alterations and Exemptions below). The essential elements are:

1. statement about the project that indicates:

a. it is a research project
   b. an explanation of the purpose of the research
   c. expected duration of the subject's participation
   d. description of the procedures to be followed
   e. identification of any procedures that are experimental
2. description of any reasonably foreseeable risks or discomforts to the subject (required for Broad Consent)
3. description of any benefits to the subject or to others which may be reasonably expected (required for Broad Consent)
4. disclosure of appropriate alternative procedures or treatments, if any, that may be advantageous to the subject
5. statement describing the extent, if any, by which confidentiality of records identifying the subject will be maintained (required for Broad Consent)
6. for research that involves more than a minimal risk, an explanation as to:
   a. whether any compensation and any medical treatment are available if injury occurs
   b. what those elements consist of
   c. where further information may be obtained
7. explanation of whom to contact for answers to pertinent questions about the research and research subjects' rights, and whom to contact in the event of a research-related injury to the subject
8. statement that (required for Broad Consent):
   a. participation is voluntary
   b. refusal to participate will involve no penalty or loss of benefits to which the subject is otherwise entitled
   c. the subject may discontinue participation at any time without penalty or loss of benefits to which the subject is otherwise entitled.
9. (New 2018 Requirement) One of the following statements about any research involving identifiable data or specimens:
10. statement that identifiers may be removed from the identifiable private information or biospecimen and after such removal, the information or biospecimen can be used for future research or distributed to another investigator for future research, or
11. statement that the subject's information or biospecimen collected as part of the research, even if identifiers are removed, will not be used or distributed for future research studies.
12. statement that biospecimens, even if identifiers are removed may be used for commercial profit,

Additional elements that may be provided to each subject are:

1. A statement that the particular treatment or procedure may involve risks to the subject that are not currently foreseeable
2. Anticipated circumstances under which the subject's participation in the research may be terminated by the investigator without regard to the subject's consent
3. Any additional cost to the subject that may result from participating in the research
4. Procedures for the orderly voluntary termination of the subject from the research and any consequences to the subject because of that termination
5. A statement that any new findings developed during the research project that might relate to the subject's willingness to participate in the research will be provided to the subject
6. The approximate number of subjects in the research project
7. (New 2018 Requirement) A statement that biospecimens may be used for commercial profit and whether or not the subject will benefit from such profit (required for Broad Consent)
8. (New 2018 Requirement) A statement about whether or not research involving biospecimens, including individual research results, will be disclosed to subjects, and if so, under what conditions

9. (New 2018 Requirement) A statement whether the research will (if known) or might include whole genome sequencing (*i.e.*, sequencing a human germline or somatic specimen with the intent to generate the genome or exome sequence of that specimen) (required for Broad Consent).

Additional elements required for **Broad Consent** are:

1. Description of research using identifiable data or specimens including enough information to permit the type of research
2. Description of the identifiable data or specimen used for the research, whether or not it will be shared and the types of institutions or researchers that will use the identifiable data or specimens
3. The time periods that the identifiable data or specimens will be used for research and/or stored (could be indefinite)
4. A statement that the subject will not be informed of the details of the research (including purposes they may have consented to)
5. A statement regarding the disclosure of clinically relevant research results
6. An explanation of who to contact for questions regarding the use and storage of identifiable data and specimens.

Generally, the essential and additional elements that are to be transmitted to each subject will be documented in an information sheet which is included in the proposal package submitted to the IRB for approval. Once approved it is then the responsibility of the investigator to provide each subject with this sheet and obtain the signed consent form under the conditions specified in the general requirements.

Alterations and/or waivers to the requirement to obtain informed consent may be approved by the IRB when it finds and documents one of the following conditions:

- That the project is to be conducted by or is subject to the approval of state or local government officials and is designed to study, evaluate or examine the delivery, procedures, or benefits of a public benefit or service program and the research could not be carried out without the alterations or waiver; or
- that the project:
  - involves no more than minimal risk to the subjects, and
  - the waiver or alterations will not adversely affect the rights and welfare of the subjects, and
  - the research could not be practically carried out without the waiver or alterations, and
  - if the research involves identifiable data or specimens, the research could not be practically carried out without the use of such data or specimens in an identifiable format, and
  - when appropriate, subjects will be provided additional pertinent information after participation.

Furthermore, the secondary research use of identifiable private information or biospecimens would not require informed consent if at least one of the following criteria are met:

- the information or specimens are publicly available
- information is recorded by the investigator in such a way that the identity of the human subjects cannot be readily ascertained directly or indirectly through identifiers linked to the subjects, the investigator does not contact the subjects, and the investigator will not re-identify subjects
- the research only involves information collection and analysis involving the investigator's use of identifiable information for the purposes of treatment, payment and operations (as defined by HIPAA), or for public health activities and purposes
- research is conducted by, or on behalf of, a Federal department or agency using government-generated or government-collected information obtained for nonresearch.

There are several vulnerable categories of human subjects that may be involved in research projects. Because of the unique nature of each category, there are specific elements that must be included in the informed consent procedure for the category. The following references will provide the details required for each category when needed:

- Title 46.200 Pregnant Women, Human Fetus, and Neonates Involved in Research
- Title 46.300 Biomedical and Behavioral Research Involving Prisoners as Subjects
- Title 46.400 Children Involved as Subjects in Research.

There are two forms of documentation of informed consent. One of the two is required unless the IRB waives the requirement for the investigator to obtain a signed consent form from some or all subjects.

They are:

- The long form written consent document that includes each of the essential and additional and vulnerable category of subject requirements appropriate to the research project. The investigator may read the material in the document to the subject or subject's representative, but must give the subject or subject's representative adequate opportunity to read it personally before it is signed; or
- The short form written consent document which states that the elements which would have been included in the long form above have been presented orally to the subject or the subject's representative. When the short form written consent document is used, the following requirements must be met:
    - A witness must be present for the oral presentation
    - The IRB must approve a written summary of what is to be orally presented to the subject or subject's representative
    - The subject or subject's representative will sign only the short form
    - The witness will sign both the short form and a copy of the summary
    - The person obtaining the consent will sign a copy of the summary
    - The subject or the subject's representative will be given a copy of the signed short form and the signed summary.

HHS and FDA regulations permit the flexibility of using electronic and paper informed consent methods independently or in combination throughout the course of the research study. The FDA and the Department of Health and Human Services' Office for Human Research Protections (OHRP) issued joint guidance on the use of electronic informed consent (eIC). The final guidance replaces a draft FDA-only question and answer guidance released in March 2015.

The IRB may waive the requirement to obtain a signed consent if it finds either of the following:

- That the research presents no more than a minimal risk of harm to subjects and involves no procedure for which written consent is normally required, or
- That the only record linking the subject with the research would be the consent form and the principal risk would be potential harm from breach of confidentiality, and the subject chooses not to be so linked to the research. In cases where the IRB waives the documentation of informed consent requirement, they may require the investigator to provide the subject with a written statement regarding the research.

Likewise, access to a study's data or biospecimens may be approved by an IRB without signed consent for the purposes of screening, recruiting or determining eligibility. The appropriate procedures for this consideration are:

- The investigator will obtain information through oral or written communication with the prospective subject or legally authorized representative, or
- The investigator will obtain identifiable private information or identifiable biospecimens

by accessing records or stored identifiable biospecimens.
- Non-compliance common to the obtaining of informed consent forms includes:
- Lack of required elements
- Use of inappropriate language
- Inadequate protection of vulnerable populations
- Failure to submit research projects for IRB consideration for approval, waiver, or exemption
- Inadequate explanation of pertinent aspects of the research to subjects before obtaining consent
- Inadequate research subject confidentiality mechanisms
- Inadequate or incorrect translation into subject's native language.

Mitigation strategies addressing non-compliance in the obtaining and maintenance of informed consents include the use of:

- a consent form template for a normal project and for each vulnerable category of subject that is appropriate to the institution
- training modules (online, written, and face-to-face) for all aspects of the informed consent procedure
- review of each consent form in a proposal for research by an IRB member or IRB support staff
- auditing of research project files to ensure that informed consent forms have been completed where needed or that other required documentation is present.

Adverse Events and Protocol Deviations/Violations

Adverse events and unanticipated problems must be reported to the IRB, institution officials and the sponsor, and in certain cases to other specified government oversight bodies. Unanticipated problems that are adverse events should be reported within a very short time period. Other unanticipated problems may be reported within a longer time period.

Depending on the level of detail in a research institution's Policies and Standard Operating Procedures, it may identify and define adverse events in sub-categories with more specific criteria. These have different reporting obligations depending on 21 CFR 812 (devices) and 21 CFR 312 (drugs).

Adverse Event (AE): any untoward or unfavorable medical occurrence, although not necessarily unexpected, whether or not considered to be related to investigational product.

Serious Adverse Event or Serious Suspected Adverse Reaction (SAE): An adverse event or suspected adverse reaction is considered "serious" if, in the view of either the investigator or sponsor, it results in any of the following outcomes: death, a life-threatening adverse event, inpatient hospitalization or prolongation of existing hospitalization, a persistent or significant incapacity or substantial disruption of the ability to conduct normal life functions, or a congenital anomaly/birth defect. Important medical events that may not result in death, be life-threatening, or require hospitalization may be considered serious when, based upon appropriate medical judgment, they may jeopardize the subject and may require medical or surgical intervention to prevent one of the outcomes listed in this definition. Examples of such medical events include allergic bronchospasm requiring intensive treatment in an emergency room or at home, blood dyscrasias or convulsions that do not result in inpatient hospitalization, or the development of drug dependency or drug abuse.

Suspected adverse reaction (SAR): Any adverse event for which there is a reasonable possibility the drug caused the adverse event. Suspected adverse reaction implies a lesser degree of certainty about causality than adverse reaction, which means any adverse event caused by a drug.

Unanticipated Adverse Device Effect (UADE): any serious adverse effect on health or safety or any life-threatening problem or death caused by, or associated with, a device, if that effect, problem, or death was not previously identified in nature, severity, or degree of incidence in the protocol, instructions for use, or consent form, or any other unanticipated serious problem associated with a device that relates to the rights, safety, or welfare of subjects.

Unanticipated Problem (UP): An adverse event that is unexpected (specificity and/or severity is not consistent with the protocol or the investigator brochure (IB), informed consent form (ICF), product labeling, package insert or any other protocol related documents; or is not an expected natural progression of any underlying disease or condition), and related or possibly related to participation in the research, and places subjects or others at a greater risk of harm than previously known or recognized; *e.g.*, results in death, is life-threatening, results in hospitalization or prolonged hospital stay, results in persistent disability/incapacity, results in congenital anomaly/birth defect, or may require medical or surgical intervention to prevent these outcomes.

Unexpected Adverse Event or Unexpected Suspected Adverse Reaction: any adverse drug/biologic experience for which the specificity or severity is not consistent with any of the following:

a. Investigator brochure
b. Protocol
c. Risk information in the consent form

For example, under this definition, hepatic necrosis would be unexpected (by virtue of greater severity) if the investigator brochure only referred to elevated hepatic enzymes or hepatitis. Similarly, cerebral thromboembolism and cerebral vasculitis would be unexpected (by virtue of greater specificity) if the investigator brochure only listed cerebral vascular accidents.

Protocol deviations will be defined by the institution with criteria to determine reporting obligations. A protocol deviation is any change, divergence, or departure from the study design or procedures of a research protocol that is under the investigator's control and that has not been approved by the IRB. Some institutions differentiate among minor protocol deviations, that can be "voluntarily" reported, and major protocol deviations, which must be reported:

Minor Protocol Deviation:

a. has no substantive effect on the risks to research subjects
b. has no substantive effect on the value of the data collected (*i.e.*, the deviation does not confound the scientific analysis of the results)
c. did not result from willful or knowing misconduct on the part of the Investigator(s)
d. did not result in or require any substantive action to be taken or result in any change to the subject's condition or status (*i.e.*, did not affect the subject's participation in any way, did not result in a change to the subject's emotional or clinical condition, did not cause an adverse experience or require a change to the clinical care of the subject, etc.)

Major Protocol Deviation:

a. resulted in or required a substantive action to be taken or resulted in a change to the subject's condition or status
b. caused harm or posed a significant risk of substantive harm to research subjects
c. damaged the scientific integrity of the data collected for the study
d. is evidence of willful or knowing misconduct on the part of the Investigator(s)
e. involves serious or continuing noncompliance with federal, state or local research regulations
f. repeated minor protocol deviations
g. failure to follow action ordered to correct minor protocol deviations
h. failure to follow action ordered in accordance with the emergency action section of this policy

Additional Guidance:

a. Minor protocol deviations should be reported to the IRB at the time of continuing review.

b. Major protocol deviations that affect subject safety, increases risk or results in a serious adverse event must be reported to the IRB within 24 hours of discovery of the deviation. All other major protocol deviations must be reported within 10 working days of discovery of the deviation.
c. Major protocol deviations and their administrative resolutions must also be tabulated and reported to the IRB at the time of continuing review.
d. Investigators who also serve as the sponsor of an investigational drug, biologic or device study, must report adverse events to the appropriate federal agency within the time frame specified in the applicable regulations.

Research Project Personnel and Training

The following areas relate to the role of those staff members involved in the conduct of a research project (study). The structure of how staffing and training is established is extremely important to a solid compliance program.

Areas reviewed are:

- Principal Investigator Responsibilities
- Policies and Standard Operating Procedures (P&P)
- Research Integrity and Misconduct.

Principal Investigator Responsibilities

The principal investigator (PI) on a research study is the individual who is ultimately responsible and accountable for all aspects of the study, including scientific, financial, operational, and informational.

While not exhaustive, the following is a list of those responsibilities:

- The preparation of the proposal for the research study in conformance with the institution's Policies and Standard Operating Procedures for Research
- Obtaining written approval from the Institutional Review Board (IRB) for the conduct of the study before beginning research activities
- Obtaining Human Subject Protections and HIPAA Researcher Training (personally and for all appropriate study personnel) before performing any human subject research and maintaining certifications of that training in the study's regulatory files
- Obtaining all required informed consent forms and filing the signed forms in a secured area with limited and documented access during the term of the research and for a period of 6 years after the termination of the study
- The conduct and/or supervision of all study procedures and activities including scientific, financial, operational and informational
- Obtaining prior written approval of the IRB for any amendment or modification to the protocol or supporting materials, including (but not limited to) changes to:
  - inclusion/exclusion criteria
  - procedures
  - sub-investigators
  - sponsor funding agencies
  - informed consent documentation or procedures
  - recruiting materials
  - patient education materials unless immediately required for the protection of study subjects
- Obtaining yearly updated, documented, signed, and dated conflict of interest statements on all human subject investigators involved in the study and maintaining them in the study files
- Promptly reporting (in accordance with the P&P) any serious adverse events, unanticipated problems, or significant new findings that arise throughout the course of the study
- Complying with all IRB requests to report on the status of the study including annual reviews
- Maintaining an active IRB approval through proper submission of request for annual continuation of the study
- Complying with all requirements of the sponsor (funding organization) of the study

- Maintaining accurate and complete regulatory records of all study activities
- Filing a final report to the IRB upon conclusion of the study.

Sponsor-Investigator Responsibilities

A sponsor-investigator is an individual who both initiates and conducts an investigation, and under whose immediate direction the test article is administered, dispensed, deployed or implanted. The requirements applicable to a sponsor-investigator include both those applicable to an investigator and a sponsor. Sponsor-investigators must develop the study plan (including the protocol, statistical analysis plan, risk analysis, description and labeling of test article(s), monitoring procedures, and consent materials with document version control. Sponsor-investigators define and standardize data elements, manage data collection (CRFs or electronic data collection, spreadsheets, etc.), keep an audit trail of data edits, and verify and protect data integrity according to the data management plan. The following is a list of responsibilities for an investigator-initiated study funded by the public health system (PHS), intended to support an FDA submission, or for scientific and scholarly contributions to generalizable knowledge:

- Conduct in accordance with all institutional policies, applicable laws and regulations for HSP, IRB review, and Financial Disclosure
- Comply with all terms, conditions, reporting, and financial management requirements of the funding award (PHS) (the PHS sponsor role may be limited to funding with specific conditions so that the investigator becomes responsible for HSP safety, and the proper conduct and monitoring of PHS funded research)
- Comply with all FDA IND, IDE requirements such that it may be necessary for the investigator to obtain an IND or IDE for the research
- Comply with all requirements applicable to both an investigator and a sponsor
- Include a DSMP (data safety monitoring plan) reviewed by the IRB and in compliance with the funding agency policies (PHS); or if the research involves treatment with unknown or significant risk, or a vulnerable population (FDA and scholarly activity)
- Report adverse events to the appropriate federal agency within the time frame specified in the applicable regulations.

Policies and Standard Operating Procedures

Policies and Standard Operating Procedures (P&P), while similar for all research institutions, will vary because of the culture and operating model of each organization. Consequently, in this section we will review the types of material that should be in the P&P for a research organization rather than the particular wording of the material. A generic P&P might include the following:

- Policy statement that indicates what is covered and who has authority over the process
- A set of Standard Operating Procedures to effectuate the policy statement
- Practice aids or guidelines for critical steps in a research study
- Forms and templates to aid the IRB and PIs in carrying out their responsibilities.

The policy statement should indicate that the IRB is the authoritative body for authorizing and overseeing research studies. In addition, it will usually specify:

- The exact authority or charter of the IRB, including whether or not it will act as the privacy board
- The proposals for research that are covered by this authority
- The criteria for acceptance of proposals as research studies
- The pre-conditions for performing research, such as training and certifications.

The Standard Operating Procedures table of contents should include at least the following categories:

- Review and approval of studies

- Full review
- Expedited review
- Exempt
- Criteria for the acceptance of studies
    - Required documentation
- Training of research personnel
    - Initial
    - Refresher
- Ongoing monitoring and reporting
    - Changes
    - Adverse events
- Continuation reviews
- Special situations
    - Sabbaticals and leaves of absence
    - Research at collaborating institutions
    - Research contracts and pricing
    - Research integrity and misconduct
    - Use and disclosure of PHI in research
    - Research conflict of interest
- Documentation and records retention
    - Informed consent forms
    - Scientific information
    - Financial information
    - Reports.

Practice aids or guidelines should be prepared for any activity that has special and unique requirements. This will enable consistency of treatment across many researchers and make review by the IRB and other oversight organizations easier. Usually these aids or guidelines fall into two categories: study procedures and study populations. A sample list of each follows:

- Study procedures
    - Surveys/questionnaires/interviews
    - Oral history activities
    - Private data, human specimens and cells
    - Data protection
    - Audio taping/videotaping
    - Research involving deception
    - Research that may affect privacy of healthcare information
    - Payments/costs involving subjects
- Study guidelines
    - Students as subjects
    - Students as investigators
    - Minors as subjects
    - Subjects with limited comprehension
    - Subjects with limited ability to read, hear, or see
    - Non-English speaking subjects
    - Other vulnerable subjects.

One of the most effective ways to ensure that all forms needed to approve and conduct research are properly constructed and contain the required information is to develop a set of standard forms and templates to be used by all PIs. This tactic reduces the time required of the IRB to review and approve both individual document content and the proposal to conduct research. For the PI, it provides a simple solution to what is required. A list of possible standard forms and templates follows:

- Application for Approval to Use Humans as Experimental Subjects (exempt)
- Application for Approval to Use Humans as Subjects (standard)
- Checklist for Standard Application Form
- Continuing Review Questionnaire
- Application for Changes to an Approved Protocol
- Consent to Participate in Biomedical Research
- Consent to Participate in Non-Biomedical Research
- Consent to Participate in Interview
- Assent to Participate in Research (for minors)
- Authorization for Release of Protected Health Information (PHI).

Examples of actual policies, procedures, guidelines and forms and templates may be found on the web page of most institutions conducting research.

Research Integrity and Misconduct

Research integrity includes both the avoidance of misconduct and the performance of the hallmarks of good scholarship, namely rigor, carefulness and accountability. Integrity in research is the responsibility of every faculty member, staff member and student involved in the research enterprise. It is supported and nurtured by a strong organizational ethical culture. Specific activities that foster intellectual honesty and integrity in research are:

- Open publication and discussion
- Institutional and departmental emphasis on quality of research
- Appropriate supervision at all levels of the research enterprise
- Maintenance of accurate and detailed research procedures and results
- Appropriate assignment of credit and responsibility for research and publications
- Clear and documented policies and procedures for the conduct of research, including pre-defined consequences for non-compliance
- Appropriate avenues for all stakeholders to report misconduct in research
- An established procedure to respond to allegations of misconduct.

It is clearly the responsibility of the institution conducting the research to ensure the presence of research integrity and to take appropriate action on all allegations of misconduct in research. As noted above, research integrity is much broader than the avoidance of misconduct. Consequently, an institution can have many policies that deal with integrity. These will be unique to each institution.

Misconduct generally means fabrication, falsification, plagiarism or other practices that seriously deviate from those that are commonly accepted within the scholarly and scientific community for proposing, conducting and reporting research. Misconduct does not include honest errors or differences of judgments or interpretations of data.

Sponsoring organizations would expect institutions performing research to bear primary responsibility for prevention and detection of research misconduct including the following:

- Developing and maintaining procedures to respond to allegations of research misconduct to include:
  - Appropriate separation of responsibilities for inquiry and investigation and for adjudication
  - Maintenance of objectivity
  - Due process
  - Whistleblower protection
  - Confidentiality
  - Timely resolution
- Initiating prompt inquiries into allegations of misconduct
- Conducting investigations, if warranted
- Taking action(s) necessary to ensure the integrity of research, to protect the rights and interests of research subjects and the public, to ensure the observance of legal and contractual requirements
- Providing appropriate safeguards of the subject of allegations and the informants.

In addition, sponsoring organizations would also expect prompt notification should the institution become aware during an inquiry or investigation that:

- Public health or safety was at risk
- The sponsor's resources, reputation or other interests needed protecting
- There is reasonable indication of possible violations of civil or criminal laws
- Research activities should be suspended
- External action may be necessary to protect the interests of a subject of the investigation or someone else potentially affected
- The scientific community or the public should be informed.

Research Finance

Billing

The Office of Inspector General (OIG) has exercised enforcement of research billing compliance, giving researchers a new incentive to look closely at cost calculations for clinical research, time and effort reporting for grants, budget negotiations and third-party billing practices. In addition, there is arguably some obligation to manage the business aspects of research activity to the extent that organizations establish financial reporting controls and maximize their potential investment return by making informed research enterprise decisions.

The Federal government holds a person or entity liable for knowingly submitting a false claim for payment or using a false record or statement to obtain payment or causing a third party to do the same, and can result in monetary penalties of $5,000–$11,000 (discretionarily adjustable) per false claim plus three times the damages sustained by the government.[6] In addition, a person or entity that knowingly and willfully makes or causes to be made a false statement or representation on any claim with the intent to fraudulently secure overpayment can be subject to 5 years imprisonment and/or a $25,000 fine.[7] Suspension and disqualification from participation in government-sponsored programs such as Medicare or Medicaid is also a possible adverse outcome.

The liability and risks associated with clinical trial billing were highlighted with the first false claims settlement related to billing for routine services provided during clinical trials announced in December of 2005. The one million dollar settlement acknowledged overbilling Medicare for services already paid by another entity and under billing Medicare for services assuming that there was an alternative primary payor. In addition, "the U.S. attorney also (said) that some or all of the physician and hospital inpatient and outpatient services charged to Medicare and Medicaid were not reimbursable because they were not considered routine care associated with clinical trials."[8] This case of false claims submissions is a key area of financial risk in clinical research and suggests that clinical trial sites should become increasingly more familiar with billing statutes, regulations and guidelines. (See also, Chapter 11 Clinical Research Billing Compliance.)

The Federal False Claims Act applies also to recipients of federal research grants who contractually agree to perform the stated project activities in exchange for a government commitment to pay for the expenses attested to in the grant application. "When (a government agency) awards a grant, the grantee institution has the responsibility to ensure that grant funds are expended only for allowable costs under the award as budgeted. When a grantee requests payment for costs not budgeted, even though incurred, it is submitting a false claim in violation of the False Claims Act."[9] (See also, Chapter 12, Grant Management.)

Private insurers may have policies and coverage criteria for clinical trial services that must also be adhered to. Obtaining payment from a commercial payor by means of false presentations is fraud and could also result in imprisonment and fines.[10] Medicare is, however, the largest single payor for medical services in the United States, and CMS (Centers for Medicare and Medicaid Services) provides the most detailed clinical trial billing guidance and enforces the most severe penalties for fraud and abuse. For these reasons, research billing determinations are often based on Medicare guidance:

Key areas of financial risk in clinical research include:

- **Overcharging.** Receiving payments from pharmaceutical/medical device sponsors that significantly exceed the costs of the research, especially for Phase 4 marketing studies, could be construed as a violation of the anti-kickback law.
- **Undercharging.** Conducting clinical studies without receiving adequate reimbursement for the costs of the study. This is primarily a financial (business) risk but may be a concern for not-for-profits if the under-recovery of costs could be viewed as a subsidization of a for-profit enterprise such as a pharmaceutical or medical device company.
- **Mischarging.** Billing patients or their insurance carriers for the costs of research, especially where those costs have already been covered by the sponsor of the study.[11]

Overcharging. The Office of Inspector General (OIG) has indicated in their guidance to pharmaceutical manufacturers that, "Payments for research services should be fair market value for legitimate, reasonable, and necessary services" and must support bona fide research activity.[12] Sites should scrutinize studies generated by sales departments for clinical or statistical merit to validate that payments are not associated with sham "research" designed to encourage product use. An analysis of study expenses should provide detailed support for study payments consistent with fair market value for the work performed. Excessive industry sponsor payments could be a compliance risk if there is a perception that an individual or entity is receiving remuneration in exchange for purchases or referral.[13] Thus, it is important to document legitimate reasons for accepting enrollment incentives, recruitment bonuses, finders' fees and excessive or disproportionate benchmark payments. Sponsor benefits such as meals, honoraria, conference travel or educational funding should also be considered with caution.

Flowing sponsor payments through to investigators must be in accordance with fair market value compensation for investigator services. Excessive investigator payments can otherwise be perceived as a kickback to induce physician referrals. In addition, sponsor payments should not be used to support subject deductibles or co-insurance to the extent that providing this form of remuneration to the subject could be perceived as an inducement for study participation.

Overcharging a federal agency can occur as a result of false certifications in grant applications, budgeting unallowable costs or submitting overstated time and effort reports and is a violation of the False Claims Act. Violating certain federal laws and regulations can result in civil monetary penalties, criminal fines and/or imprisonment, loss of licensure, special considerations in the form of integrity agreements and possibly exclusion from participation in federal programs including Medicare, Medicaid and federal granting opportunities.

Undercharging and Fiscal Accountability. Analyzing a research study for an accurate assessment of cost establishes an expense justification to support and develop a budget for a grant application as well as negotiate sponsor payment contracts. It is important to define and communicate business tolerance in reference to clinical trial funding and to establish consistent and accurate cost calculation and funding thresholds that force business decisions. While a project may be financially underfunded, studies that align with a specific mission or service line may have merit or value that compensates for the monetary shortfall. As a matter of compliance, undercharging for clinical services and labor required in conducting clinical research must be considered within the context of tax laws. Tax exempt organizations cannot take on clinical research activity at a financial loss resulting in a substantial private benefit to another individual or entity. Documenting a value statement supporting equal consideration or benefit comparable to the financial loss may be a strategy to avoid jeopardizing tax exempt status.

Institutions should develop pricing standards to support standardization in budget development as well as a minimum level of payment expectation. Budget negotiations with a sponsor are then based on verifiable and consistent costing principles with logic that provides added leverage to the funding requests. This type of process and strategy facilitates responsible and fiscally sound research decisions.

Mischarging. The overriding statute governing Medicare billing for patient care items and services performed in the context of clinical research is the Social Security Act. Title XVIII of this statute specifically states that such services must be "reasonable and medically necessary for the diagnosis or treatment of illness or injury or to improve the functioning of a malformed body member."[14] A section of the act is specific to research, stating, "Notwithstanding any other provision of this title, **no payment may be made** under Part A (hospital and skilled nursing services) or part B (doctor's services and outpatient care) **for any expenses incurred for items and services**—in the case of research conducted pursuant to section 1142, **which is not reasonable and necessary** to carry out the purposes of that section...."[15] The Social Security Act requires that specific coverage decisions include input from the Agency for Healthcare Research and Quality (AHRQ) to recommend the standards and processes that would be most likely to ensure that the requirements of the Social Security Act would be met. Whether externally or internally generated, National Coverage Decisions, or NCDs help ensure that access to advances in health technologies that may result in improved healthcare are available to Medicare beneficiaries when those items and services are reasonable and necessary. NCDs may also be used to bar payment for specific items or services that are not reasonable and necessary as described in the Medicare Act. The NCD process facilitates the rapid and uniform diffusion of beneficial technologies, items, and services.

Billing Compliance. On June 7, 2000, the President of the United States issued an executive memorandum directing the Secretary of Health and Human Services to explicitly authorize [Medicare] payment for routine patient care costs... and costs due to medical complications associated with participation in clinical trials. The Health Care Financing Administration (now the Centers for Medicare & Medicaid Services, or CMS) responded to the executive order with the clinical trial policy NCD issued on September 19, 2000. The NCD for routine costs in clinical trials was implemented through the CMS NCD process and determined the circumstances under which certain items and services would be reasonable and necessary when provided to Medicare beneficiaries in clinical trials. The Clinical Trials Policy (CTP) NCD was reopened for revision July 10, 2006. On April 10th, 2007, CMS issued the first proposed decision memo outlining recommended policy revisions followed by an additional public comment period. In response to the voluminous feedback, CMS issued a second proposed reconsideration memo and issued a final decision memorandum on July 9, 2007 that preserved the status quo of the 2000 CTP with minimal changes. On October 17, 2007, CMS closed the reconsideration with a final decision memorandum that retained the July 9, 2007 policy.[16]

Category B Device Regulations. The Category B Investigational Device Regulations are part of the Federal Register and address the criteria and procedures for extending Medicare coverage to certain devices and related services. Title XVIII prohibits Medicare from providing coverage for the use of devices that are not "reasonable and necessary for the diagnosis and treatment of an injury or illness or to improve the functioning of a malformed body member."[17] Consequently, prior to the category B regulations, Medicare denied any and all reimbursement for experimental devices and associated costs due to the absence of medical necessity that cannot be established when the safety and effectiveness of a device are unknown. A device the Food and Drug Administration (FDA) categorized as investigational was presumed to be experimental, including devices being studied under investigational device exemptions (IDE). An IDE allows an investigational device to be used in a clinical study in order to collect safety and effectiveness data required to support a Premarket Approval (PMA) application or a Premarket Notification [510(k)] submission to FDA. A medical device required FDA approval for marketing (post marketing approval, also PMA), the device's safety and effectiveness having been established, to qualify for payment consideration.

There was increasing recognition that there are devices that are refinements of existing technologies or replications of existing technologies that could be viewed as "reasonable and medically necessary" if devices were categorized into those that are "experimental" and those that are "investigational." On November 1, 1995, Congress enacted legislation that now permits coverage of some investigational devices. The resulting interagency agreement established an FDA risk assessment that would assist CMS in determining Medicare coverage for devices. The FDA now places all approved IDEs into one of two categories. Category A devices are typically novel, innovative first-generation products determined to be experimental in addition to investigational, given that the FDA has insufficient evidence to determine whether these device types can be safe and effective. Category B devices are investigational but usually similar to another approved device type for which safety and efficacy has already been established. CMS acknowledges this FDA risk assessment and has indicated that category B devices may be eligible for coverage consideration. The final coverage decision is made by Medicare and their contractors, who must authorize billing for these devices (and related patient services) prior to any claims submissions. Medicare payment may also be made for patient care services related to the use of a Category B device as well as services required to treat complications related to the device.

While not explicitly stated in the category B regulations, the underlying principle and federal intent would indicate that investigational devices provided free of charge by the sponsor are not considered a billable item or service because the cost of the device has already been covered by the sponsor of the study. When the study sponsor intends to charge the investigator or facility for the device, the final decision to reimburse for an investigational device and related services is not based on the FDA category B status, but rather, on the Medicare contractor review of the claim. The category B regulations state, "Medicare coverage of a non-experimental/investigational (Category B) device will be subject to the same process and criteria used by Medicare contractors when making coverage decisions for legally marketed devices. Coverage of the device is dependent on it meeting all other Medicare coverage requirements contained in the statute, regulations, and instructions issued by HCFA."[18] In addition, the charge "should not exceed an amount necessary to recover the costs of manufacture, research, development, and handling of the investigational device."[19] CMS updated the IDE regulations so that effective January 1, 2015, coverage of devices and related clinical trial items and services are subject to centralized review. An approval of a Category A device study permits coverage for routine care, but the Category A device itself remains statutorily excluded from coverage. Study sponsors may request coverage by submitting a letter describing the scope of the IDE study and a dossier (FDA category A or B letter, NCT registration number, IDE protocol, etc.) to facilitate CMS review. Claims for IDE clinical trial services should not be submitted until the study is identified on the CMS website as approved.[20]

Medicare may cover those FDA-approved devices with modifications (developed after marketing approval) determined by an Institutional Review Board (IRB) to pose a "non-significant risk" (NSR) to patients. Effective January 1, 2015 (revision to the Medicare Benefit Policy Manual chapter 14) Medicare contractors are to "apply the same coverage criteria...to these devices as are applied to FDA-approved Category A and B IDE devices."[21] This revision to the Medicare Benefit Policy Manual chapter 14 also imposed IDE study criteria very much like the "qualifying trial" criteria cited in NCD 310.1 (clinical trials policy NCD). The purpose of the study must test for improved health or therapeutic outcomes, the study is to be scientifically rigorous (appropriate methodology and N value) and registered on clinicaltrials.gov; should not duplicate existing knowledge; and have a protocol description of the method and timing of release of results and how those results impact Medicare beneficiaries. Non-significant risk devices are billable only if they are "reasonable and medically necessary for the diagnosis or treatment of illness or injury or to improve the functioning of a malformed body member."[22] More often, non-significant risk devices are typical diagnostic tools and would not meet these "treatment" criteria.

The current Medicare CTP established as an NCD in 2000 evolved out of an executive memo issued by former President Clinton directing Medicare to pay for "routine costs" in certain clinical trials. The CTP, as it applies to investigational drug studies, states that "routine costs" of "qualifying" clinical trials are billable so long as those costs are reasonable and medically necessary, they are generally available to Medicare beneficiaries, they are not statutorily excluded and there is no national noncoverage decision.

When a clinical trial meets the criteria of a "qualifying trial" as defined by the CTP, it means that routine care services delivered in the course of the study may be considered for Medicare coverage. The CTP states that the subject or purpose of the trial must be supported within a Medicare benefit category, the trial must have therapeutic intent, and trials of therapeutic interventions must involve diseased subject populations and trials of diagnostic interventions may include healthy subjects as a control group. In addition, the trial should test an intervention that potentially improves subjects' health outcomes, be well supported by medical information, should not duplicate existing studies, should have scientific merit and design, and should be sponsored by a credible organization with the capacity to execute the trial in compliance with federal human subject protection regulations. The CTP specifically identifies some trials as automatically "qualified." They include studies funded by specified federal granting agencies such as the NIH and any cooperative groups supported by such federal agencies, trials conducted under an IND application and drug studies determined to meet the criteria for IND exemption.

Pharmaceutical companies sponsoring investigational new drug (IND) studies typically provide the test article free of charge. Often times, the sponsor also provides payment for frequent subject visits that exceed what would be considered "reasonable and medically necessary" for the patient's condition. In these situations, only the services that are *not* already paid by the sponsor can be billed to Medicare or any other third-party payer. In addition, any item or service provided solely to collect data for the study is also not billable. A specific example mentioned in the CTP is that of serial CT scans required at scheduled intervals or more frequently than would usually be required for the stated condition. Items and services required to administer the test article, monitor for side effects of the test article or treat complications arising from participation in a clinical trial are billable services under the CTP.[23]

Effective July 9, 2007, CMS extended coverage under the current CTP for certain items and services "for which there is some evidence of significant medical benefit, but for which there is insufficient evidence to support a 'reasonable and necessary' determination." This coverage provision is in reference to the Coverage with Evidence Development (CED) standards within CMS's National Coverage Determination (NCD). The purpose of coverage with evidence development is to generate data on the utilization and impact of the item or service evaluated in the NCD, so that Medicare can:

a. document the appropriateness of use of that item or service in Medicare beneficiaries under current coverage
b. consider future changes in coverage for the item or service
c. generate clinical information that will improve the evidence base on which providers base their recommendations to Medicare beneficiaries regarding the item or service.

Adding coverage for items and services furnished to Medicare beneficiaries considered reasonable and medically necessary under CED allows Medicare coverage for services that would have otherwise been non-covered. For example, PET scanning is a billable and covered procedure for specified indications. CMS has determined that the evidence is sufficient to conclude that a PET scan for other cancer indications not previously specified is reasonable and necessary only when the provider is participating in, and patients are enrolled in, either an FDA approved IDE clinical trial or a PET clinical study that is designed to collect additional information at the time of the scan to assist in patient management. In the latter case, the CED affords coverage for a PET scan that would have otherwise been a non-covered service. NCDs that require CED are listed on the CMS website.[24]

Affordable Care Act 2014. Beginning January 2014, the Affordable Care Act (ACA), Public Health Service Act section 2709(a) established by the 10103(c) of the Reconciliation Act provides for coverage for Individuals Participating in Approved Clinical Trials. A qualified individual (eligible for the trial and referring clinician is a participating provider or the individual provides medical and scientific information supporting participation) has coverage consistent with the CTP for "routine costs," including all items and services consistent with the coverage provided in the plan that is typically covered if not enrolled in the trial.

Financial Tracking and Reporting

Study sites must have sound financial tracking and reporting mechanisms to validate fiscal stewardship. It is prudent business practice to track earned revenue and reconcile sponsor payments. In addition, the Code of Federal Regulations uniform administrative requirements for federal awards specifically cites minimum grant recipient standards for financial management systems. These include:

- The capacity to relate financial data to performance data
- Accurate, current and complete financial status reporting
- Records that identify the source and application of funds
- Evidence of accountability for all funds, property and assets
- Budgetary control
- Federal cash management procedures
- Written procedures for determining reasonableness, allocability and allowability of costs, and
- Cost accounting records supported by source documentation (i.e., time and effort reports, purchase records.)[25]

An institution should consider the following policies and SOPs as critical to risk management for research finance and billing compliance:

- Research Pricing and Fair Market Value Considerations
  - Discount pricing for physicians
  - Service fees and reimbursement
- Research Budget Negotiation
  - Cost and coverage analysis – Drug studies
  - Cost and coverage analysis – Device studies
  - Device authorization requirements from the Medicare Administrative Contractor (MAC) or Fiscal Intermediary (FI)
- Research Financial Accounting and Reporting
- Research Subject Registration and Billing
- Grant Processing Authorization
- Time and Effort Reporting.

Clinical Research Legal Considerations

(Note: This discussion is limited to clinical trial agreements with primarily industry sponsors. Refer to Chapter 12, Grants Management for specific legal commentary in reference to grants, cooperative agreements and government contracts.)

It is reckless to employ or contract with debarred individuals or companies. Suspension and debarment actions protect the government from doing business with individuals, companies or recipients who pose a business risk to the government. Before entering into a legal contract to conduct research, institutions should assure by a search that sponsors and key study personnel have not been debarred or excluded from participation in federal programs. Debarment or Exclusion lists are available at:

- **Disqualified/restricted/assurances lists for clinical investigators:** http://www.fda.gov/ICECI/EnforcementActions/ucm321308.htm

- **FDA Debarment List:** http://www.fda.gov/ICECI/EnforcementActions/FDADebarmentList/
- **Excluded Parties Listing System:** https://www.sam.gov/portal/public/SAM/
- **Exclusions Database, Office of Inspector General–HHS:** http://exclusions.oig.hhs.gov/.

Federal regulations require research sponsors to establish written agreements that ensure that the research will be performed. Three basic questions need to be answered in order to establish the appropriate parties to the contract:

- Who is the sponsor as defined by the regulations and ICH Guidelines for Good Clinical Practices (GCP)?
- Who will own the data?
- Who is the funding source?

Clinical trial agreements are then drafted to define and direct the scope of work and length of term, protect the rights of the engaging parties, protect the confidentiality of proprietary science and subject information, establish payment amounts and schedule, and describe accountability and provisions for errors, research misconduct, and subject injury.

Clinical trial agreements typically include the following sections:

- Recital—identifies the parties to the agreement and assigns roles
- Scope of Work—describes what work will be done, by whom, and special rules and conditions
- Length of Term—effective dates, process for extending or early termination, special procedures for delays, *force majeure* (uncontrollable events preventing compliance, *i.e.*, war, flood, civil unrest, disputes)
- Payments (most often as an exhibit to the agreement)—per subject, benchmark or milestone amounts; schedule of payments; pass-through payments that require invoice; one-time, startup, administrative and IRB fees; contingent charges; close-out payments; refunds; and demographics for payment exchange
- Indemnification—identifies who the sponsor holds harmless (*i.e.*, academic institution, investigator, sub-investigator, and/or IRB); describes exceptions for protocol noncompliance or negligence; assigns scope of indemnification, who controls defense of lawsuits and pays legal fees, insurance requirements and survival of obligation to indemnify. (Research involving a Contract Research Organization or CRO drives the additional considerations to require both the sponsor and the CRO as parties to the agreement with signature lines or a letter of indemnification from or authorizing the CRO to bind the sponsor.)
- Federal exclusion validation
- Publication rights—description of institution/investigator rights to publish or present; access to multi-site data, rights to publish early for reasons of public health, safety, or public welfare; sponsor's right to review and edit within a stated time frame; authorship determinations for publications resulting from multi-site trials
- Confidentiality—identifies parties with access to data and binds them to state and federal privacy laws
- Intellectual Property—defines scope, disclosure, ownership and licensure of data, inventions, discoveries, patents and improvements
- Governing law and termination.

This is not an exhaustive list of legal terms to think about when negotiating clinical trial agreements with industry sponsors. Sites should consider the different types of research activities occurring at their institutions and develop template agreements consistent with their risk tolerance and inclusive of all minimally expected institutional liability protections. As study-specific agreements are negotiated, institutions should frequently assess which terms and conditions prolong negotiations. Understanding the institutional thresholds for legal terms that are ideal, desirable and "deal breakers" can help move discussions forward to an endpoint. Model clinical trial agreements and budget exhibits can be found on Model Agreements and Guidelines International's website.[26] This must be integrated well into a process for compliance, as having the contract process independent will cause problems in many areas for the research team.

Models of Research Compliance

While human subject protection and Institutional Review Board policies and procedures have been recognized as integral to a research compliance infrastructure for quite some time, it is only recently that research billing risk and Stark and Anti-kickback laws have prompted thoughts of new models for research conduct and oversight. It is well known that research activity and data collection for the purposes of contributing to generalizable knowledge requires review by the IRB for human subject protection and usually involves an in-depth assessment of the protocol, data collection tools and consent documents as an element of research compliance and accountability. It is also typical research process to establish a legal arrangement with a sponsor and include a mutually agreed upon budget for reimbursement. In most settings, IRB review and study approval is an isolated practice with little or no consideration for the final versions of negotiated and executed budget and legal documents. The validity of the IRB review conducted in such a vacuum comes into question when their review could not assess any assurances that subject confidentiality has been secured by an appropriate legal agreement or that study payments are appropriate for the study expenses and not coercive to enrollment. There is further increased compliance risk associated with this type of disconnected review when legal agreements are inadequate to support any litigation and final documents contain inconsistencies that could raise questions about research payments and billing as well as full disclosure to subjects. An effective research project review should assure that research conduct is expertly reviewed for:

- Scientific merit and human subject protection
- Contractual arrangements that minimize legal risk
- Research services billable to a third-party payer, and
- Funding appropriate and adequate to cover study cost.

Upon completion of these reviews, all documents related to the research study should be in harmony with one another. For example, subject compensation for study related injury and subject responsibility for costs associated with the research project should be uniformly addressed in the consent document and the clinical trial agreement. Subject compensation or stipends acknowledged in the consent document should be included in a cost analysis and covered by the study budget. Study budget exhibits should be consistent with billing regulations, reflect sponsor payment for all items and services required solely to accommodate the protocol, and provide the reference to assure appropriate billing. And, a legal agreement should assure human subject confidentiality and protect the investigator and institution from serious litigating consequences.

An ideal project approval should evolve out of a concurrent review process defined by published policies. Upon submission of a research proposal, a physician/statistician should solicit expert clinical review by an appropriate physician specialist relevant to the subject population and analyze the study design for statistical merit before the project is placed on an IRB agenda. The documentation of this evaluation should be included in the IRB materials to assure that, in accordance with the regulations, risks to subjects are minimized "by using procedures which are consistent with sound research design."[27] The IRB should hold and abide by the terms of their Federal Wide Assurance (FWA) and should be organized to comply with the regulatory requirements for membership by including representation on behalf of community attitudes, institutional commitments and state laws and standards applicable to their review of human subject protection issues relevant to the research project.

Synchronous with this IRB processing, the research protocol and all submission documents should be distributed to the finance and legal reviewers to initiate those concurrent assessments.

A "project steward" familiar with the clinical aspects of the protocol should provide a risk assessment of the study to the contracts attorney who will negotiate the legal terms of the clinical trial agreement. A modification of this process should be applied to scholarly research activity being conducted as a requirement of medical education, data collection studies, and nursing and alternative health research projects. All institutional employees conducting research within their scope of employment are held accountable to the institutional Code of Conduct, HIPAA and general compliance standards and all research team members not employed by the institution should be bound to research regulatory compliance and Good Clinical Practices by signing a "research services agreement."

The legal department within a concurrent review research infrastructure should further evaluate key issues to be considered in research contracts including protection of confidential information, the project liability and required indemnification, subject injury provisions and protection against third party claims and data ownership, publication rights and intellectual property considerations. The contracts attorney should be negotiating the terms of the clinical trial agreement while the IRB is reviewing the protocol for human subject protection, and at the same time the finance department should be collaborating with the project steward and the investigator to assess the financial aspects related to the study conduct. Legal or financial outliers that could potentially affect human subject protection should be brought back to the IRB to determine risk and consider any consent revisions to assure full disclosure. For example, sponsor budgets that cannot be negotiated to reimburse based on actual deliverables may result in "back ended" payments that could appear to create a financial incentive to the investigator if he or she can keep subjects in a study. The IRB should be asked to determine if the payment structure in such a situation is a human subject protection risk.

Government billing and financial risk has been reviewed at length in reference to the CMS guidance documents. Recent expert publications indicate that the creation of an infrastructure specifically designed to support clinical research is key to managing compliance risks especially in the areas of clinical trial billing. The ideal research compliance model requires financial review and process implementation by finance analysts familiar with hospital and facility cost accounting and billing systems, grants management experts, ancillary staff responsible for invoicing and payment reconciliation and clinicians familiar with research billing regulations. A matrix communication with patient financial services should be established to facilitate appropriate identification of research subjects involved in patient care activity within the facility and a similar relationship with the Health Information Management (HIMS) department should be established to assure appropriate coding for healthcare claims involving research items and services.

In December of 2005, Rush University Medical Center in Chicago settled the first false claims case since CMS established billing guidelines for routine services provided during clinical trials in the CTP. Double billing was the original issue identified, but a more detailed audit revealed that patient consent forms used in the clinical trials indicated that the research sponsor would cover the cost or provide certain services for free, yet these services were included on third party claims submitted for payment. In addition to double-billing, subjects involved in the research study were either misinformed of the true financial arrangements or wrongly held accountable for insurance claims inclusive of services already purported to be paid by the sponsor.

A research compliance infrastructure should assure that checks and balances are established to verify that there is uniformity in the documentation. Appropriate representation from each area of expert review should meet regularly to air out issues and concerns relevant to their analysis of the project. The IRB should be informed of all coverage findings and made aware of any proposed budget issues with regard to study costs at the time of their review so as to assure appropriate consent disclosure. A template legal agreement should include all minimum content legal terms to be used as a point of reference to elevate any difficult negotiations requiring less than desirable compromise or liability to another level of business and ethical review.

All references to financials in a legal agreement are best limited to a budget exhibit or attachment reviewed by finance prior to signature. And, no IRB approval letter or consent document should be released to the investigator until all final documents are cross referenced for consistency.

Conclusion

Operationalizing research compliance, whether it is in the corporate world or in a hospital, takes an interdisciplinary approach and collaboration by the entire infrastructure of the institution or organization. There is no "cookie cutter" model that will suit every institution or facility. Regardless of how many staff or how many people are involved, there must be one responsible party who has the authority to make difficult decisions in research compliance. Making research compliance a priority where it's visible, consistent and transparent takes solid support from upper management and attention towards education, training, auditing and monitoring. The first step is awareness of the risks and being ready to accept what those are. Then, a concerted effort must be paid in order to integrate a program from its inception to acceptance. Once a program is started, there must be constant process improvement with metrics to enhance and maintain the order for research compliance. Nobody does it perfectly but applying effort towards it speaks volumes to others while ensuring patient safety throughout the life cycle of a study.

Chapter 15 Endnotes

1. **Wendy Schroeder, BSN, RN, CCRC** is Director of Research and Regulatory Programs at VisionGate, Inc. in Seattle, WA.
2. 45 C.F.R. 46.
3. 83 F.R. 2885.
4. 83 F.R. 28497.
5. Compliant with 45 CFR § 46.114.
6. Civil False Claims—31USC §§ 3729-33.
7. Criminal False Claim 42 USC § 1320a-7a(a).
8. "Rush Resolves Landmark Case on Clinical Trial Billing for $1 Million ," *Report On Medicare Compliance*, Dec. 19, 2005.
9. Coleen M. Roberts, "A Summary of Fraud and Abuse Issues Affecting Clinical Research Programs," *QRC Advisor*, 14, no. 12 (October, 1998): 9-12.
10. Health Care Fraud—18 U.S.C. Section 1347.
11. Staman, Matthew W. Staman, "Infrastructure for Clinical Research—Managing Financial Risks. The Bureau of National Affairs," *Medical Research Law & Policy Report*, 3, no. 8 (2004): 313-316.
12. OIG Compliance Program Guidance for Pharmaceutical Manufacturers, 68 Fed. Reg. 86 (May 5, 2003).
13. Federal Anti-kickback Statute 42 USC § 1320a-7b(b).
14. Social Security Act § 1862(a)(1)(A).
15. Ibid.
16. The policy is available for review at http://www.cms.gov/medicare-coverage-database/details/ncd-details.aspx?NCDId=1&ncdver=2&fromdb=true.
17. Social Security Act § 1862(a)(1)(A).
18. 60 CFR 48417.
19. 21 CFR 812.7(b).
20. U.S. Dep't of Health and Human Services, Centers for Medicare and Medicaid Services, Approved IDE Studies, https://www.cms.gov/Medicare/Coverage/IDE/Approved-IDE-Studies.html.
21. U.S. Dep't of Health and Human Services, Centers for Medicare and Medicaid Services, Medicare Benefit Policy Manual, Chapter 14, (revised November 6, 2014) https://www.cms.gov/Regulations-and-Guidance/Guidance/Manuals/downloads/bp102c14.pdf.
22. Social Security Act § 1862(a)(1)(A).
23. NCD for Routine Costs in CLINICAL TRIALS (310.1).
24. U.S. Dep't of Health and Human Services, Centers for Medicare and Medicaid Services, Coverage with Evidence Development, https://www.cms.gov/Medicare/Coverage/Coverage-with-Evidence-Development/.
25. Uniform Administrative Requirements, Cost Principles, and Audit Requirements for Federal Awards, Performance measurement, 2 C.F.R., §200.301, and Financial management, 2 C.F.R., §200.302, https://www.ecfr.gov/cgi-bin/retrieveECFR?gp=&SID=0caf094a996036c52f8ce8b4db68fbb&mc=true&n=pt2.1.200&r=PART&ty=HTML#_top.
26. MAGI Best Practice Standards, https://www.magiworld.org/forms/Overview.aspx.
27. CFR, Title 21, § 56.111(a)(1)(i).